THE POWER TO SAVE

'Robert Davey's *The Power to Save* ... should be prescribed reading
for Christians in the Western world'
(from the foreword by Sinclair Ferguson)

'Despite all opposition, and in answer to the prayers of many
generations, God is at work. This thrilling account encourages us to
pray again for such mighty acts of God even here in the West'
(Faith Cook)

'Bob Davey is to be deeply thanked for this succinct, deeply helpful
overview of the progress of Christianity in China'
(Michael A. G. Haykin)

'In the future there will be millions of Chinese who will value this
history of how they have emerged through the last two hundred
years to become a mighty spiritual army'
(Erroll Hulse)

'I will heartily recommend this book... Read, study and relish it, and
be awakened and revived for Christ and for the souls of men in
China and beyond'
(Jack Sin)

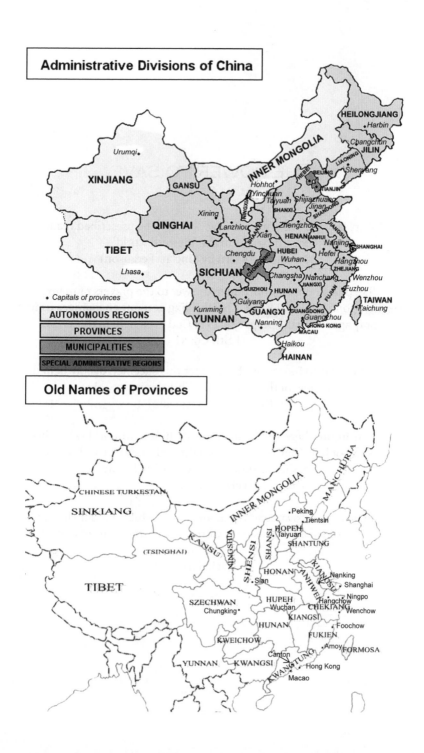

Administrative Divisions of China

HEILONGJIANG
Harbin
Changchun JILIN
INNER MONGOLIA
LIAONING
Shenyang
Urumqi
BEIJING
XINJIANG
GANSU
Hohhot HEBEI TIANJIN
Yinchuan
NINGXIA
Taiyuan Shijiazhuang
Xining SHANXI Jinan
QINGHAI SHANDONG
Lanzhou Zhengzhou
Xian SHAANXI HENAN ANHUI JIANGSU
Nanjing
TIBET HUBEI Hefei SHANGHAI
Chengdu CHONGQING Wuhan Hangzhou
Lhasa SICHUAN Changsha Nanchang ZHEJIANG
GUIZHOU HUNAN JIANGXI Wenzhou
FUJIAN Fuzhou
Kunming Guiyang GUANGDONG TAIWAN
YUNNAN GUANGXI Guangzhou Taichung
Nanning HONG KONG
MACAU
Haikou
HAINAN

• Capitals of provinces

| AUTONOMOUS REGIONS |
| PROVINCES |
| MUNICIPALITIES |
| SPECIAL ADMINISTRATIVE REGIONS |

Old Names of Provinces

CHINESE TURKESTAN
INNER MONGOLIA
MANCHURIA
SINKIANG
Peking
Tientsin
KANSU NINGSHIA SHANSI HOPEH
Taiyuan
SHENSI SHANTUNG
(TSINGHAI)
HONAN Nanking
Sian KIANGSU
ANHWEI Shanghai
TIBET HUPEH Ningpo
SZECHWAN Wuchan Hangchow CHEKIANG
Chungking KIANGSI Wenchow
HUNAN
FUKIEN
KWEICHOW Foochow
Canton Amoy FORMOSA
YUNNAN KWANGSI Hong Kong
KWANGTUNG
Macao

The Power to Save

A HISTORY OF THE GOSPEL IN CHINA

Bob Davey

 BOOKS

EP Books
Faverdale North, Darlington, DL3 0PH, England
e-mail: sales@epbooks.org
web: www.epbooks.org

EP Books USA
P. O. Box 614, Carlisle, PA 17013, USA
e-mail: usasales@epbooks.org
web: www.epbooks.us

First published 2011

British Library Cataloguing in Publication Data available

ISBN 13: 978 0 85234 743 0   ISBN: 0 85234 743 X

Printed and bound in the UK by Charlesworth, Wakefield, West Yorkshire

DEDICATED TO MY DEAR WIFE

HILARY

Acknowledgements

With grateful acknowledgement to the following, without whose help this book would not have been written.

Firstly, to Erroll Hulse, editor of *Reformation Today* magazine, who encouraged me to complete the book by publishing a series of my articles on the history of the gospel in China.

Secondly, to Peter Isaac of Polperro, whose library supplemented my own and furnished much important material.

Thirdly, to the Evangelical Library, whose resources also furnished much-needed material.

Finally, to OMF International, who kindly let me search their archives for pictures and gave their permission to use them to help illustrate the book.

Contents

Illustrations

Foreword

It is both an honour and a privilege to have the opportunity to commend Robert Davey's *The Power to Save*. It should be prescribed reading for Christians in the Western world.

During the precise period covered by these pages, the impact of the Enlightenment and the Laodicean character of so much church life have left the misimpression that the gospel has failed and that the hope that 'Jesus shall reign where'er the sun doth his successive journeys run' was simply a pipe dream of Western political expansion. Robert Davey tells a different story. Here is a vivid record of the way in which, from the day of Robert Morrison's arrival in Macao (Macau) in September 1807 until the present time, God has done great and mighty works throughout the vast landmass of China. Christ has built His church in a way that defies merely human explanation.

The Power to Save combines a bird's eye view of these wonderful works of God with thumbnail sketches of many of the individuals who — with countless unnamed others — have been instruments of heaven.

On my bookshelves stand a number of lengthy, carefully researched and learned tomes on China. This book, however, tells the story these larger works omit; it reveals what they conceal: the story of a work of grace that cannot be described in terms of historical cause and effect, and of men and women who, Esther-like, have 'come to the kingdom [of God!] for such a time as this'.

Reading these pages has left me with two distinct impressions, the first general and the second more personal.

The first is that *The Power to Save* is a manageable length 'must-read' for Christian teenagers and young adults in the West. In former days physicians would send some of their patients abroad for the good of their health (admittedly only those who could afford it). The south of France and the pure air of the Swiss Alps were seen as wonderful aids to restoring health and vigour. This book will serve as a spiritual parallel for any younger Christian who feels that the culture in which he or she lives is so debilitating that survival is a struggle and that discouragement is the order of the day. A visit abroad, and a journey through two hundred years of the church in China, will do more good than reading a shelf full of the 'How to get the best out of being a Christian' literary genre that currently floods the evangelical world and feeds unsuspecting minds. Here, instead, is the kind of authentic spiritual pick-me-up that we so often find in Scripture: the God who did this kind of thing there and then is our God here and now!

The second impression left by these pages is more personal, yet perhaps not untypical for a Christian from the generation of the 'baby boomers'. We — certainly I — have lived in the West all our Christian lives. A few of us have visited China; some have walked on the Great Wall. Yet the story of many of our Christian lives has been influenced and shaped in all kinds of ways by the purposes of God for his people in China.

Until reading this survey I do not think it struck me how true that is of my own life. I suspect that may be true for many others, too. For a remarkable number of those whose names are mentioned in these pages (and some unmentioned but who were no less a part of the story) were instruments of encouragement, instruction and challenge to Christians

throughout the second half of the twentieth century. I doubt
that I am altogether untypical.

The physician who gave me spiritual counsel the night I
came to faith in Christ had been a missionary doctor in China
with the China Inland Mission. Like many a youngster in the
'swinging sixties', one of the first Christian books I was given
was Watchman Nee's *The Normal Christian Life*. As a school-
boy I remember taking a bus journey from the east end of
Glasgow to the west end to hear Bishop Frank Houghton
speak. He would never have imagined the impact his hand-
shake at the church door and his few words of encouragement would have on a sixteen-year-old boy. It was possible in
the 1960s to meet men whose lives had been impacted by Eric
Liddell (whose real greatness lay not in movie reinterpret-
ations but in hidden, sacrificial, Christ-honouring living in
China). And then there was the ever-to-be-reverenced name
of William Chalmers Burns, of whom I first read in *The
Memoirs and Remains of Robert Murray M'Cheyne* — and
from whom I hope I learned the lesson that greatness, or
usefulness, is not measured by numbers of converts but by
obedience to the Lord's calling. For here was the young man
who, having been God's instrument in the awakening that
took place in M'Cheyne's congregation, had then virtually
disappeared in obedience to God's call to go to China.

Here too are men and women whose life stories became
the staple biographical reading of a teenage student: Hudson
Taylor, Pastor Hsi, John and Betty Stam, John Sung — and,
perhaps most impactful for me, the story of James Fraser and
his 'prayer of faith' for the Lisu people. Then again, there was
'the small woman', Gladys Aylward, from whose lips I first
learned of the martyrdoms of young Chinese Christians, and,
in addition, some whose names are less well known. I think of
my first meeting with another CIM figure, Henry Guinness
(less well known in the Christian world than his son Os
Guinness would become). Can I ever forget my first encounter
with a man who had taken the trouble to find out the name of

a shy eighteen-year-old before he crossed the room to introduce himself?

So these pages do not tell the story of a separate world, a
part of the body of Christ with which we in the West have no
connection. If you are a Christian this is the story of your
family, the spiritual anatomy of part of the body of which you
are a member. It is not an identical part — it belongs to the
east rather than the west side — its struggles have been
different from ours; it has felt more of the burning fire of
persecution than the rising damp that has rotted the church
of the West; its life has been shaped much less by church-
building programmes and far more by hidden conventicles; it
has survived, and witnessed within, the struggle to apply
biblical principles in a world of Marxist totalitarianism, not
within a democratic system. Its story must not be read by us
on the assumption that we have 20-20 spiritual vision, but
through biblical lenses. If we are able to do that we will learn
much.

Among the lessons we will learn is one that the men and
women from the Western part of the body of Christ whose
stories are recorded here all knew well. Shortly before reading
these pages I remarked to a friend on a word that seems to
have dropped out of the basic vocabulary of contemporary
Christian life but was central to the vocabulary of a former
generation The word? 'Sacrifice'. I can still see in my mind's
eye that one-word title on a second- (or was it third-?) hand
copy of an old Inter Varsity Press book, *Sacrifice* by Howard
Guinness. Revealingly, a web search offers me second-hand
copies of it at prices ranging from £3.00 to £44.81, but few
contemporary books on the subject. How could this fail to be
a major theme in a Christian community where some seventy-
nine CIM missionaries — and countless Chinese believers —
had been killed in the Boxer Uprising of 1900?

Perhaps, then, these pages will serve as a sobering, but
also liberating, reminder to ourselves as Western Christians
that God has not sidelined the principle of fruitfulness which

His Son both exemplified and taught: 'Except a grain of wheat fall into the ground and die it abides alone; but if it dies it will bear much fruit' (John 12:24). Nor should it be only apostles who can write, 'We have this treasure in jars of clay, to show that the surpassing power belongs to God and not to us ... always carrying in the body the death [literally 'dying'] of Jesus, so that the life of Jesus may also be manifested in our bodies. For we who live are always being given over to death for Jesus' sake, so that the life of Jesus also may be manifested in our mortal flesh. So death is at work in us, but life in you' (2 Cor. 4:7,10-12).

There are many kinds of 'death' to be died by believers; some are literal and physical; others involve the choices we make, the marginalizing we experience, the demeaning by society and the 'shame of the cross' we are willing to endure, the commitment we are willing to make to give ourselves to prayer, to holiness in an unholy world, to witness in a hostile environment, to put Christ before career ... and so on.

The Power to Save is far more than a spiritual 'pick-me-up'. It is a sobering historical narrative and a thrilling story of men and women 'of whom this world was not worthy'. But it also carries a radical challenge to the part of the body of Christ to which most readers of its pages belong.

I pray that reading this book will stimulate deep thanksgiving to God for his amazing grace, a sense of fellowship with the whole family of God, an appreciation for Christians who have sought to be faithful citizens of China while even more fundamentally citizens of the kingdom of Christ, and a fresh consecration to trust, love, obey and serve the Saviour. May 'his kingdom stretch from shore to shore 'til moons shall wax and wane no more'!

Sinclair B. Ferguson
First Presbyterian Church,
Columbia, South Carolina

Preface

In 2008, at the Beijing Olympic Games, China was the centre of world attention. In the twenty-first century, China will occupy an increasingly central role in world affairs. It could hardly be otherwise. In an ever more inter-dependent world, China is the most populous nation on earth, and one whose more than 1,300 million people are well known for vitality and industry. The iron hand of the atheistic Communist regime ensures stability, though at the cost of much repression, corruption and limitation of human rights.

The Chinese rightly pride themselves on being the heirs of a great civilization which stretches back to the Bronze Age of the Shang dynasty of 1600 BC. This civilization was itself built upon an occupation stretching back to much earlier times. For some centuries China led the way, outpacing the rest of the world in both the arts and sciences. Paper, porcelain, gunpowder, the compass and printing (both block and movable type) are all Chinese inventions.

THE PURPOSE OF THIS BOOK

This book tells the story, which is still unfolding, of the mighty acts of God in China — a story that needs to be told.

It has become clear since the 1970s that God has done something special in China. The spiritual awakening and turning to Christ compare in magnitude to anything in the whole history of the church. This has the potential to be very important for China and the rest of the world.

The gospel went to China and took root there because of the profound love and dedication of many Christians from all parts of the world. Their fundamental motivation was the power of the love of Christ that constrained them. Their goal was not political but spiritual — the salvation of souls and the planting of an indigenous, self-supporting church able to propagate itself by the power of the biblical gospel. That this has been achieved against all the powers of hell and in spite of much human weakness should be a matter of real encouragement to believers the world over. It ought also to be a matter of great praise and thankfulness to God for his mercy and grace towards the Chinese people.

Every single Chinese person is created in the image of God with an immortal soul, as is every other human living on this planet of ours. The gospel declares that Christ died as a sacrificial punishment for sin. He rose from the dead to achieve eternal salvation from sin and judgement with His infinite power, love and endless life. Salvation is the receiving of the free gift of eternal life through repentance towards God and trust in the Lord Jesus Christ. The new birth is Christ indwelling the soul. This living and personal relationship transforms the life and character. Everything works by love. As the apostle Paul says, without love we are nothing (1 Corinthians 13:1-3). This gospel (good news) is to be preached and offered to every living person, in loving obedience to Christ's own great missionary commission (Matthew 28:18-20; Mark 16:15). That is why the gospel had to be taken to the Chinese.

Biblical Christianity, otherwise known as evangelicalism, is found in confessional form in the various Reformation confessions of faith. The *Chinese Confession of Faith* of 1998 is in that tradition. It is reproduced in Appendix V and commented upon in chapter 20. It is pleasing to see that the leaders of the house churches have a clear biblical view of the fundamental doctrines of salvation.

Two other matters need explanation. Firstly, I have employed the old names of Chinese places and people, in the forms used by the English-speaking world, until 1949. I have then used the modern names, currently employed by the Chinese, after that date. The alternative name is often added in brackets for helpfulness. Appendix I is a guide to the old and modern names with respect to the provinces of China.

Secondly, some may be surprised at how little attention is given to the story of the Roman Catholics in China (though a summary is given in chapter 2). The reason is simple. This author does not believe the Reformation in Europe was a mistake. The system of belief and practice of the Roman Catholic Church is fundamentally unbiblical, especially in the doctrines concerning the nature and the way of salvation. The original Protestant missionaries, and the majority thereafter, clearly believed this to be so. The Chinese authorities have always regarded Roman Catholicism as a separate religion altogether from Protestantism.

My fervent prayer is that our Chinese Christian brethren will continue to prosper spiritually and be used by God to change their great country morally by the renewing power of the gospel. I pray also that they, in their turn, will in the coming years be called of God to send out many missionaries of the gospel to the rest of the world.

Soli Deo Gloria.

Bob Davey
Looe, Cornwall, England

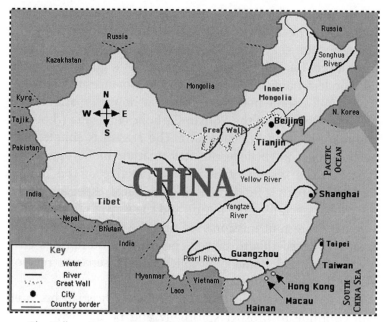

The Yellow, Yangtze and Pearl Rivers and the Great Wall of China
Note that modern Beijing = Peking
Guangzhou = Canton
Macau = Macao
Tianjin = Tientsin

1. China's roots

GEOGRAPHY

Much of China proper is in the valleys of two great river systems. These are the Yellow (Huang) and Yangtze Rivers, with their tributaries. These two rivers have their rise in the great plateaux and mountains in central Asia, where other major rivers, including the Mekong of Indo-China, are also born.

The Yellow River is in the north and is so called after the vast amounts of yellow sediment that it carries and which blankets much of the north China plain. As a result of its frequent and disastrous flooding, it has been known as 'China's sorrow'. It is the sixth longest river in the world. It rises in the high plateau in west China and flows 3,010 miles into the Bohai Sea, south of Tianjin. Between Lanzhou and Zhengzhou the river makes a large loop north.

The Yangtze River is also known as the Chang Jiang (Long River). It is the third longest river in the world and flows west to east across central China. From an elevation of 16,500 feet (a little over 5,000 metres) at its source on the Tibetan plateau, the river flows into the sea 3,915 miles away at Shanghai.

A view of the Yangtze River in Yunnan province

Between the Yellow River and the Yangtze River there is a dividing mountain system. The Yangtze is navigable from the sea for 1,800 miles. Its upper and lower courses are divided from each other by a range of mountains through which the river cuts its way in deep gorges, now tamed by the Three Gorges Dam.

In the far north, along the boundary of Mongolia, is the Gobi Desert, which extends to the western boundary of China along the Junggar Desert and Tarim Basin. Along here was the famous silk trading route.

The coast, south of the Yangtze, is bounded by mountains and is indented, in some places deeply, by estuaries which provide inviting harbours. In the south is the Pearl River system, the tributaries of which join up to flow into the South China Sea in the Zhu (Pearl) Estuary at Guangzhou (Canton), Hong Kong and Macau.

The coast to the north of the Yangtze has more coastal plain than the south. These plains stretch north to Tianjin and Beijing (Peking). North-east of Beijing, beyond the Great Wall, is historic Manchuria, which now constitutes the three

Chinese provinces of Liaoning, Jilin and Heilongjiang. These border with Korea, Mongolia and Russia.

So extensive a country has every kind of climate: from the steamy jungle of the south-west to the biting wind and snow of the north; from sub-tropical rice-bowls to dusty wheat-lands in the north and centre. These wheat-lands have suffered greatly at times from either drought or flood, both of which brought the calamity of famine. The coast is buffeted annually by the China Sea typhoons.

China's geography has lent itself naturally towards a unified state. Apart from the periods of Mongol and Manchu domination from the north, north-west and north-east, China has been free from landward invasion and always free from foreign settlement on any massive scale. Indeed, it was Manchuria and Inner Mongolia that were to become settled in any massive numbers by the Han Chinese in the twentieth century. The same fate appears to be happening now to Tibet. In the main, the Chinese have been self-sufficient and their culture has chiefly been their own creation. A major cultural influence came from their greatest philosopher, Confucius (551–479 BC). Much of the mindset of the Chinese, both conscious and unconscious, is indebted to him.

THE PEOPLES OF CHINA

The Han Chinese are the largest ethnic group of 1.2 billion. They constitute no less than 92% of the population. In addition to the Han there are fifty-six officially recognized ethnic groups in China, only two of which are over ten million persons in number. The south-west provinces, an exotic part of China with spectacular scenery, are home to most of these small Chinese minorities.

The largest minority in China are the Zhuang people from the south-west, estimated at eighteen million persons (1.2% of the total population). They live mostly in the Guangxi autonomous region in south-west China. The West River runs through the middle of this province eastward down to the sea at Guangzhou (Canton). The Zhuang are of Tai origin, a people who migrated south from central China. Long struggles with the Han Chinese (they were considered 'barbarians' by the Hans) led many Tais to migrate south around AD 1100 to avoid the destruction of their race. They created the Lao, Thai and Shan peoples of Indo-China.

The second-largest minority in China are the Manchu people, who live in Manchuria, estimated at 10.6 million persons (0.75% of the total population). Manchuria has largely been assimilated by the Han Chinese. Manchuria consists of today's provinces of Heilongjiang, Jilin and Liaoning. Ancestors of the Manchu were tribes from the Mongolian steppes. Their heyday was in the seventeenth century, when they brought down the Ming dynasty and set up their own Qing (Ching) Manchu dynasty. This elite group then ruled China from AD 1644–1912. They were the last of the imperial dynasties.

It is surprising to learn that the Mongols are only 5.8 million in number and the Tibetans only 5.4 million. Both are less than one half of one per cent of the total population of China.

The strength and size of China's regions, with their differing characteristics, has meant that at times the country has resembled a federation. There have also been many fluctuations over time in the struggle for power between the regions and the central authority.

OLD CHINESE SCHOOLS OF THOUGHT

The religion of Taoism (Daoism)

The roots of Taoism lay in primitive animism, which is the superstitious fear of the forces of nature. This developed into a hotchpotch of spiritism, exorcism, magic, dreams, divination and the search for immortality through an elixir of life.

Chinese alchemy, astrology, traditional medicines, feng shui and many folk tales have their roots here. Taoism is later linked with the name of Laozi (Laotze), meaning 'Old Master', who traditionally lived in the sixth century BC and was said to have been a contemporary of Confucius. The ethics of this kind of Taoism, familiar now as yoga, were concerned with personal self-negation, pursuit of tranquillity of spirit and of good health. It advocated the simplest society possible. Ethical codes of any kind were rejected. Later, under the influence of Buddhism, Taoism developed a pantheistic system of temples and priestcraft. Reverence for nature and ancestor spirits is common in popular Taoism.

Confucianism

Confucius (551–479 BC) did more to shape his people than any other individual in the nation's history. He made a lifelong study of history and had a love of ceremonial and music. He was deeply disturbed by the disorder he saw around him. He was dignified, courteous and affable, a statesman and a teacher of ethics. He attracted loyal disciples who recorded his words and actions. Optimistic about human nature, he sought to produce cultivated men of superior culture patterned on the way of the ancients.

He aimed particularly at the ruling classes, whose good example would, he believed, produce an ideal society. He propounded a code of conduct for every man, from emperor to slave. The result was a highly ethical civil code. He had little regard for religion, except as a system of protocol. He was living just as the golden age of Greek philosophers was to blossom, of whom Socrates springs to mind.

Scholars who built upon the foundation of Confucius were Mencius (373–288 BC) and Xunzi (c. 300–230 BC). In AD 605 imperial administrators were recruited through civil service examinations, open to all, in which the writings of Confucius constituted the core curriculum. During the Song dynasty (AD

960–1279) Confucianism was reformulated, combining with it Buddhist and Taoist ideas. Zhuxi (AD 1130–1200) was the outstanding synthesizer. This Neo-Confucianism became the backbone of the annual examinations for scholars right up to 1905! The educated classes were known as the literati, or mandarins. They constituted a great conservative influence in China.

Mohism

Mozi (Mo Tzu, Micius) lived around 470–391 BC. Though from the lowest class, he became an accomplished engineer, craftsman and an active pacifist, teaching universal love as 'the way to heaven'. Though Mozi's school of thought faded into obscurity after the Warring States period, he has been studied again in more recent times by the republican revolutionaries of 1911, especially by Sun Yat-Sen. They, and the Communists since, have seen in Mozi a surprisingly modern thinker whose thought had been stifled by Chinese history. Mozi was a utilitarian, appealing to enlightened self-interest. Though respecting the past, he taught that we are not to be bound by it. However, he did also believe in the power of ghosts or spirits. He had little time for art or music.

Legalism

Towards the end of the Zhou era (1122–246 BC) there was a period known as the 'Contending States'. China was being torn by wars among the states, and people became disillusioned with the idealistic Confucian way of a good moral example. Legalism, or the School of Law, was a pragmatic political philosophy which did not speculate about other questions. It said that people are fundamentally the same and need stringent laws and harsh punishments to keep them in order. No one, apart from the emperor, was to be above the law. Legalism turned the Qin from a backward state into becoming a strong, though short-lived, dynasty in China (221–

206 BC). Aristocracy was swept away, to be replaced by a meritocracy, especially in the military. The harsh penal system still operates in China to this day. The philosophy of imperial China was to become a sugar-coated Confucianism covering a hardcore legalism.

Buddhism

The introduction of Buddhism into China occurred along the Silk Road during the Han dynasty in AD 67, but it did not gain popularity for a number of centuries. Much of it was alien to Chinese feelings. Concepts such as monasticism and individual spiritual enlightenment, for example, directly contradicted Confucian ideas about family and emperor. It was questioned how the life of a monk seeking personal nirvana could possibly benefit the state.

It was in the north that Buddhism finally established itself and grew in popularity. Only after AD 589 was Buddhism absorbed into the Chinese way of life. It became the prominent religion in China during the Tangs (AD 618–907) after its adoption by the royal family. Chinese Buddhists made their way to the central shrines in India and returned with extensive Buddhist literature, much of it for popular reading. Buddhism also had attractive temples and images. Its colourful public celebrations were popular. It received a major setback in AD 845 when the Tang emperor Wuzong persecuted Buddhism and destroyed 4,600 monasteries and 40,000 temples. Yet Buddhism recovered, and Tibetan Buddhism became the official religion of the Qing (Ching) court (1644–1912).

CHRISTIANITY

The seventh century AD saw Nestorian Christians in China. Their communities did not survive beyond the sixteenth century, however. Our story begins with them.

2. Christianity in China up to AD 1800

The first definite introduction of Christianity to China was achieved by Nestorian missionary monks and traders.

THE NESTORIANS (ASSYRIAN CHURCH OF THE EAST)

Nestorius (AD 381–451) was a famous preacher/monk in the biblical city of Antioch in Syria. He became patriarch of Constantinople in AD 428 but was condemned by the Council of Ephesus in AD 431 for heresy and banished. Nestorians held that Christ had not only two distinct natures (divine and human) but was also two distinct persons — a divine Son of God indwelling the human son of Mary. The orthodox insisted that, although Christ had the two distinct natures, these were united in the one person, Jesus Christ. Nestorius died in exile, but his views found favour with churches in Assyria and Persia (modern-day Iraq and Iran). Their churches also repudiated the worship of Mary as the 'mother of God' and, at that time, the use of images.

The Nestorians, with missionary zeal, diffused their doctrines along trade routes as far as Arabia, India, Scythia, Mongolia and China, from the fifth century AD onwards. The system of belief and practice of the Nestorians was fundamentally weak from a biblical point of view. All the contemporary Christian confessions of faith, and earlier ones, lacked any clear statement on the doctrines concerning the nature and the way of salvation, such as, for instance, justification by grace alone through faith alone. It was this failing that contributed much to the growth and popularity of the monastic and ascetic way of life in the Christian church.

Tradition has an early date for the entrance of Christianity into China, but there is no evidence for this. The third-century Christian writer Arnobius (c. AD 400) mentions a people known as the 'Seres' as having been evangelized by his time, and this is taken by some to refer to the Chinese. The earliest plausible date for the entrance of Christianity into China would be about AD 505, with the arrival of Nestorian missionary monks in China. It was they, it is said, who first brought back silkworm eggs to Constantinople in AD 511.

The first definite date showing a Nestorian presence in China is a monument standing in the Forest of Steles Museum in Xian in the province of

The Nestorian Tablet, AD 781

Shaanxi. It dates from AD 781 and reviews the history of Nestorianism in that part of China from its introduction in AD
635. It also contains a summary of some of their doctrines
and practices. The monument itself states that it was carved
by the monk Jingjing of the Da Qin monastery. The site of the
Da Qin monastery, about fifty miles south-west of Xian, was
rediscovered by the Englishman Martin Palmer in 1998. The
church building had been obliterated by Mao Zedong's
fanatical Red Guards, but a pagoda has been left standing.

There is little trace of the survival of Nestorianism in
China from these early times. After a period of severe persecution and proscription of all forms of monasticism in AD
845, the Nestorians seem to have died out in China by 900.

NESTORIANS UNDER THE MONGOLS AND THEREAFTER

Nestorianism had taken root in Mesopotamia and central and
north-eastern Asia. In AD 1007 the Keraits, a Turkish tribe
living south-east of Lake Baikal, became Christian. Nestorian
Keraits were in the high service of Genghis Khan (c. 1162–
1227) and his successors. A Kereyid Nestorian princess,
Sorghaghtani (c. 1198–1252) was married to the fourth son of
Genghis Khan. She was the mother of three brothers, Mongke
Khan, Hulagu (Guyuk) Khan (who overran much of west
Asia, conquered Baghdad and founded a dynasty in Persia)
and Kublai Khan, who became emperor of all China in 1279.
Sorghaghtani became the moving spirit behind the throne
and was responsible for many of the trade openings and
intellectual exchanges. This was made possible by her place
in the largest contiguous empire known in the whole of world
history to this day. She was the most competent and powerful
woman in the Mongol empire.

The Yuan dynasty in China (1279–1368) was established by
Kublai Khan but lasted less than a hundred years. Under the
Mongols, the Nestorians found favour. By about 1330 it is

recorded that there were 30,000 Nestorians in Cathay (China). Monasteries and churches were recorded in at least five provinces. A Nestorian metropolitan, or archbishop, had his seat at Khanbaliq (present-day Beijing).

Rabban Bar Sauma (c. 1220–94) was a Turkic/Mongol born near Beijing. He became a Nestorian monk and diplomat. He travelled on a pilgrimage to Jerusalem with his student Rabban Marcos. As a result of military unrest they never reached their destination, but instead spent many years in Baghdad. Marcos became the patriarch of the Church of the East in AD 1281. Rabban Bar Sauma was sent on a mission as Mongol ambassador to Europe in 1287. The mission bore little fruit, but he did meet King Edward I of England at Bordeaux and also Pope Nicholas IV in 1288. On his return to Baghdad, Rabban Bar Sauma wrote up a keenly observed account of all his travels. His account has been translated from the Syriac into English and gives a fascinating extra viewpoint to Marco Polo's account of his travels to China. Rabban Bar Sauma died in 1294.

When the opportunity came, the Chinese threw the Mongols out. In 1368, the Mongols were replaced by the native dynasty of the Mings. Since the majority of Nestorians were of Mongol stock, they too were evicted. The native Christians remaining were severely persecuted and curtailed. By the late sixteenth century there were no traceable Nestorians left in China.

THE TRAVELS OF MARCO POLO

With the rise of the Mongol dynasties, travellers, traders and diplomats arrived at the courts of the khans in central Asia and north China. The Franciscans Giovanni di Plano Carpino and Willem de Rubruk were sent by the pope and made official contact in 1246 and 1254 respectively. The Italian brothers Niccolo and Maffeo Polo set out on business affairs from Constantinople in 1259. They eventually arrived in 1266 at the seat of the Grand Khan at Khanbaliq. They returned bearing letters from Kublai Khan to the pope asking for a hundred teachers of science and religion to be sent to instruct the Chinese in the learning and faith of Europe. In 1271, armed with letters from the pope, the Polo brothers returned to China accompanied by only two Dominican monks and Niccolo's seventeen-year-old son Marco Polo. The monks, however, turned back because of the dangers. The Polo family arrived at Kublai Khan's summer palace at Shang Tu (Xanadu) in 1275 and stayed in China for seventeen years. Marco Polo took service with Kublai Khan and was entrusted with diplomatic missions and travelled extensively in China. He was even made governor of Yangzhou on the Grand Canal for three years. On the return of the Polo family to Venice in 1295, Marco Polo published a delightful narrative of his experiences, which was soon translated into many European languages. A heavily annotated copy of the book was in the possession of Christopher Columbus on his voyage of discovery to America. He was aiming for China.

THE FIRST ROMAN CATHOLIC MISSION IN CHINA

A Franciscan monk, Giovanni of Monte Corvino, arrived in Beijing (Khanbaliq) in 1294 with a letter from the pope. He was kindly received and stayed until his death around 1329. He was allowed to build two churches in Beijing and claimed to have baptized about six thousand converts by 1305. The pope sent further help and also appointed him Archbishop of Cambulac (Khanbaliq, Beijing) with a diocese of much of East Asia! By his death it was claimed he had 30,000 converts. The Great Khan sent to the pope for a replacement legate. Giovanni of Marignolli did not arrive until 1342. He returned after three years with a glowing report of progress. In Europe the plague of the Black Death distracted attention and reduced the manpower available for distant missions. On the fall of the Mongol dynasty in 1368 their successors, the Chinese

Mings, destroyed both the Nestorian Church and the Roman Catholic Church. Christianity completely disappeared from China.

THE SECOND ROMAN CATHOLIC MISSION IN CHINA: ITS ESTABLISHMENT (1601—1700)

Ironically it was under the later Mings (Ming dynasty, 1368–1644) that, in the year 1601 at Beijing, a new Roman Catholic Jesuit mission was established in China. The approach was not, as before, from the landward route, but by sea. Navigation of the eastern waters was now under the control of the Catholic countries of Portugal and Spain. In 1557 a Portuguese settlement in the peninsula of Macao (Macau) in southern China was approved by the imperial court. This foothold in the country became the only European settlement allowed by the Chinese in the whole of China. Nearby Canton (Guangzhou) became, in due course, the only port through which trade with the West was permitted until the nineteenth century.

The Jesuit Francis of Xavier died on his way to China on an island just off the coast of China in 1552. Alessandro Valignani became the superintendent of Jesuit missions in the East and went to Macao in 1579. He recruited the Italian Jesuit Matteo Ricci, who managed to settle in Chaoch'ing (Zhaoqing) on the mainland in 1583. An astonishingly talented and prudent man, by 1601 he had moved in stages to Peking (Beijing). Ricci had made himself very proficient with the Chinese classics. He dressed as a literary man and gained much influence with court scholars with his display of Western scientific learning and technology. He translated Euclid's *Geometry* into Chinese and won approval by his skill in making and repairing clocks, drawing maps and compiling reliable calendars. He gained an official position. He also had a number of converts. Ricci restated Christianity in Confucian thought and terminology while opposing Buddhist and Taoist concepts.

When Matteo Ricci died in 1610 his able Jesuit successors, such as the German Adam Schall von Bell (1599–1661) and the Belgian Ferdinand Verbiest (1623–88), continued his eclectic programme. Between 1620 and 1629 nineteen Jesuits joined the staff and they had missionary centres in six provinces. Schall von Bell was appointed court astronomer in the new Qing (Ching) dynasty (1644–1911) and Verbiest, the most influential of all, was president of the Board of Mathematics and also court astronomer. By the time of the death of Verbiest in 1688 it was reckoned that there were more than 300,000 Roman Catholic proselytes living in 1,200 communities in spite of some periods of persecution. In 1692 the emperor Kangxi granted toleration for Christianity by an edict. This increased the opportunities for missions. The future looked very bright for Roman Catholicism.

THE RITES QUESTION AND THE DOWNFALL OF THE SECOND ROMAN CATHOLIC MISSION IN CHINA (1700–1800)

What destroyed the Roman Catholic mission in China was the jealous rivalries that arose between the Jesuits, on the one hand, and, on the other, the Spanish Dominicans and Franciscans who had made their way to China from the Philippines towards the middle of the seventeenth century. The Dominicans and Franciscans were not slow to accuse the Jesuits of compromising the faith. They objected to Matteo Ricci's contention that the ceremonial rites of Confucianism and ancestor reverence were primarily social and political in nature and could be practised legitimately by converts. To them, all these rites were idolatrous. This controversy became known as 'the Rites Question'.

In 1697 the pope asked the Inquisition to look into the Rites Question in order to bring it to a conclusion. However, the Jesuits in China believed they already had papal authority to do what they thought best and they approached the

Chinese emperor, Kangxi, for his opinion. He confirmed and backed the Jesuit position. This proved disastrous because in 1704 the Inquisition found against the Jesuits and the decision was confirmed by a papal bull in 1715. This reduced the issue in China to a simple matter of supremacy — pope or emperor. The emperor expelled the papal legate and ordered out all missionaries who did not follow the Jesuits. Later, in 1724, edicts of expulsion and confiscation of property were issued against the whole Roman Catholic Church, the four churches in Peking excepted. Chinese Christians were ordered to renounce their faith. These and subsequent decrees were not enforced with equal vigour over the entire empire.

The comparative failure of the Roman Catholic mission up to this time was due to the dominant role of the foreign priesthood, the emphasis on political patronage and social status and, above all, because of its primary allegiance to a foreign authority. This was anathema to any Chinese emperor. After 1724 heroic priests stayed on as best they could, always in grave danger. In spite of all, the Roman Catholic Church still survived in China and in 1800 it is reckoned that there were up to 150,000 baptized Roman Catholic community members in China, half of the number that there had been in 1688. In 1807 there were recorded 1,800 adult Roman Catholic baptisms in China. This was the year that the very first Protestant missionary, Robert Morrison, arrived in China.

POSTSCRIPT: ROMAN CATHOLICS IN CHINA TODAY

The French Revolution and Napoleonic wars (1789–1815) threw Europe into confusion and crippled any efforts on the part of Roman Catholic missions towards China. Only after 1840 were recruits sent to China from Europe in any large numbers. Roman Catholicism's fortune in China then roughly paralleled that of the Protestants during the missionary era, without experiencing any of the spiritual revivals. Today they number around sixteen million in China and are known as *Tianzhu jiaotu* (Lord of Heaven religion followers).

The system of belief and practice of the Roman Catholic Church has always been fundamentally unbiblical, especially with regard to the doctrines concerning the nature and the way of salvation and the question of where authority lies for the Christian. The original Protestant missionaries, from Robert Morrison in 1807 onwards, clearly believed this to be so and studiously distanced themselves from the Roman Catholics in their dealings with the Chinese authorities. So do evangelical Christians in China to this day. The Communist authorities in China today treat Roman Catholicism and Protestantism as separate religions.

THE BIBLICAL GOSPEL UNKNOWN IN CHINA

The biblical gospel had never been introduced to China. This was why Robert Morrison was sent as a missionary to China by the London Missionary Society in 1807. The gospel he brought to China was both Protestant and evangelical. His first task was to translate the Bible into Chinese.

3. Robert Morrison, the pioneer of the gospel to China, 1807

In 1800 there had been no gospel work east of India. Robert Morrison was *the* pioneer of the gospel to nearly a quarter of the world's population.

Just over two hundred years ago, on the 4 September 1807, Robert Morrison, aged twenty-five, arrived on the American ship *Trident* at Macao (Macau), the Portuguese colony on the coast of China. Having presented his credentials, he immediately departed for Canton (Guangzhou) where he arrived on 7 September 1807.

Robert Morrison had been sent to China by the London Missionary Society with the task of learning the Chinese language in order to translate the Bible into Chinese. He was also to compile a Chinese grammar and an Anglo-Chinese dictionary. Being alone in this task, he was given full freedom to act 'on every occasion according to the dictates of your own prudence and discretion'. It had been intended to send two or three men with him, but it had proved impossible to obtain them.

China had shut itself away from the rest of the world. The west was bounded by the mountains of Tibet and by desert; the north was protected by a wall 1,300 miles in length; the east and south were protected by the sea. China, haughty and

self-sufficient, had almost one quarter of the world's population, then as now. Determinedly a closed country for
foreigners, China had not the slightest wish to allow the
'barbarians' to penetrate her shores, and only the most
tenuous links for trade were allowed. Teaching Chinese to
foreigners was outlawed on pain of death.

EARLY LIFE AND CONVERSION

Robert Morrison (1782–1834) was born on 5 January 1782 in
Bullers Green, near Morpeth in Northumberland, in the
north-east of England. His father James was a Scot who
married a godly girl from Northumberland named Hannah
Nicholson. Robert was the youngest of eight children and his
mother's favourite. The family moved to Newcastle-upon-
Tyne in 1785 for James to start a business. He made tools for
the footwear trade and was both hard-working and a success.
He was a godly man of Presbyterian views and joined a
church of that persuasion in Newcastle. He went on to
become a worthy elder in that church. James also took pains
to hold daily family worship and catechized his children.

Robert was a serious boy with a good deal of the dour
Scots character. He received only an elementary education
and showed no obvious talents, except dogged determination
and a very good memory. When he was twelve, one Sabbath
evening in church, he repeated from memory all 176 verses of
Psalm 119 without a single mistake. He went to work for his
father when he was nearly fifteen and was very diligent,
working from six in the morning until seven or eight in the
evening.

According to his own testimony, Robert was converted in
1798 at the age of sixteen. He had a very real sense of sin in
his life and yielded himself decidedly to Christ in repentance
and faith. He sought church membership and joined a prayer
meeting which met on Monday evenings in his father's
workshop. From the time of his conversion, Robert would

settle down in the work-shop after work in order to study the Bible. He also set up his bed there. He had a desire for wider learning and studied all he could, as much as his limited time and opportunities would allow. Certainly, Sabbath days were a delight for him and he sought every opportunity for spiritual fellowship. He visited the sick and instructed the

Robert Morrison

children of the poor. He regularly borrowed the *Missionary Magazine* from a friend.

As a matter of interest, from childhood Robert Morrison was a friend of Robert Stephenson, the future inventor of the first public railway steam engine. The families were neighbours. Robert Stephenson regularly visited Robert Morrison at his workshop and learned the trade as a hobby. What influence these two have had in the history of the world, both secular and spiritual, will only be fully revealed at the Day of Judgement.

The call to be a missionary

At the beginning of 1801, Robert Morrison knew, without a shadow of doubt, a call to the ministry of the gospel. His parents opposed his call. He set himself to learn Latin (in order to gain access to higher education) and also Greek and Hebrew. He paid for lessons out of his earnings, little as these were. It was clear that he had an exceptional gift and love for learning languages. After the death of his mother, Robert applied for entrance to Hoxton Academy, London, on 24 November 1802. This was a training college for Congregational ministers. He was accepted at once and he set sail from Newcastle to London.

This was against the wish of his father, who had come to rely on Robert in the family business. No sooner was Robert settled into his studies than he received a heart-rending summons from his father and family to return home. His letter in reply has survived. Expressing the tenderest affection and respect for his father and family, Robert goes on to say:

> What can I do? I look to my God and my father's God ... my father, my brothers, my sisters, I resign you all and myself to His care, who I trust careth for us. Are not our days few? ... You advise me to return home. I thank you for your kind intentions, may the Lord bless you for them ... having set my hand to the plough, I would not look back. It has pleased the Lord to prosper me so far and grant me favour in the eyes of this people.

His family were still not satisfied with his decision and continued their opposition. It was very painful for Robert, and a running sore, but he was clear in his mind where his first duty lay.

For a year and a half Robert Morrison studied at Hoxton Academy. Dr Clunie, a fellow student at the time, later wrote that he was an exemplary student and said concerning him:

> Few have ever entered more fully into Martin Luther's great axiom, 'to pray well is to study well'. Others possessed more brilliant talents, a richer imagination, a more attractive delivery or more graceful manners, but there was no one who more happily concentrated in himself the three elements of moral greatness — the most ardent piety, indefatigable diligence, and devoted zeal in the best of causes.

It was during this time of study and prayer that a definite and ruling purpose for foreign missionary work developed in Robert Morrison.

His tutors sought to dissuade Morrison from this purpose, by representing to him the arduous nature of the work. This only persuaded him all the more. They noted the great opportunities for him in the home field, even promising to help him obtain a place in a Scottish university. They advised him to think carefully and pray over the matter. He did so — and offered himself for work in the foreign mission field. Morrison wrote on 27 May 1804 to the London Missionary Society (LMS), at that time called the Missionary Society.

The (London) Missionary Society had been founded less than ten years earlier in 1795, by a group of evangelical Anglicans and Nonconformists, as a non-denominational missionary society. The famous Congregational minister David Bogue wrote the appeal in the *Evangelical Magazine* that led to its formation. The society was formed along the non-denominational lines of the Anti-Slave Society. After the Church Missionary Society was founded in 1799 by Anglicans, the (London) Missionary Society became largely Congregationalist in outlook and personnel. Its first fields of operation were islands in the South Pacific and then Africa. The change of name to its full title took place in 1818.

The committee called Robert Morrison to an interview and he was at once accepted without the customary second examination. He was to be sent immediately to the Missionary Academy at Gosport, on the south coast of England, which was presided over by Dr David Bogue himself. Robert Morrison set off that very night, after a united meeting of the students at the Hoxton Academy for prayer on his behalf. No time was to be wasted. Morrison had no idea where his eventual field of service would be, but his inclination was towards Africa.

THE CALL TO CHINA

It is at this point in time that we see the extraordinary providence of God at work. The great modern missionary movement springing up towards the end of the eighteenth century
was still in its infancy and there had been no great attention
paid to the needs of China. Yet a quarter of the world's population were there, all without knowledge of the gospel and the
way of salvation. But there was one man, a Congregational
minister named Dr William Willis Moseley, who for the six
previous years had tried to form a society for the translation of
the Bible into Chinese. Dr Moseley discovered a Chinese folio
volume of transcript manuscripts dated 1737 and 1738 hidden
away in the British Museum. It was found to be a large part of
the New Testament, obviously the work of a Roman Catholic
missionary of earlier times. Moseley approached bishops,
clergy and ministers of all sections of the Protestant church,
all in vain. Everyone was interested in his project and sure that
it was a good and necessary thing to be done, but they did not
see how it was possible. The problem of translation seemed
almost insuperable as there was no knowledge of Chinese in
the institutions of learning, and even if there were, the cost
would be very great, and far more than could be spared.

Eventually the LMS, at the behest of Dr Bogue, took up the
idea of sending suitable men to China. The idea was for them
to learn the language and translate the Bible out there in
China. Dr Bogue already saw in Robert Morrison a young man
with the right qualities for the task, and recommended him to
the LMS, who accepted him. So it was that in August 1805
Robert Morrison was on his way back to London to gain useful
knowledge in medicine, astronomy and to learn as much of
the Chinese language as he could before going to China.

Once again we see another extraordinary providence of
God at work. A chance meeting by Dr Moseley in a City of
London street with a young mandarin Chinaman led to Yong
Sam-tak's agreeing to teach Robert Morrison the Chinese

characters. Yong Sam-tak had come to England to learn English, so Morrison and he would be able to help each other! It was not going to be easy, for Yong Sam-tak had a fierce and domineering spirit. But Morrison bore all patiently because he was determined to forge ahead. It was agreed that Robert Morrison and Yong Sam-tak should transcribe the whole of the manuscript found in the British Museum and also that of a Latin-Chinese dictionary belonging to the Royal Society. These were intended for use in China.

After a brief visit to his family in the summer of 1806, Robert Morrison was ordained to the work of the ministry of the gospel in the Scots Church, Swallow Street, London, on 8 January 1807, three days after his twenty-fifth birthday. Now he was ready to go to China even though no helpers had been found to go with him.

TO CHINA

The British East India Company was opposed to all missionary work and flatly refused even to give him passage in any of their ships. What they feared was loss of their lucrative trade with China, because all missionary activity and all unauthorized personnel were banned, and the Chinese authorities strictly enforced this ban. The company dared not compromise its position. So Robert Morrison had to travel by ship to New York, then around Cape Horn to China.

The stopover in New York was providential, because he found powerful friends who obtained for him a letter from Mr Maddison, Secretary of State, asking the American Consul at Canton to help Morrison all he could. This connection was to save his mission in China.

The journey to China took seven months in all. On more than one occasion the sailing ships were in danger of shipwreck from violent storms. However, Robert Morrison arrived on 4 September 1807 at Macao and produced his letters of introduction. One was from Joseph Banks, the

Canton, the trading area for foreign nations.

President of the Royal Society. He then continued upriver to arrive at Canton on 7 September 1807.

GETTING A FOOTHOLD

Canton is seventy-five miles up the Pearl River from the island of Hong Kong (which had no importance at that time). At Canton was the trading area known as the Factories (from 'factor', meaning 'trader'). It was situated outside the city walls on mudflats beside the river. It consisted of the buildings and living quarters of the various permitted trading companies — American, Danish, English, French, Spanish and Swedish. With the buildings also of the Chinese hong-merchants, the trading area was known as the Thirteen Factories. This was the only trading post in China and even then trading was only allowed during the trading season, which consisted of the six months of the year between September and March. Only six favoured nations were allowed to trade. Britain traded under the name of the East India Company, who had an exclusive charter to trade. No women were allowed to live there. Hostility and insults constantly surrounded the traders. No foreigner was permitted to stay there unless he was a *bona fide* member of staff of one of the factories. Permanent residences for traders and their families were at Macao, the peninsula ninety miles to the south-west and controlled by the Portuguese. For a Protestant missionary to live in Macao was deemed impossible, owing to the vigilance and extreme hostility of the Roman Catholic clergy. In Canton, exposure meant death.

With timely help from two American individuals, Robert Morrison managed to gain a precarious foothold in Canton, in almost complete seclusion. He adopted Chinese dress, customs and food, but soon learned that this was a mistake, attracting unwelcome attention. The financial cost for lodgings, books and servants was enormous as the servants cheated him. His health was in danger from the climate and lack of hygienic conditions. Yet all the time he worked tirelessly at his studies, learning Mandarin and Cantonese Chinese. He made remarkable progress. Two young Roman Catholic men helped him. One was Abel Yun, who could speak Latin and Mandarin Chinese (the official language) but could neither read nor write. The other was Teacher Li (Lee Sêensang), who could read and write, yet spoke only Cantonese. These two ran the real risk of death in helping a foreigner to learn Chinese. We know that at least one of them carried poison to use in preference to the horrors of a Chinese prison. They were willing to help because of their faith, and they did also have some protection as a result of being with the traders.

Morrison thought seriously of leaving Canton and Macao to go to Penang (Pinang), or elsewhere in Malaysia, where he could work unmolested among expatriate Chinese. The LMS was actually to adopt this policy as the only feasible option. Even at this stage, Morrison managed to collect over a thousand books and booklets in Chinese. After nine months in Canton, he became ill and had to move back to Macao.

A view of Macau (formerly Macao) today

MARRIAGE

Robert Morrison became acquainted with a Dr Morton and his family, who were newly arrived at Macao. They attended a service of worship in English that Morrison regularly held. Not only did his witnessing lead to the conversion of the son and daughter, but he also married the daughter, Mary Morton. The marriage took place on 20 February 1809 and for her sake they were planning to move to Penang. However, once again, another remarkable act of providence occurred that led them to change their minds and stay on. On the very day of the wedding, Robert received an official offer to become Chinese Secretary and Translator to the British East India Company. The salary was to be £500 per annum — the exact sum that he had spent during his first year in China. In all, Robert Morrison had been in China less than two years! His honest and cautious character, tireless work and absolute genius at language learning had become evident to all, including the highest officials of the company. Robert recognized the hand of God at work in this and he accepted the post, subject to LMS approval. His official status would make his position in Canton and Macao safe; his duties would help him considerably with the Chinese language; and he would be less of a financial burden on the missionary society, leaving more for the literature work. The LMS readily approved.

The Morrisons were to have three children. The first, a son, James, died at birth in March 1811. Then came Rebecca (born July 1812) and John Robert (born April 1814). Mary Morrison eventually died in June 1821, after twelve years of marriage and much ill-health.

GETTING TO GRIPS WITH HIS LIFE'S WORK

The appointment to the staff of the East India Company turned out to be a mixed blessing. It was very much a full-time job and very demanding, on account of the care needed for official communications. This left only a limited amount of time for his missionary work. Morrison did not spare himself and worked constantly late into the night on the Chinese Grammar, the Anglo-Chinese dictionary, the translation of the Bible into Chinese and writing tracts. In 1812 Robert's official workload was increased, and his salary doubled. The Chinese grammar was completed in 1812 and sent to Bengal for printing. It was so well thought

Robert Morrison translating the Scriptures with two assistants

of that the company paid for it. It had taken three years, but it was an excellent production in every way.

At last, on 4 July 1813, Robert Morrison received much-needed help from the LMS with the arrival of the Rev. William Milne (1785–1822), who was accompanied by his wife Rachel and their infant son. From this time onward things moved rapidly. At the end of 1813 the New Testament in Chinese was ready and 2,000 copies were printed.

William Milne

William Milne was unable to get permission to stay in either Canton or Macao, so it was seen as the right time to expand the work by going on a visit to Java and the chief Chinese settlements in the Indonesian archipelago, to find a suitable location to set up a missionary college and a safe place for printing. This tour Milne undertook in 1814. He took with him the 2,000 copies of the New Testament, 10,000 tracts composed by Robert Morrison and 5,000 copies of a catechism in Chinese. It all had to be arranged very secretly for fear of the Roman Catholic authorities at Macao. If they found out, they would take action and destroy the literature, as they had done before. The Chinese authorities had also woken up to the existence of the Christian printing work at Macao. Morrison narrowly avoided dismissal from the East India Company. The reason that he was not dismissed from his post was the fact that he was indispensable!

During his tour in 1814, William Milne found time to help in the work of translating the Old Testament. On his return,

Milne and his family were sent to Malaysia to set up a missionary college in the British Straits Settlements of Malacca (Melaka). There he opened a Chinese free school, set up a printing press, published a magazine in Chinese and held religious services in Chinese. The foundation stone of the Anglo-Chinese College, of which Milne was principal, was laid on 11 November 1818.

JOYS AND SORROWS OF A PIONEER MISSIONARY

While William Milne was away on his tour, Robert Morrison had the joy of baptizing the first Chinese convert, Tsae Ako (Xai Afu), on 16 July 1814 'at a spring of water issuing from the foot of a lofty hill by the seaside' at Macao. He wrote:

> Oh that the Lord may cleanse him from all sin by the blood of Jesus, and purify his heart by the influences of the Holy Spirit! May he be the first fruits of a great harvest — one of millions who shall come and be saved on the day of wrath to come.

This prayer for a great harvest has been answered.

On 21 January 1815, Mary Morrison, suffering from an incurable disease, was forced to go to England for five years with her two surviving children. In 1816 Robert Morrison had the opportunity to travel through inland China with the unsuccessful embassy to Peking by Lord Amherst, of which he was a member. In 1817, volume 1 of the Anglo-Chinese dictionary was published by the company, and the University of Glasgow honoured Robert Morrison with the degree of Doctor of Divinity in acknowledgement of the great value of his labours as a philologist and as a Christian teacher. This was followed on 25 November 1819 by the completion of the whole Bible in Chinese. In 1820 the University of Glasgow also honoured William Milne with the degree of Doctor of Divinity for his part in the translation of the Old Testament.

Mary Morrison returned from England with the two
children in 1820, only for her to die on 10 June 1821. By 1822,
the perils of the eastern climate had taken a full toll. Mary
Morrison and both William and Rachel Milne were all dead.
Robert Morrison wrote:

> I have been fifteen years in this country and one-half
> of these years quite alone, but God has borne with my
> infirmities and has blessed the labour of my hands. I
> did not at first suppose I should live as long as I have. I
> hope I, too, shall die at my post.

He also wrote:

> My parents have all been long dead — all of you [his
> family] are far from me. Those I loved have been taken
> away. The heathen around me are inhospitable and
> void of affection for strangers. Yet, oh how much I have
> to be thankful for... I enclose £300 for the benefit of my
> dear children. I wish to adopt little Robert Milne as my
> son and support him with my own [John] Robert. This
> must be arranged with the executors.

FURLOUGH

Early in December 1823 Robert Morrison sailed for England,
visiting Malacca and Singapore on the way. It was to be a
well-earned two-year break. He took with him his Chinese
library of over 10,000 books and, at last, the printed complete
Anglo-Chinese dictionary in six large volumes. In London, he
was presented to King George IV, who accepted a copy of the
Bible in Chinese. Robert Morrison was elected a Fellow of the
Royal Society (FRS). He was so much in demand around
Britain, in Ireland and in France that he worked as hard as he
had in China. He still found time, however, to court and
marry Elizabeth Armstrong (1795–1874) by whom he was to

have five more children. While in London, Robert Morrison formed what was eventually to lead to the School of Oriental Languages, which inherited his Chinese library. It is now part of the University of London.

He returned to China with his new wife and his two surviving children from his first marriage, Rebecca and John Robert, arriving on 19 September 1825. A mutiny on board ship had been quelled by Morrison's presence of mind and personal intervention.

The rest is soon told. Robert Morrison continued to work hard on many projects, not least a commentary on the whole Bible in Chinese. He died 'at his post' on 1 August 1834 aged fifty-two. On the last Sunday of Robert Morrison's life, after he had preached his final sermon, Teacher Li, one of his original helpers, made a confession of belief in Jesus. He was one of only a handful of Chinese converts seen by Morrison in his twenty-seven years in China. His son John Robert buried Robert Morrison at the Old Protestant Cemetery in Macao (now part of the Luis de Camões Garden). He was buried beside his first wife Mary and their first-born child James, who had died at birth.

FOUNDATIONS WELL LAID

Gifted like his father, John Morrison continued his father's work. He was appointed Chinese Secretary and Interpreter to the British Embassy after his father's death, although he was only twenty years old! He was engaged as chief interpreter in all negotiations with the Chinese authorities during both war and peace. He was a devoted Christian who used all his influence to forward the cause of the gospel. He was elected a member of the first Legislative Council of Hong Kong and appointed the first Colonial Secretary of Hong Kong. He died of fever on 29 August 1843, only nine years after his father.

Between 1810 and 1836, just two years after the death of Robert Morrison, 751,763 copies of tracts and books had poured from the presses at Macao and Malacca, most of which had come from the pens of Dr Morrison and Dr Milne. All these were distributed within Chinese communities and in China itself.

As far as Robert Morrison is concerned, all his immediate goals had been achieved — the translation of the Bible, compilation of a Chinese grammar and an Anglo-Chinese dictionary. Though much of his technical work was to be superseded, it might be said of him, as of the apostle Paul, 'According to the grace given me, as a wise master builder, I have laid the foundation and another builds thereon.'

There are many millions of Christians in China today, the fruit of a spiritual awakening and revival within Communist China over the past forty years. The prayer made by Robert Morrison at the time of the baptism of the first Chinese convert in China has been fully answered: 'May he be the first fruits of a great harvest — one of millions who shall come and be saved on the day of wrath to come!'

4. Charles Gutzlaff, pioneer explorer and missionary to China

Karl (Charles) Gutzlaff (1803–51) was a pioneer missionary and statesman in the first part of the nineteenth century. He was one of the first generation of Protestant missionaries to China. His abilities and achievements for the cause of the gospel were immense.

EARLY LIFE AND CALLING

Karl Gutzlaff was born on 8 July 1803 in Pyritz (Pyrzyce), Pomerania, (now in Poland) to a Prussian colonial family. He was noted for his early piety. He was a tailor's son and apprenticed to a saddler in Stettin. His natural gifts were such that in 1820 he obtained a scholarship awarded personally by King Frederick William of Prussia to study at the Moravian Missionary Institute of Johannes Janicke in Berlin. In 1823, as there was no German missionary society, he applied to the Netherlands Missionary Society. He studied medicine in Paris, France, and also in London, and qualified as a doctor. His interest in China grew after a meeting in London with Robert Morrison of the London Missionary Society while the latter was on furlough from China. Like Morrison, he was a brilliant linguist.

Charles Gutzlaff

Ordained in July 1826, Karl Gutzlaff was sent by the Netherlands Missionary Society to the Dutch East Indies, to Batavia (Jakarta) in Java. He joined the pioneer Rev. Walter Medhurst, who was a printer by trade, at the London Missionary Society's Chinese mission there. Karl was one of fewer than ten Protestant missionaries in the Far East at that time. All the others were LMS missionaries. He helped out at the printing press there and became fluent in Chinese and Malay. He saw his ministry at that time to be a distributor of tracts and portions of Scripture in Chinese to mobile Chinese traders returning to mainland China. His medical skills opened the way on to their junks. He was brilliantly successful, living among them like a Chinaman. He travelled along the coasts of Java, Borneo and among the islands. At length Gutzlaff found Bangkok in Siam (Thailand) an ideal base for this work, and from there he sent out, with skill and insight, no less than twenty-three large boxes of books of literature in Chinese for distribution within China. He also learned the Thai language.

By 1829 Karl Gutzlaff had become an independent missionary because he saw the scope of his work as extending beyond the Dutch colonies. He travelled to Malacca (Melaka) in Malaysia, where he temporarily took charge of the LMS work there. While there, he met and married Miss Mary Newell, an English lady who was the first single Protestant woman missionary to East Asia. She was a teacher with the LMS. Karl anglicized his name to Charles. He returned with his bride to Bangkok in February 1830. A year later both she and their baby were dead.

Traveller

In his grief Charles Gutzlaff poured out his soul to God for the conversion of China. Not only that, he did something about it! He took on the lifestyle of a Chinaman and signed up as cook and surgeon on a 250-ton junk bound from Bangkok to Tientsin (Tianjin), a city in north China. He was the only one of fifty on board who did not use the opium drug. As a 'barbarian', Gutzlaff was in constant danger of his life. He says:

A traditional Chinese junk

I was suffering much from fear and sickness. I found rich consolation in the firm belief that the gospel of God would be carried into China whatever might be the result of the first attempts. The perusal of John's Gospel, which details the Saviour's transcendent love, was encouraging and consoling though as yet I could not see that peculiar [special] love extended to China; but God will send the word of eternal life to a nation hitherto unvisited by the life-giving influences of the Holy Ghost. In these meditations I tasted the powers of the world to come and lost myself in the adoration of that glorious name, the only one given under heaven whereby we must be saved.

Neither was he backward in warning the crew of the judgement of God against their vices. The crew cursed him — until the day when lightning split a mast of the ship! More than once during his travels, Charles Gutzlaff's medical skill, so useful to those around him, saved him from the hands of malicious men.

Arriving at Tientsin in June 1831, he wanted to travel inland to Peking (Beijing) but was unable to do so. From Tientsin his junk went up the coast to the Great Wall of China. He distributed Christian literature wherever he went. It was dangerous work, but God's hand of protection was upon him.

Charles Gutzlaff was back at Macao before Christmas 1831. Here he once again met Robert Morrison, the pioneer missionary to China, who was not only amazed but also deeply encouraged to learn at first hand that his Christian publications (off the presses at Malacca and Batavia) were known and being read all along the Chinese coast and also inland, including at the court of the emperor.

A SUMMARY OF TWENTY-FIVE YEARS OF GOSPEL MISSION, 1807–32

At this point it will be helpful to summarize the state of the gospel mission to China in its first twenty-five years from the arrival of Robert Morrison in 1807. As was noted in the previous chapter, his bases of operations were at Canton, on the mainland of China, and at the Portuguese colony of Macao, ninety miles distant and set on a peninsula. In 1832 China was still closed and as hostile as ever towards foreigners. Trade was still allowed only at the one port of Canton, and then only for male official staff and was limited to a trading season of six months in the year. Robert Morrison alone of the missionaries had official status there from Britain. There was one LMS mission station, with a school and printing press, at Malacca in Malaya run by Samuel Dyer (1804–43), and another press in Java run by Walter Medhurst (1796–1857) at Batavia. Robert Morrison had by this time compiled an Anglo-Chinese grammar and an Anglo-Chinese dictionary in six volumes, and had translated the whole Bible into Chinese with some help from William Milne, who had died in 1822.

By 1832 there were still fewer than ten active Protestant missionaries, including two American missionaries and Charles Gutzlaff, in the whole of East Asia. The Americans were Elijah C. Bridgman (1801–61) and David Abeel (a missionary to seamen) who had both arrived at Macao in 1830, much to the delight of Morrison. They had been sent by the American equivalent of the LMS called the American Board of Commissioners for Foreign Missions (ABCFM). Bridgman was able to stay, though Abeel was to move on.

To these we must add the illustrious name of Liang Afa, who, with his wife, was among the ten baptized during the first twenty-seven years of mission. Liang Afa was a printer and Chinese helper at the Malacca mission. He turned out to be not only a strong Christian but also a fine leader and

evangelist. He had been ordained as evangelist/pastor for the
LMS by Robert Morrison in 1823.

That E. C. Bridgman was able to stay on in Canton was
owing to the hospitality of an American trader, D. W. C.
Olyphant, who has been called 'the father of the American
mission in China'. He furnished a house rent-free in Canton
for the mission and provided free passages for missionaries.
His rooms in the American Factory were dubbed 'Zion's
Corner'.

MORE TRAVELS AND AUTHORSHIP

Back to Charles Gutzlaff. After his first voyage in 1831 he
based himself at Macao. In 1832 and 1833 he made two more
voyages up the Chinese coast distributing Scripture and other
Christian literature. On his return he immediately published
in English, and then in German, *A Journal of Three Voyages
along the Coast of China in 1831, 1832 & 1833 with notices of
Siam, Corea and the Loochoo Islands.* We know the Loochoo
islands as the islands of Ryukyu, south of the main islands of
Japan, of which Okinawa is the main island. The book proved
to be a best seller in Britain, America and Europe, arousing
intense interest everywhere among political, commercial and
religious people. Gutzlaff was at that time advertising the
needs not only of the Chinese for the gospel, but also those of
the whole of East Asia. This was over a third of the world's
population in all. Inspired by reading Gutzlaff's *Journal*, David
Livingstone offered himself to the LMS for service in China.
But, with the future there unpredictable at that time, he was
sent instead to join Robert Moffatt in Africa.

In 1834 Charles Gutzlaff married for the second time. He
married Mary Wanstall, who was a cousin of Harry Parkes,
the future British Minister at Peking. Mary ran a school and a
home for the blind in Macao. She died in 1849.

Gutzlaff made seven missionary voyages in all, even
visiting Japan. As a missionary/explorer, Charles Gutzlaff

became as famous and as highly regarded in his time as David Livingstone of Africa was to become later in the century. Writing in the *Missionary Register*, Gutzlaff made the plea:

Are the bowels of mercy of a compassionate Saviour shut against these millions? Before him, China is *not shut!* He, the almighty conqueror of death and hell, will open the gates of heaven for these millions. He *has* opened them. Neither the apostles nor reformers waited until governments were favourable to the gospel, but went on boldly in the strength of the Lord. We want no gentleman missionaries here but men who are at all times ready to lay down their lives for the Saviour and can wander about forgotten and despised, without human assistance but only the help of God.

His plea for the gospel to be taken to China continued in his optimistic book *China Opened*, published in 1838. It was from Macao that in 1838 Gutzlaff sent two of his Chinese assistants inland on a mission to preach. Their report on their return was very encouraging. However, the outbreak of the Opium War interrupted further attempts to repeat and expand this kind of work.

THE FIRST 'OPIUM WAR'

Among the woes of the first half of the nineteenth century was the iniquitous and illegal opium trade carried on openly by Western traders in collusion with corrupt officials. The cost to China was a massive increase of drug addiction throughout the land and a large outflow of silver from the treasury. The source of the opium was British India. In 1839 the emperor sought to stop this trade. Britain went to war with China to protect this lucrative trade. In this First Anglo-Chinese War (1839–42), also known to us as the First Opium War, China was ill-equipped to fight and was humiliatingly defeated as a result of the British navy's vast superiority.

STATESMANSHIP AT WAR AND PEACE

God used Charles Gutzlaff in this far-reaching historical setting and drama. He was engaged as an official Chinese interpreter by the British government and, with John Robert Morrison, helped in the drafting of the peace treaty, the Treaty of Nanking (Nanjing), which was signed on 29 August 1842. According to the provisions of this treaty there were to be five treaty ports on mainland China in which foreigners were allowed to trade. In each port they could settle and live in an allotted area known as a 'settlement'. They would not be answerable to Chinese law, but to the consuls appointed and resident in each of the treaty ports (these were the infamous 'extra-territorial rights'). The ports were Canton (Guangzhou), Amoy (Xiamen), Foochow (Fuzhou), Ningpo (Ningbo) and Shanghai. Foreigners were also allowed to travel inland within a day's journey of a treaty port. The barren island of Hong Kong, ninety miles from Canton and forty miles east of Macao, was ceded to Britain and it became the natural base for missionary outreach to mainland China.

It must be remembered that in those days the missionaries were the only source for Chinese translators and interpreters, and as such they were involved in political issues. The position was ideal neither for missionaries nor for governments and the situation was remedied as speedily as possible. Both traders and governments had no love for missionaries. Traders hated their morality and opposition to the slave and opium trades; the governments saw them as a burden and nothing but trouble. At best the missionaries were tolerated.

In 1844 a decree by the Emperor of China gave toleration for Christianity in China for Chinese subjects. It was also decreed that a missionary caught outside of the permitted limits of travel must not be punished by the Chinese authorities. He must be returned to his consul in the treaty port, who was responsible for punishing him. Of course, if a missionary did dare to take the risk of travelling beyond the limits, he was also in danger of being stabbed and killed, or even stoned to death by an enraged mob.

By 1845 Hong Kong had 600 European settlers and 23,000 Chinese. The rapid coming of Europeans was helped by the development of the steamship, the beginning of modern globalization. Soon railways and the telegraph were to follow worldwide. As a direct result of the Treaty of Nanking, merchants and about twenty missionaries arrived with the consuls at the new treaty ports. At a stroke, in the providence of God, the walls of the 'bamboo curtain' were beginning to fall.

Charles Gutzlaff was appointed governor of Chusan Island, off the Shanghai coast, for nine months and was then recalled to Hong Kong in October 1843 to become Chinese Secretary to the Governor of Hong Kong. He held this post until his death in 1851. During this period of official occupation in Hong Kong his missionary work did not abate. Official work and missionary work were in separate spheres and were kept apart. A typical day's work would begin with a Bible exposition in Hokkien (the dialect of the Fujian province) to scores of Chinese between 7 and 8 a.m. From 8.30 to 9.30 he taught in Hakka or another dialect. Then started the day's official work. After that was completed, he would go into the Chinese town and adjacent villages to preach, or else work at home on his personal correspondence and on his own translation of the Old Testament from the Hebrew.

LITERARY OUTPUT AND ITS INFLUENCE

Gutzlaff's literary output was large. His publications were in all: sixty-one in Chinese; two in Japanese, including the Gospel and Epistles of John; one in Siamese; five in Dutch, seven in German; and nine in English, plus many articles in periodicals. His correspondence was voluminous. In all this he still poured out his soul for the conversion of China to Christ. He also called for missionaries to be sent, not only for the conversion of China, but for all Eastern Asia, including Japan, Korea, the Philippines, Tibet and Chinese Turkestan — all countries hermetically sealed against the missionary. His success in this regard can be seen by the fact that over a period of ten years no less than seven missions in Britain and Europe were formed, attributable to organizations founded by Gutzlaff. Not for nothing has Charles Gutzlaff been called the 'Pied Piper of Missions'. It is an honourable title.

Between 1840 and 1847 a group of four men, Charles Gutzlaff, John Robert Morrison, Walter Medhurst and Elijah Bridgman, co-operated to translate the Bible into the more classical version of Chinese (i.e. into High Wen-li or Traditional Chinese). Gutzlaff translated most of the Hebrew of the Old Testament. This version was 'marvellously correct and faithful' to the original. However, Gutzlaff issued an amended version in a more colloquial form. This 'Gutzlaff' version became famous when a British sloop was sent up the Yangtze River in 1853 to make contact with the leaders of the Taiping Rebellion. To their astonishment they found printers were churning out, by thousands, portions of Gutzlaff Bibles under the personal supervision of the rebel leader Hong Xiuquan. Reports of this apparently Christian movement electrified the Christian public in the West with hopes for the success of missionary work in China. These hopes were disillusioned as the true nature of the rebellion became evident.

EVANGELIZING INLAND CHINA

In 1844 Charles Gutzlaff founded the 'Chinese Union' (Fuhanhui). This was a mission for Chinese Christians, designed to be under Chinese management only. The mission was to evangelize the whole of China by the Chinese Christians themselves. The mission was based in Hong Kong and grew out of Gutzlaff's daily Bible teachings. Recruits were to go forth, two by two, into inland China as colporteurs and evangelists. They were to distribute the Scriptures, tracts and also an essay on the nature of saving faith. Each had to learn whole chapters of the Bible, the Ten Commandments and the Creed. The principles of the mission were advanced for their day. These were as follows: China could only be evangelized fully by the Chinese themselves. The function of foreign missionaries was only to train, as servants of the Chinese church (tuition, not tutelage). Foreign missionaries must dress and live like Chinese as far as possible and must live and work among them. Chinese churches should be autonomous from the beginning. Anglo-Saxon Christian culture, including church denominations, must not be imposed on the Chinese churches. Charles Gutzlaff urged Christians everywhere to pray for a thousand native evangelists to reach all China.

This visionary programme was strongly criticized and opposed by some of the missionaries already in China. Gutzlaff pleaded the apostolic example of missionary work in the early church as the divine pattern for his programme. The scriptural pattern for missionary work was to go out in obedience to a divine call, preach the gospel and plant autonomous indigenous churches.

One severe critic of this programme was the scholar James Legge, DD, LLD (1815–97), of the London Missionary Society. He believed that the only sane course for the church to adopt was to win the Chinese for Christ by education and steady church institutional programmes. Legge came to China in 1839 to become the principal of the Anglo-Chinese College, Malacca (later in Hong Kong). He became a famous translator of the Chinese literary classics and finally Professor of Chinese at Oxford University from 1877 until his death in 1897.

Gutzlaff had high standards, as befits the work of God. He chose the original colporteurs carefully and travelled with

them when he could. But, true to his principles, as the work
developed, he took more of a back seat and put the tried and
tested Chinese workers in the forefront to lead and organize.
Regarding the colporteurs he wrote:

> As no worldly prospects are attached to their pro-
> fession, we have had very few hypocrites ... one of the
> most necessary things to introduce true Christianity is
> to keep the idol of the world — money — entirely out
> of view. Lying and falsehood are ingrained in the Chi-
> nese character and can only be expelled effectually by
> the Holy Spirit of truth. Though there have been disap-
> pointments, still the great body has proved beyond
> contradiction that the Lord is with us.

Gutzlaff also had high standards in the quality of the
Chinese Union literature used in evangelism. With the Bible
and Bible portions there was also a history of the Bible and a
history of the church. There was the Anglican *Prayer Book*,
the *Augsburg Confession* (Gutzlaff was a Lutheran) and two
expositions of Christian doctrine. There were booklets on the
birth, death and resurrection of Christ. There were also
booklets on *God the Creator*; *Who is Jesus?*; *The Lord of All
Things*; *The Saviour of the World*; *Moral Principles in the Bible*;
God's Love to Mankind, and so on. There was also a general
history and a general geography.

The priorities of Gutzlaff concerning the Chinese mission
were clear from his own words:

> Nothing can be done without the Spirit of God, and
> unless the prayer for His powerful assistance is con-
> stant and earnest there can be no success... The love of
> Christ in and through us must actuate all our thoughts
> and actions ... it must be love from first to last, real,
> ardent, never-failing love, flowing from the great foun-
> tain, Jesus Christ.

'People who do not show here [in Hong Kong] a paramount interest in the gospel will not do so at a distance,' he wrote. 'Those who cannot on the spot readily communicate Christian doctrines will not do so when far away.'

In Germany one enthusiastic supporter of Gutzlaff's work was Christian G. Barth of Wurttemberg in his magazine *Calwer Missionblatt*. This support bore fruit when Theodor Hamberg (d. 1854) and Rudolph Lechler (1824–1928) of the Basel Missionary Society and Ferdinand Genahr (d. 1864) and Heinrich Koster of the Rhenish Missionary Society were assigned to the Chinese Union. They arrived in Hong Kong in March 1847. Lechler was to be in China until 1899.

Between 1844 and 1850, 200 colporteurs/evangelists were reported as having been sent and every province, bar one, was said to have been reached. Baptisms were reported in the hundreds — no less than 655 in 1847. At a time when converts elsewhere within and immediately around the treaty ports were numbered in tens or in single figures, this success was regarded as outstanding. These reports fuelled enthusiasm in Britain and Europe.

EUROPEAN TOUR

In September 1849 Charles Gutzlaff set out for a European tour, handing over direction of the Chinese Union to Theodor Hamberg while he was away. His object was to gain support for the Chinese mission. His personal vision was for pioneer missionaries, committed to go into the interior of China, who would take with them between twenty or thirty Chinese evangelists. The pioneers would set an example in 'preaching Christ' from village to village, from city to city, wherever hearers might be found. Gutzlaff also called for women missionary recruits for China, as being invaluable for reaching into Chinese families and for educational work among women and children.

Gutzlaff's first stop was England. Arriving in January 1850, he conducted a blitz tour of England and Scotland. This had the aura of romance and fame. He had time to form two associations in Scotland and one in England, the Chinese Association, later to be called the Chinese Evangelisation Society. George Pearse, a London stockbroker, was invited to act as honorary secretary of the Chinese Association. Organization was left in the hands of Richard Ball, a capable businessman, who was to launch a monthly periodical, *The Gleaner in the Missionary Field*, in March 1850. This magazine circulated news, not only about China, but about missions worldwide. It was popular with the emerging Christian Brethren movement and their sympathizers, as their principles were similar to those of the magazine. While in England, Charles Gutzlaff married Dorothy Gabriel. His second wife had died the previous year, taken ill when visiting Singapore.

Moving on to the continent, Charles Gutzlaff visited Holland, Germany, Belgium, Switzerland, Finland, Denmark, Sweden and Austria-Hungary. Everywhere he was fêted. But disquieting news began to emerge. Then incontrovertible news broke that Charles Gutzlaff had been mercilessly imposed upon by fraud. An investigation had found that the majority of the colporteurs and their reported baptisms did not exist. The opportunistic and the charlatans had taken full advantage of the rapid expansion of the work. Reports had been expertly and convincingly made up in Hong Kong and the literature, including the Bibles, had been sold back to the printers, who then resold it to the Chinese Union. This devastating revelation naturally cast a great cloud over the work. It so demolished the reputation of Gutzlaff that he and his work have not been treated kindly by posterity. Charles Gutzlaff has ended up as an unfortunate footnote in history.

The Chinese Union had to be disbanded, though twenty-one good and true Chinese evangelists were taken up. They served honourably under other missionaries, including Theodor Hamberg and William C Burns.

HIS DEATH

The revelation of the fraud in April 1850 turned out to be literally a death blow for Charles Gutzlaff. In November 1850 he returned to Hong Kong with his new wife Dorothy. They arrived in January 1851 and Gutzlaff launched into a flurry of activity. Yet the shock of the merciless imposition upon him had further undermined his failing health and he succumbed to a fever in Hong Kong on 9 August 1851, after a rigorous preaching trip. He was aged forty-eight. His last recorded words on his deathbed, after praying fervently for China with his wife, were: 'Victory, victory.' He was truly a man of faith to the end.

HIS LEGACY

At the time of his death Gutzlaff's own church in Hong Kong was made up of twenty-six loyal Chinese Christians at the time when the total in China was about 350 communicants. The church prospered and within five years had trebled to eighty-seven baptized members.

Four support organizations survived and became sending societies to China. They were the Berlin Missionary Society for China, the Berlin Women's Missionary Society for China, the Berlin Foundling House of Hong Kong and the Chinese Evangelisation Society.

The Basel Mission found that the seeds sown by the literature that had been distributed and the ministry of faithful Chinese Union members like Jiang Jiaoren did indeed bear spiritual fruit. When Basel missionaries were able to go inland, the welcome they received in places was such that they were able to build solid spiritual works, especially among the Hakka people. In 1862 a Basel missionary found in one place 170 believers located in some twenty hamlets, the fruit of one faithful Chinese Union evangelist named Zhang Fuxing. A strong Hakka church developed in their heartland in Kwangtung (Guangdong) province, and even today some ninety congregations have survived and continue to meet in this region.

POSTSCRIPT

God in his merciful and gracious providence has given a remarkable postscript to the story. Among the subscribers to *The Gleaner* from the very first was the Taylor family, living in Barnsley, Yorkshire, in the north of England. The eldest son of the family, James Hudson Taylor, set sail for China under the auspices of the Chinese Evangelisation Society on 9 September 1853, just over two years after the death of its founder, Charles Gutzlaff. Hudson Taylor was in his turn the founder of the great China Inland Mission (CIM). He always regarded Charles Gutzlaff as the 'grandfather' of the CIM and put into practice most of his principles. This is a worthy epitaph for a great man of God whose fault — a fatal fault on the mission field — was that, in his zeal for the cause, he was too trusting.

5. Liang Afa, the first Chinese Protestant evangelist and pastor

Liang Afa (1789–1855) was the first Chinese Protestant minister of the gospel and evangelist. He was ordained by Robert Morrison of the London Missionary Society in 1823. Later, Liang Afa was the first pastor of the Chinese Church in Canton. To this day he is regarded as one of the most notable Chinese Christians of all time. He willingly suffered much for the cause of the gospel of Christ.

Liang Afa was born to a poor farming family in the Ko Ming (Gaoming) district to the south-west of Canton in 1789. Coming from a poor family, he left the village school at fifteen years of age. He went to work in Canton as a pen-maker and then as an apprentice block printer. By 1810 Liang Afa had come into contact with the gospel in Macao. Robert Morrison had sought his help in printing the Chinese version of the New Testament which he was in the process of translating. Initially hostile towards the gospel of Christ, Afa slowly began to show an interest, and his understanding grew steadily.

CONVERSION AND EARLY WORK

In April 1815 Liang Afa went with William Milne to Malacca, where Milne was to continue his missionary work among the

Liang Afa

expatriate Chinese and also set up a printing press. This move for Liang Afa was not only to use his printing skills, but also for his protection from the ever-increasing suspicions of the Chinese authorities. It was a capital offence in China to teach foreigners Chinese and to assist in any way in the printing and distribution of Christian books. Afa was baptized by William Milne on 3 November 1816. He was the second convert in the LMS mission, nine years after the arrival of Robert Morrison in 1807.

Liang Afa returned to his home village in 1819 to build a house for his father and also to marry. He had written a tract of thirty-seven pages to explain his Christian beliefs to his clan. It was seized by the police. Before the magistrates, Afa pleaded that the pamphlet exhorted to virtue. But under the law against fraternizing with rebels and enemies, he was fined, beaten on the soles of his feet until the blood ran down his legs and then imprisoned. The money intended for his bride price was taken, as were his savings for the house. Even his clothes were confiscated. However, Liang Afa refused to turn his back on Christ amid all these pressures. Robert Morrison made the observation: 'It is not impossible that this land must be watered with the blood of many martyrs before the gospel prevails generally.' This has indeed proved to be the case.

The marriage also took place. It was a long and happy one in spite of many enforced separations.

ORDINATION AND WORK

After his release from imprisonment, Liang Afa was sent back to Malacca for safety. Whenever he returned to see his wife and family, he continued boldly and fearlessly the work of colporteur and evangelist. His Christian character, understanding and zeal were exemplary. Following the death of William Milne in 1822, Liang Afa went to Macao with his wife and young son to see Robert Morrison and to testify to his wife's conversion to Christ. She and their young son A-te (A-de) were baptized on 20 November 1823. Here was the first Protestant family in China. Before Robert Morrison left for England in December 1823 on a two-year leave of absence, he ordained Liang Afa as evangelist/pastor in association with the London Missionary Society and left him in charge of the work of the small mission at Canton.

On his return to China in 1826, Robert Morrison reported to the LMS:

Liang Afa has been most faithful and diligent in the discharge of the important duties with which he had been entrusted. Afa presented me with a small Chinese volume containing explanatory notes to the Book of Hebrews, also a small essay in favour of the Christian religion entitled *The True Principles of the World's Salvation*. He gave a most interesting account of conversations he had held with his countrymen. One of these took place in a passage boat. Afa happened to be reading the Evangelist Mark. A fellow passenger took up the book and cast his eyes over chapter nine, verse nine, 'until the Son of man be risen from the dead'. The enquirer asked what the rising from the dead meant. Afa declared the death and resurrection of Jesus to make atonement for the sins of man, confessed his own faith, and preached salvation for all who would believe on His name. He also spoke of the miracles of mercy done by Jesus. His companion asked if he had seen these miracles with his own eyes. 'No,' said Afa. 'They are related in the sacred books which were published in the land of Judea, situated in the Western world, and many nations believe them to be true.' 'Have you never read', said the critic, 'what the sage Mang-tse said — it would be better for mankind to have no books, than to believe everything contained in books? Although the Western nations believe these books, it is not necessary that we Chinese should believe them. Do you believe them?' To this Afa replied, 'Although I never saw the things recorded, I most firmly believe the principles and doctrines contained in the Bible. I know that I have been a very wicked man, and if there be no Saviour to make atonement for sin it would be impossible for me to escape the righteous judgement of God.'

In 1828 Liang Afa opened a small school in his home district. It was not a success and was soon closed because of suspicions and prejudice against the teaching of foreign ideas. Afa continued to preach and teach from house to house and distribute literature. All this was done at great risk because Christianity was still outlawed in China.

Two years later, in 1830, back in Canton, Afa saw the conversion of a young printer, Keuh Agong (Qiu Agong). Together they read through the whole Bible in ten days! They then printed tracts as fast as they could. Some of these were written by Afa. Supplied with these and the Scriptures, the two men set out on an expedition to win young Chinese literati to Christ.

It was a remarkable providence that opened up this amazing opportunity. Agong had a relative in the literary chancellor's retinue which toured the province holding public examinations for literacy and the civil service. Literacy and good prose and poetic style were, and still are, highly valued in Chinese culture. Agong and Afa obtained permission to join the retinue and hand out literature among candidates leaving the halls. On this 250-mile trip into the interior of the province, they distributed literature in the towns along the way. Three literati came to faith as a result of this work. Back in Canton they did the same, without permission, hiring coolies to carry the books into the hall and handing them out, as fast as they could, to 20,000 students as they left the imperial examinations.

One examination candidate who took a set of tracts in Canton, including one written by Afa called *Good Words to Admonish the Age*, was Hung Hsiu-chuan (better known as Hong Xiuquan), an ethnic Hakka. His quasi-Christian Taiping Rebellion was to dominate events in China from 1851 to 1864 and almost unseated the Manchu Ching (Qing) dynasty.

THE RISE OF THE TAIPING

After continual failure in the examinations, Hong Xiuquan (1814–64) had a breakdown and suffered delirium and hallucinations for about forty days in 1837. He experienced vivid visions of demon conflicts and appearances of venerable sages and an 'Elder Brother' to instruct him. In these visions he was commanded to exterminate demons and reform society. He recovered his health but, after his fourth examination failure in 1843, Hong reread Afa's tract. This time it made some sort of sense to him. He 'understood' his visions and destiny. The chief sage was God the Father, the Elder Brother was Jesus and the demons were idols. He and his cousin baptized themselves and preached to their families who, as a result, turned from their idols.

After two years' preaching he met the American Baptist missionary Issachar J. Roberts (1802–71), who taught him for a few months. This did nothing to deflect Hong from his path and in 1845, in Kwangsi (Guangxi) province, the 'Society of God Worshippers' (Worshippers of Shangdi) was formed. It was a spontaneous mass messianic movement with Hong

Xiuquan as the 'true ordained son of Heaven' and 'Heavenly King, Monarch of the great principle Quan'.

At baptism, new followers confessed their sins by reading aloud a written prayer of repentance and burning it. This was a common practice in popular religion, where 'memorials' were sent to the gods in flames. They honoured the Bible. Saturday was kept as the Lord's Day, with compulsory worship twice. Daily meetings started with the doxology and hymns in honour of the triune God. There was reading of Scripture and recital of an orthodox Christian creed. A sermon was preached and the Lord's Prayer said by all. Monogamy was enforced, as was a strict moral code. They destroyed all idols. Followers promised not to worship demons and vowed to keep the Ten Commandments. Yet, at the same time, they offered up animal sacrifices and practised shamanistic trances, visions and prophecies. The poor were cared for and private property respected. This made followers of the movement popular with the common people.

All this created a popular Chinese messianic cult religion with more than a little mixture of Protestant religion added. It was Chinese in its nature but Christian in its vocabulary. The cult rapidly gained in numbers, which alarmed the authorities. Local hostilities began in 1848. At this stage no one had an inkling of the holocaust about to devastate China.

In 1851, the year of the death of Charles Gutzlaff, 20,000 'worshippers of Shangdi' proclaimed the Taiping (great peace) heavenly kingdom, under Hong Xiuquan as emperor. Open rebellion against the hated Manchu dynasty had started.

THE BRITISH STRAITS SETTLEMENT AT MALACCA, MALAYSIA

Back to Liang Afa. In 1833 he was publicly denounced in a decree as a traitor, and the 'vile and trashy publications of the outside barbarians' were once again denounced and prohibited for printing or sale. Liang Afa continued his work undaunted and managed to evade arrest for a time. However, the next year saw him betrayed by a false convert who sold Afa and his family to the authorities. Afa was arrested at the American mission press at Canton, but escaped and fled to the American missionary, Elijah Bridgman, who put him on a ship to Malacca, via Singapore. His family escaped punishment, but Afa's travelling companion received a hundred lashes to the body and a hundred more to the face. He survived to continue his gospel work with undaunted spirit.

By this time there were still only ten baptized Chinese from the Canton and Macao mission, most of whom had been baptized by Liang Afa. Yet strong foundations for the future gospel work had been laid with the translation of the Bible into Chinese, the literature work and the work among expatriates in the East Indies, where there were already a few professing Chinese Christians.

The vision of the dozen foreign Protestant missionaries in East Asia was the conversion of the whole world to Jesus Christ, in accordance with Scripture promise. This was their understanding of Scripture teaching. They knew they were pioneers, ploughing up virgin ground. It would be left for others to water the seed sown. Their fundamental motivation was love for the glory of God. They had a strong conviction that God would give the increase of a great harvest for the gospel in China and the whole world, but only in His own good time. Liang Afa fully entered into this view.

At Malacca all was peaceful. Liang Afa struck up a close friendship with Samuel Dyer, the LMS printer, who encouraged him to continue to write. Dyer reported that Afa had written nine very good tracts. In addition, Afa had plenty of scope to preach and pastor among the emerging church of Chinese there. Apart from the worries about his family (who were being well looked after back in China) Afa was happy. He was seeing the good development of the work with which he had been involved at its very beginning. Twenty Chinese and one Siamese were baptized at Malacca in April 1838, and ten more Chinese in May. By this year also, the number of missionaries in East Asia was on the increase, approaching the twenty mark. Many of these new missionaries were Americans.

PASTORATE AT CANTON (1839–55)

Apart from one brief surreptitious visit home, Liang Afa was not to be reunited with his family in Canton until 1839, at the dawn of the infamous first 'Opium War' (1839–42). He did not support this war in any shape or form: 'If Britain wages war, the Chinese will not believe in the Bible nor ever listen to British missionaries.' Certainly the war added fuel to hatred of the foreigner, especially after the humiliating defeat and the terms of the peace treaty. This was the first of what the Chinese call 'the unequal treaties'. Missionaries later became known as 'the running dogs of the imperialists'. This identification of the missionary with official political policies was almost inevitable as a result of the absolute reliance of the authorities on missionaries as translators during the first half of the nineteenth century.

During the war, the leadership of the small group of twelve Christians in Canton fell to Liang Afa and he became the first Chinese Protestant pastor of a church in China. He was left in peace by the authorities because his son Liang Ade was employed by the imperial commissioner as a translator. Liang Afa served this church in Canton until his death. He refused invitations to live and work in Hong Kong, not least because of his antipathy towards the foreign arrogance which was rife there.

In 1845 Afa barely escaped with his life when a mob smashed his rented house in a Canton suburb and destroyed his possessions. He joined Dr Peter Parker as an evangelist at his hospital in Canton. Dr Parker (1804–88), of the American Board Mission, had started this work in 1835. He was the first medical missionary in China. He was also for a time an

American chargé d'affaires in China. The first time Liang preached at Parker's hospital, eighty attended. The next time there were 180. Dr Parker reckoned that in three and a half years over 1,500 people heard the gospel in Afa's meetings. When the London Missionary Society hospital of 'Merciful Love' was opened in Canton in 1848, Afa, a LMS worker, was transferred there. He preached daily to congregations of 250 persons. But to the end he saw very few outward results from all his many years of effort and suffering for the gospel.

One encouragement Afa did see was the emergence of Ho Tsun Shin as a Chinese Christian leader for the next generation. He was the son of one of Afa's former printers and was a graduate teacher in the Anglo-Chinese College. Ho Tsun Shin was now transferred to Hong Kong with the Anglo-Chinese College in 1843. Ho could read the Old and the New Testaments in the original Hebrew and Greek and was an eloquent preacher. He became the first pastor of the Chinese Church in Hong Kong (now Hop Yat Church on Bonham Road, where there is a marble plaque of him and his wife Lai She).

Liang Afa published, in Chinese, tracts both long and short. Some of the titles are: *Simple Explanations to the Questions and Answers to the Truth*; *Seeking the Source of the True Way*; *The Essentials on Mastering Theology*; *On Souls*; *On Heresy* and *Prayers and God-praising Poems*. In addition he published one of China's first magazines entitled *The Monthly Total Record of the Inspection of the Worldly Customs*.

Liang Afa died on 12 April 1855 at Honam, a suburb of Canton. On his deathbed he exhorted his son to serve the Lord and held his eight-year-old granddaughter's hand as he talked about a golden sedan chair coming to carry him to the King's palace. In 1905 Liang Afa's remains were reburied at a place of honour in the centre of Canton Christian College campus on Henan Island, which became the Lingnan University, now Zhongshan University.

6. Hudson Taylor: the making of a pioneer missionary, 1832–53

For the opening of mainland China to the saving gospel of Jesus Christ, no one man was more used of God than James Hudson Taylor (1832–1905). He is popularly known just as Hudson Taylor. His personal leadership, from the front, established what was to become the largest and most influential Christian mission in China.

HUDSON TAYLOR'S SPIRITUAL BACKGROUND

Spiritually, Hudson Taylor was a child of the great Methodist Revival of the eighteenth century in Great Britain. On 1 February 1776 his great-grandfather James Taylor, a stonemason by trade, had come under a great conviction of sin on the morning of his wedding day. He could do nothing but sink to his knees in prayer. He arose only when he had in his heart the seal of assurance of sins forgiven as he yielded himself to Christ. Then, to his dismay, he realized he was late for the wedding!

Afterwards his new wife Betty scolded him for his new-found faith, day after day, until James could endure it no longer. He carried Betty upstairs, knelt by the bed holding her beside him and then poured out his soul to God in audible prayer. His earnestness solemnized Betty and, though she would not show it, she came under conviction of her sinfulness. The next evening, as James read the Scriptures and prayed with her in family worship, Betty's heart was strangely warmed and she entered into peace with God.

It was a wonderful movement of the Spirit of God into which James Taylor and his wife were thus introduced, in a remote corner of Yorkshire in the north of England. All over Great Britain and Ireland similar conversions were taking place throughout all classes and backgrounds. Amid much opposition and open persecution the gospel was salting the nation, slowly but surely, by dedicated Christian lives. After setting up a Methodist meeting in their cottage in Barnsley, James himself was pelted with stones and refuse for attempting to preach in the open air. On another occasion two men rubbed a mixture of ground glass and mud into his eyes. Apart from the excruciating pain and danger of permanent blindness, it was a full three months before James could resume work. He refused to prosecute the men. In 1786 the Taylors had the joy of giving John Wesley himself the hospitality of their humble home, after he had preached in the open air in their town.

The little Methodist society seems to have grown rapidly after John Wesley's visit and steps were taken to build a chapel on Pinfold Hill, near the busiest part of town. Among the first to be received into fellowship in the new building in 1795 was the family's eldest son, young John Taylor. He too was an artisan, a linen-reed maker for the rapidly expanding linen trade at Barnsley. John married into the family of one of John Wesley's early preachers in 1799.

Following the example of Robert Raikes of Gloucester, one member of the society started a Sunday school for untaught children of the streets. No fewer than 600 crowded in at the opening — a testimony not only to the need but also to the widespread eagerness to learn to read and write. The Bible was the reading manual. By 1810, a capacious building had been built for this work and also an enlarged chapel for the society.

John Taylor, Hudson Taylor's grandfather, prospered in business and ensured an education for his four sons. One took up his father's business; another became a minister of the gospel and a third became a stockbroker. As for the fourth son, James, the father of Hudson Taylor, the divine hand was upon him from an early age. He was quick in mind, an omnivorous reader and methodical in all his habits. Next to the Bible, theology became his favourite study. James Taylor spent seven years as an apprentice to an apothecary (part chemist, part doctor) in Rotherham. He became a local preacher at the age of nineteen. Then he fell in love with the minister's daughter, Amelia Hudson. With his father's help, James set up business successfully in Barnsley. He married Amelia on 5 April 1831.

BIRTH OF JAMES HUDSON TAYLOR

James and Amelia Taylor continued as class leaders in their chapel. Early in 1833 they were privileged to see a large number of young people converted during a period of revival there. Their first-born son, James Hudson Taylor, was a mere babe in arms during this precious time of spiritual harvest. He had been born on 21 May 1832. James and Amelia had together already dedicated their first-born to God's service, if the child should be a son. They prayed for him to be a missionary 'with the great unevangelized land of China in mind'. How their hearts' desire and prayers were to be answered! (The object of their consecrated prayers was not to learn of this dedication until much later in his life.) Two brothers were to die in infancy, but two sisters, Amelia and Louise, survived.

For the children, schooling was to be at home. Their father taught arithmetic, French and Latin; their mother, a trained governess, taught English, music and natural history. It was a happy home. The children all loved books, especially anything to do with travel and foreign missions. Industry, discipline and perseverance were taught them by happy example. Family worship was conducted by the father regularly after both breakfast and tea. They were also taught heart-to-heart fellowship with the Lord by the happy example of their parents. The habit of regular private times for Bible reading and prayer was instilled at an early age.

Once every three months, the drawing room above the shop at 21 Cheapside was filled with preachers from the local Methodist circuit. They were invited to tea after circuit business. And how the children loved to hear them talk! Theology, sermons, politics, the Lord's work at home and abroad — all were discussed with much earnestness and intelligence. It made a great impression upon the children, especially little Hudson. He would often be taken by his father to the various country chapels where James was preaching Sunday by Sunday. Thus Hudson witnessed the year 1839 to be a special year of spiritual blessing. It was the centenary year of the birth of the great revival known as the Methodist Revival, or the Evangelical Awakening. In this centenary year, a religious revival broke out during the communion season at Kilsyth, Scotland, under the ministry of William C. Burns,

James Taylor, father of Hudson Taylor

who had been ordained only five months previously. The influence spread as far as Yorkshire. Many were converted in the Methodist chapels, and this was witnessed by seven-year-old Hudson. It was said of him that often his face glowed with delight when men were blessed and saved. Burns and Taylor were later to meet in China and work together for a time. What holy, happy and profound fellowship they were to have, to their mutual benefit, and for the advance of the gospel in China!

CONVERSION

At the age of thirteen Hudson began to work in his father's shop. He became keenly interested in compounding and dispensing medicines and studied hard. When he was fifteen years old, he went to a bank in Barnsley in order to acquire a business training which was to prove highly useful to him in his future career. Unfortunately, Hudson had to give up after only nine months because of health problems. The time at the bank had also had a disastrous effect on his spiritual life, which had fallen away under the bad influences of fellow clerks. He stopped praying, doubted God's existence and determined to get rich. This period lasted for over a year and caused pain to his family. His mother and his sister Amelia agreed together to pray specifically for Hudson's conversion.

One afternoon in the summer of 1849, Hudson picked up a tract to while away the time. In his own words:

> I was struck by the phrase 'the finished work of Christ' ... light was flashed into my soul by the Holy Spirit, that there was nothing in the world to be done but to fall down on one's knees and, accepting this Saviour and His salvation, praise Him for evermore. Little did I know at the time what was going on in the heart of my dear mother, 70 or 80 miles away! She arose from the dinner table that afternoon with an intense yearning

for the conversion of her boy. She went to her room and turned the key in the door, resolved not to leave the spot until her prayers were answered. Hour after hour did that dear mother plead, until at length she was constrained to praise God for that which the Spirit taught her had already been accomplished, the conversion of her only son.

Hudson's sister Amelia, too, had prayed every day, including that day, for his conversion.

When his mother returned to the house a fortnight later, Hudson was the first to greet her at the door and tell her the glad news. 'I know, my boy,' she replied. 'I have been rejoicing for a fortnight in the glad tidings you have to tell.' Hudson Taylor remarks, 'It would be strange indeed if I were not a believer in the power of prayer.' It was upon this belief in the power of 'believing prayer', and also in its practice, that the future China Inland Mission was built and maintained itself consistently for a century

Mrs Amelia Taylor, Hudson's mother

of mission in China. There can be no doubt that when God determines to work through His consecrated servants He can put the desire for a specific prayer into the heart and then the conviction of its definite answer. This is called 'the prayer of faith'. It is in no way related to a mere human wish whipped

The young Hudson Taylor with a book

up into a 'belief' by an undue reliance on 'a promise of God' and which justly only ends in disappointment.

It was at this point that the unspeakable value of years of steady spiritual discipline, both in a Christian home and in chapel, became apparent. These foundations now came into their own. Hudson's spiritual growth was rapid and deep, laying the foundations of his life's work. On one occasion, during an afternoon of private prayer, the presence of God became so over-whelmingly real that he stretched himself on the ground, lying there with unspeakable awe and joy in unreserved consecration for service to God. A deep consciousness of acceptance by God took possession of him 'which', he later wrote, 'has never since been effaced'. However, the devil soon afterwards attacked this faith and Hudson was gripped with spiritual agitation over times of painful deadness of soul and disappointment in the struggle with indwelling sin within the heart. He longed for the regular cleansing and sanctifying power of the Holy Spirit.

CALL TO CHINA

On 2 December 1849 Hudson wrote to his sister Amelia, 'Pray for me. I am seeking entire sanctification. The earnest desire of my heart is that He will sanctify me wholly and make me useful in His cause.' That night, on his knees in prayer, a mighty battle took place in Hudson's soul. Absorbed in his own need, the lad was longing for true holiness, but the Lord had other things in view as well — the needs of China! The struggle intensified until in a great climax Hudson renounced his all for God. He would go anywhere, do anything, suffer whatever Christ's cause might demand, with nothing held back, if only God would deliver him from his burden and answer his cry for a victorious Christian life. He wrote:

> Never shall I forget the feeling that came over me then. Words can never describe it. I felt I was in the presence of God, entering into covenant with the Almighty. I felt as though I wished to withdraw my promise, but could not. 'Your prayer is answered; now go for me to China.' And from that time the conviction never left me that I was called to China.

In a brief postscript to the letter to Amelia written in the morning, Hudson wrote:

> Glory to God, my dear Amelia. Christ has said 'seek and ye shall find' and, praise His name, He has revealed Himself to me in an overflowing manner. He has cleansed me from all sin, from all my idols. He has given me a new heart. Glory, glory, glory to His ever-blessed name! I cannot write for joy. I open my letter to tell you.

Blessed are those who hunger and thirst after righteousness, for they will be filled (Matthew 5:6).

PREPARATION FOR CHINA

From that time, Hudson was committed heart and soul to preparing himself to go to China. His family were united with him in support. His parents were now beginning to see the answer to their prayers, in which they had dedicated their son to the Lord's service before his birth. They told Hudson nothing of this, however, but quietly encouraged him with level-headed counsel. He would need to develop fitness of body as well as mind and soul.

Hudson continued to learn the trade of a dispensing chemist. When he went to China he took with him equipment enabling him to perform a chemical analysis of Chinese drugs and to make and process his own photographic plates. He read everything about China he could find and started to learn the written characters of the language. Also, from this time on, he used a polyglot Bible with English, Hebrew and Greek together.

1850 saw the visit of Charles Gutzlaff to Britain from Hong Kong and the setting up of the Chinese Association, later known as the Chinese Evangelisation Society. This association was designed to promote missionary work in China. In March, the magazine called *The Gleaner in the Missionary Field* was launched, to supply news from Dr Gutzlaff's workers in China and other missionary news. Hudson Taylor subscribed from the beginning. This magazine introduced him into a new world of Christian endeavour, both on the continent of Europe and in Britain. This was the developing network of the fast emerging movement of the Christian Brethren (also known as the Open Plymouth Brethren). From the magazine, Hudson learned of the work and principles of George Müller of Bristol, who insisted on trusting only in God for supply of all needs for his orphanages. Public appeals for money, or offerings taken at meetings, were not permitted.

The Brethren movement was non-sectarian, and international in its interests for the gospel. The strengths of the movement were its faithfulness to a biblical (evangelical) faith and the insistence on a living faith for the individual, based on conversion and a full consecration to Christ. The Brethren sought to regain the simplicity of New Testament Christianity without the historical accretions of human tradition. Into this mould Hudson Taylor was schooled of

God and felt most at home. The Brethren movement has been influential in the history of modern missions, thanks to such agencies as the China Inland Mission, which Hudson Taylor was later to found.

Within two years, Charles Gutzlaff was dead, with much of his work apparently in tatters. But this young man, Hudson Taylor, was to take up his mantle, as an Elisha to Elijah. And like Elisha, he was granted a double portion of God's blessing for the task.

On 21 May 1851, on his nineteenth birthday, Hudson Taylor left home to gain further medical and surgical skills at a medical practice in Hull. He was there for sixteen months and then in London for a year, where he studied at the London Hospital, Whitechapel. During this latter period Hudson passed through stern, self-imposed spiritual discipline and training. The foundations of a great pioneer missionary and visionary leader were being laid. Three things in particular show us the man.

Firstly, in close contact with poverty and suffering, Hudson Taylor began to give away up to a third of his small income. He practised rigid economy and self-denial, as a preparation for the life he would have to live in China. In London he would walk eight miles a day to and from the hospital rather than pay for public transport. He lived off a diet of brown bread, apples and water.

Secondly, during this period Hudson Taylor set out to prove that he could rely on God alone to supply all his needs. His only resource was prayer. Time and again, in small ways and large, he found that his needs were met. Only on this basis could Hudson justify his going out to a dark and distant country where the sole resource on which he could rely would be the faithfulness of God in answer to prayer. This was indeed a life of faith.

Thirdly, Hudson Taylor fostered a strong spiritual base of fellowship and friendships that were to last a lifetime. In Hull, he joined the meetings of the Plymouth Brethren led by

Hudson Taylor as a young man

Andrew Jukes and, through this connection, he was brought into touch with George Müller of Bristol. Müller was famous for his large orphanage and mission work supported through prayer and without appeals for funds. On a visit to London to meet Mr Pearse, the secretary of the Chinese Evangelisation Society, Hudson attended the Brook Street meetings at Tottenham. There he met the Howard family. This family was to become very influential in the support and development of the China Inland Mission. (As a sixteenth birthday treat for his sister Amelia, they went for a day's visit to the Great Exhibition of 1851, which was being held in London at that time.)

THE TAIPING REBELLION

In 1851, as recounted in the previous chapter, Hong Xiuquan had declared the 'Taiping Heavenly Kingdom' with the intent of overthrowing the Manchu ruling dynasty. Over the next two years, the Taiping conquered much of Central China, inexorably destroying idols wherever they went. In March 1853 they captured the former Ming capital of Nanking (Nanjing) and slaughtered 40,000 Manchu 'demons' trapped inside the city walls. Hong made it his capital and renamed it Tianjing (Heavenly Capital). This quasi-Christian sect then set up a utopian regime based on the Ten Commandments. They sought to create a perfect world of equality, morality and material prosperity. Bans were placed on opium smoking, prostitution, gambling, dancing and alcohol. Land was to be distributed equally among all the inhabitants, with public granaries. Community life would be regimented, highly centralized and hierarchical. The basic unit was to be a unit of twenty-five families.

Hong Xiuquan published his *Annotations to the New Testament*, in which he sought to maintain that his 'heavenly kingdom' was that of the last two chapters of the book of Revelation. This was a millennial hope based on Christian eschatology. Taipings expressed it in more traditional Chinese terms: 'Our Heavenly King [Hong Xiuquan], having personally received God's mandate, shall eternally rule over mountains and rivers ... thousands and hundreds of generations of boundless happiness, founded for eternity.'

Hong Xiuquan personally supervised the printing of thousands of 'Gutzlaff' Bibles and many more Scripture portions. Distribution of these prepared the ground for Christianity in Central China.

DEPARTURE FOR CHINA

In 1853 events moved fast in England. When news broke that the Taiping Rebellion in China had seized Nanking (Nanjing) it caused a sensation among the Christian public. It appeared that the door was opening in China for the gospel, for which many had prayed for a long time. On 4 June Hudson Taylor was asked to go to China without delay, under the auspices of the Chinese Evangelisation Society. He sailed on 9 September 1853 for Shanghai from Liverpool. He was aged twenty-one, the only passenger on a small sailing ship of 470 tons. In his own words:

> Never shall I forget that day. As we passed through the dock gates and the separation really commenced, never shall I forget the cry of anguish wrung from my mother's heart. It went through me like a knife. I never knew so fully until then what 'God *so* loved the world' meant and I am quite sure my precious mother learned more of the love of God for the perishing world in that one hour than in all her lifetime before.

7. Hudson Taylor: up to the formation of the CIM, 1854–65

When Hudson Taylor set foot in China at the treaty port of Shanghai on 1 March 1854, he found that he was in a war situation, in a strange country and with no one to meet him. He had no acquaintances and only three letters of introduction to guide him. Of the three persons to whom these introductions were addressed, one was dead and another had left Shanghai but, happily, the third, Walter Medhurst of the London Missionary Society, was still there. Taylor was introduced by Medhurst to the small band of pioneer Protestant missionaries based in the foreign settlement. This was outside the walls of the ancient city of Shanghai. It was enough. Hudson Taylor had a toehold in China.

Shanghai was in the hands of local triad rebels (the Red Turbans) who were under siege from 50,000 imperial troops. The triads were criminal secret societies devoted to restoring the Chinese Ming dynasty by the destruction of the ruling foreign Manchu dynasty. The Taipings disowned them for their opium smoking, idolatry and criminal activities. Day and night there were dangers from cannon fire and there

were daily sights of the calamities of war. Within a month of
Taylor's arrival there was a bloody and inconclusive battle.

From the start, Hudson Taylor felt acute embarrassment
at his reliance on the good offices of his fellow missioners.
They had no advance notice of his coming and had no confidence in the Chinese Evangelisation Society, which had sent
him. They saw how inadequately financed he was and how ill-
prepared he was to stand on his own, not least because of his
lack of knowledge of the Chinese language. Also Hudson
Taylor was not connected with any particular denomination,
he had not been ordained and had been hurriedly sent out by
the CES before his medical course was finished. It is not
surprising that the existing missionaries thought his coming
ill-advised, though they were too polite to say so and they
helped him with much kindness.

Until Hudson Taylor found his feet in China, he was
kindly looked after in the home of Dr and Mrs Lockhart.
William Lockhart (1811–96) of the LMS had been the first
English missionary doctor in China, arriving in 1839. In 1843
he had moved from Canton to Shanghai with Walter Medhurst, whose distinguished missionary service had begun as
long ago as 1817 as printer for the LMS press at Malacca. This
was when only Robert Morrison and William Milne were in
the mission field for China. Rev. Walter Medhurst DD (1796–
1857) was a most remarkable man, and at this time was in
charge of the massive LMS presses at Shanghai which were
powered by bullocks and buffaloes. Proficient in ten languages and with over ninety publications in them, Bible
translator Medhurst also had the heart of a true pioneer
missionary. Following the example of Charles Gutzlaff, he had
made a journey up the coast of China in 1835 and made a trip
inland in disguise in 1845. His book *China: Its State and
prospects*, published in England in 1838, had been obtained
and devoured by the youthful Hudson Taylor.

Hudson Taylor buckled down to learn Chinese for five
hours a day. Because of the war it was impossible to find and

rent living quarters of his own. There was no correspondence from home to greet him on arrival; nor did he receive any for the space of four months. Mail from England took two months to arrive, and folk back at home had waited to hear from him before writing!

He made several excursions with older missionaries into the populous plain around Shanghai and was impressed by the welcome they received and the friendliness of the people. This cemented the desire to take the gospel inland and to live among the people. Summer heat and dust gave him a constant headache, inflamed eyes and dysentery.

At last, after six months, Hudson Taylor came into possession of a spacious native house away from the settlement near the north gate of the city. Its availability was the result of two factors — its ramshackle condition and the fact that it was situated between, and within the range of, the guns of the two warring parties! The dangers were very real and the house was indeed hit by a cannonball. Bullets also hit it on more than one occasion.

In September 1854 the house was opened as a medical dispensary. Hudson Taylor also had a new teacher of Chinese, an earnest Chinese Christian who was able to take morning and evening worship, to which all were invited. Mr Si was an invaluable help for Hudson Taylor when seeing patients, entertaining visitors and attending to housework. On Sundays they went out together to distribute tracts and to preach. Soon a small day school was added for both boys and girls. Teacher Si had to give all his time to these activities, so a new teacher was engaged for Hudson Taylor's language lessons.

Also in September 1854 Taylor went downriver with two colleagues to distribute Testaments and tracts on the big junks which came from the far north and the south of China. This was in the tradition of Gutzlaff. 'In every instance we were well received.' Hudson Taylor was finding his feet.

Hudson Taylor was so single-minded in his calling that he had no taste for the clannish and insular mode of British expatriate life. He was in no way boorish in such company, but he had no appetite for it. He was never happier than when mixing with the Chinese, learning from them and praying for them. This was not understood by the majority of the closely linked British trading community. The British authorities were not enamoured with him either, on account of his seeking to live among the Chinese.

EVANGELISTIC JOURNEYS AND WEARING CHINESE DRESS

From February 1855 onwards, the horrors of the war increased steadily around Shanghai, culminating in a crescendo of barbaric frenzy when the town fell to the imperial force. By this time Hudson Taylor's sights were on inland China. After nearly fifty years of Protestant missionary effort, there were still only eighty-six missionaries in China. They all lived within treaty-port areas or in Hong Kong. Hudson Taylor did not want to be confined to the treaty ports, or to the limit of one day's travel inland allowed to foreigners under the Treaty of Nanking. Though he had been badly let down by his sending missionary society, Taylor refused to allow adversity to paralyse his activities. Between December 1854 and the autumn of 1855 he went on no less than eight evangelistic journeys inland around Shanghai, either alone or with others. The British and Foreign Bible Society (the Bible Society) supplied him with as many Scriptures in Chinese (New Testaments and portions of both Old and New) as he could distribute. The society paid the larger part of his travelling expenses.

In September 1855, Hudson Taylor became the talk of the foreign settlement and the butt of ridicule, scorn and anger. For his eighth evangelistic journey he had worn full Chinese dress, including the queue, or pigtail, and he continued to do so. He had done this after much thought and prayer. He also had the approval of the very experienced missionary Walter Medhurst. But the white community in Shanghai were appalled. He was breaking white solidarity of dress and habits, the marks of imperial society. 'Traitor' was not too harsh a word to describe him in their opinion. This nobody, this pauper, without a university degree, without ordination, without accreditation by any recognized church authority, was a disgrace to the respectable society he had entered! Decorum mattered. Chinese respect for the dominant Westerner would be eroded! Unfortunately this kind of thinking was echoed by some of the twenty or so missionaries in Shanghai. In defence of this step, Hudson Taylor said:

> The missionary may claim the status of a foreigner or may assimilate himself in appearance, home and language to those around him. Nothing is easier than to find objections to the latter course but it was the course that Jesus did take and we are persuaded would still take. The Master says, 'I have given you an example that you should do as I have done to you... If ye know these things, happy are ye, if ye do them.'

Whenever he was in China, Hudson Taylor never deviated from wearing Chinese dress whenever it was appropriate. The missionary community remained divided on this issue throughout the next century.

WILLIAM CHALMERS BURNS

It was at this time that Hudson Taylor providentially met up with William Chalmers Burns, of revival fame back in Scotland in 1839. The apostolic and saintly Burns had consecrated his life to serving as a missionary to China and had arrived in Hong Kong in November 1847. He had been set apart as a missionary to China by the same English presbytery in

William Chalmers Burns

Newcastle as Robert Morrison had been. William Burns went to the treaty port of Amoy (Xiamen) in July 1851 and, after a number of preaching tours in the area, settled for a few months in the market town of Pechuia outside Amoy. 'God so remarkably opened the door in this place,' he wrote, 'that we found it our clear duty to remain and make that place our headquarters.' The spiritual depth of this work in Pechuia was evidenced by a family destroying their idols and ancestral tablets and another man refusing to open his shop on a Sunday. These people openly sided with the gospel and soon a church of about twenty was gathered. This included two whole families, each of six members. This church went on from strength to strength, having fifty-two strongly established members by 1854. The elders were elected by the congregation, a step also taken in the congregations in Amoy and Chio-bey. When the church in Amoy set apart two Chinese evangelists in 1859, their support was guaranteed by the local congregation. This little group of churches was well on the way to becoming indigenous.

In August 1855 William Burns was sent by his mission, the English Presbyterian Mission, to Shanghai in order to try to make contact with the Taiping rebels who were up the

A traditional water village near Shanghai

Yangtze River at Nanking. This turned out to be impossible. So he engaged in a water-borne ministry along the rivers and canals around Shanghai, living on a riverboat for three months. He met Hudson Taylor and they teamed up. Burns soon adopted Chinese dress like Hudson Taylor, while Hudson Taylor profited immensely from the profound experience, godliness and doctrinal strength of William Burns. They spent a month together on an evangelistic trip, going as far as a hundred miles west of Shanghai. How deeply their hearts were knit together in love, fellowship, prayer and hard work!

Back in Shanghai, Captain Bowers, a Christian, was putting before the missionary community the wickedness of the trading in humans (the coolie trade) and in opium that was being carried on by white traders at the port of Swatow (Shantou). This was 800 miles to the south, between the ports of Amoy and Canton. Not being a treaty port, Swatow was, strictly speaking, 'off limits' to the missionaries. However, both Hudson Taylor and William Burns independently felt called of God to take the gospel there. When they confessed

their call to each other, both were overjoyed that their partnership in the gospel could continue. Captain Bowers gave
them free passage on his ship.

On 6 March 1856, just over two years after Hudson Taylor
had arrived in China, they sailed for Swatow: 'We go, having
no plans. Pray for us; pray for us, that we may be kept from
sin and used of God in the conversion of sinners.' Eschewing
the foreign settlement on Double Island, the indomitable pair
of missionaries found a room above an incense shop in a
crowded corner of the mainland town. Here they set up their
mission headquarters. Few in the town could read, so priority
was given for Burns and Taylor to learn the Tiejiu dialect well
enough to preach. It also became clear that medical work
ought to be started. For this, Hudson Taylor would have to
return to Shanghai for instruments and supplies. As two
Chinese Christian helpers arrived from Hong Kong, and a
devastating typhoon made work in the countryside impossible for a time, Hudson Taylor returned to Shanghai in
July 1856 for medical supplies. He was not to know that God
was closing the door of service for him at Swatow.

William Burns carried on, but by the time he handed over
to Rev. George Smith in 1858 he could not point to a single
decided convert. Yet a successful mission was to be established in that place. Within five years of his departure, thirty-
nine converts were received into church fellowship and by
the end of the century Chinese Christians in Swatow, from all
the different works there, were numbered in a few thousand.

When severe persecution arose against the church at
Pechuia in 1861, Burns was called on by his mission to approach the British Consul on their behalf. He did so successfully, but what had happened locally could happen generally,
so he was sent to Peking in 1863 to bring the matter before
the British Ambassador. Hudson Taylor's view differed from
that of Burns on this issue. It was his conviction that missionaries should not appeal to the secular authorities for protection, but should leave it to God.

William Burns remained in the north, and engaged in rural tours until his death on 4 April 1868 at Niuchwang (Yingkou) near the Korean border. It was once said of this 'Greatheart' of China, 'He is the holiest man alive.'

MARRIAGE

When Hudson Taylor arrived back at Shanghai he learned that a fire had destroyed most of the medical supplies. So in August 1856 he had to go to Ningpo (Ningbo) for replacements, where a CES colleague, Dr William Parker, was busy establishing a hospital. Ningpo was a treaty port about a hundred miles south of Shanghai and had a fine group of fourteen missionaries by this time. They worked remarkably well together. War between Britain and China loomed (the Second Opium War, 1856–60) and it was no time to be travelling unnecessarily. So Hudson Taylor stayed at Ningpo and made it his base. There he met Maria Dyer, daughter of pioneer LMS missionary Samuel Dyer. Maria had been orphaned at nine years of age and had returned to China to teach in the girls' mission school in Ningpo. When Hudson proposed marriage he was acutely aware that he had no settled home, no regular income, no prospects, had not completed his medical course and had recently resigned from the Chinese Evangelisation Society. He told Maria right up to the time of the wedding that she must regard herself as free, if she so wanted. Her reply was, 'Have you forgotten that I was an orphan in a far-off land? God has been my Father all these years; and do you think I shall be afraid to trust him now?' Hudson and Maria were married on 20 January 1858. God gave them twelve years of happy marriage and four children before Maria was taken to be with the Lord in 1870.

At the end of August 1859 Mrs Parker died. Dr Parker returned to England for a time with his five children. Hudson Taylor had to take on the responsibility of running the

Hudson and Maria Taylor

hospital in addition to his evangelistic work in town. A small church with twenty-one members had also been established at the Taylor home in Bridge Street. With so much work, Hudson Taylor began to suffer a lot of sickness, culminating in a doctor's advising him to return to England for a complete rest, or he would die. In those days the life expectancy of a missionary in the Asian field of service was just seven years! With sad hearts the hospital was closed and passages booked for England. From Shanghai, before embarkation for England in July 1860, Hudson Taylor wrote to his sister Amelia, 'Had I a thousand lives, China should claim every one. No, not China, but Christ. Can we do too much for Him?'

BACK IN ENGLAND IN REVIVAL TIMES

On 20 November 1860 the family, together with Chinese Christian believer Wang Lae-djung, arrived in England. They made their way to London and the home of Hudson Taylor's sister Amelia and her husband Benjamin Broomhall. A doctor's verdict on Hudson Taylor was that he must abandon all thoughts of returning to China for many years, if not for ever. It was indeed to be six years before he set foot in China again, but we can clearly see the providence of God in this enforced return to England. Based in London, Hudson Taylor secured his medical degree in 1862 and gradually regained his health. He revised the Ningpo dialect New Testament in Roman script and by October 1866 had secured and sent five workers to the Ningpo mission.

Britain and Ireland were experiencing two years of revival in 1859–60 — a revival of such magnitude that it has rightly been called the Second Evangelical Awakening in Britain. The revival was extensive yet utterly free from fanaticism. According to J. Edwin Orr, over one million people were added to the membership of churches in one year, when the whole population of the United Kingdom was only twenty-seven million. The evangelical revival of the previous hundred years had been gaining in momentum in terms of church growth and this was the culminating flood tide. The revival affected all classes of the population. It did untold social good and over the next forty years also gave an effective impulse to home and foreign missionary work in terms of resources and consecrated manpower.

Hudson Taylor was to be God's man in the right place, at the right time, for China's teeming unevangelized millions.

THE SECOND 'OPIUM WAR' WITH CHINA, 1856–60

Increased commercial demands from foreign powers such as Britain, France and the USA led to war breaking out, after an incident on 8 October 1856 involving a ship from Hong Kong named the *Arrow*. It was suspected by the Chinese of piracy and smuggling and was boarded, and arrests were made.

On very dubious grounds, war was declared by Britain. France joined Britain after the execution by the Chinese of a French missionary named Auguste Chapdelaine. The USA and Russia sent envoys to Hong Kong to offer assistance to the allies. The war was short and in June 1858 the Treaty of Tientsin (Tianjin) was signed, but the Chinese court refused to ratify it. The war was subsequently recommenced, leading to an Anglo-French force taking Peking and looting and then destroying the Summer Palaces. This was an utter humiliation for the proud Chinese Empire. The Treaty of Tientsin was ratified in the Convention of Peking on 18 October 1860.

Among the provisions made, the opium trade was legalized, a permanent diplomatic presence in Peking was ceded and Britain acquired Kowloon (adjacent to Hong Kong on the mainland). In addition, Chinese Christians were granted full civil rights, including the right to own property and to evangelize. Ten more treaty ports were opened to Western trade, including Nanking and Hankou, up the mighty Yangtze River. All foreign vessels had the right to navigate the

Yangtze freely, and the restrictions preventing foreigners from travelling into inland China were lifted.

Hudson Taylor saw that the way was now opening up for foreign missionaries to travel into, and reside in, inland China under the protection of the authorities. He approached the larger missionary societies again and again to take up these opportunities, but they politely professed themselves unable to take on any greater responsibilities towards China. The time, they argued, was perhaps still not right, and anyway their priorities were elsewhere.

THE END OF THE TAIPING REBELLION, 1864

Then in 1864 the Taiping Rebellion was finally quelled. When Hong Xiuquan had claimed to be the second Son of God, 'the younger brother of Jesus', he had alienated Christian opinion, as also did the wildness of the collective leadership of spirit mediums. The Taiping army's conduct descended to the level of barbarity. The turn of the tide against the Taiping came with the help of a special elite trained force called the 'Ever-Victorious Army'. This was founded by the American F. T. Ward and led by a European officer corps. It was commanded by Major Charles George Gordon (Chinese Gordon), the same Gordon whose death in 1885 at the siege of Khartoum in the Sudan was to lead to the fall of the British government at home. Hong Xiuquan committed suicide before the fiery end of the rebellion, when General Zeng Guofan took Nanking on 19 July 1864.

Twenty million people died during the course of the Taiping Rebellion alone. The uprising had devastated much of central and southern China with famine, as the original high ideals gave way to brutality and plunder. Farther north, the Yellow River had flooded in 1851, and again in 1855. Many people were drowned. No repairs had been carried out as a result of lack of money. The flood damage, combined with a revolt, devastated the richest provinces in China that had largely escaped the Taiping ravages. All these happenings added to the woes of the Qing regime, which was crumbling into terminal decline.

THE VISION FOR A CHINA INLAND MISSION

'Surely, the end of the Taiping Rebellion leaves the way open at last to take the gospel to the needy inland areas, doesn't it?' reasoned Hudson Taylor.

As he sat in his study, with the Scriptures open on his desk and a large map of China on the wall, a vision dawned in the midst of many tears. He said later:

> I have often seen since, that without those months feeding and feasting on the Word of God, I should have been quite unprepared to form on its present basis a mission like the China Inland Mission... While in the field, the pressure of claims around me was so great I could not think much of the still greater needs of the regions far inland.

What that vision was, we know from the pamphlet he published in October 1865, *China's Spiritual Need and Claims*. It is a book in the tradition of William Carey's famous *An Enquiry into the Obligations of Christians to Use Means for the Conversion of the Heathens*. In both cases, history and facts are soberly marshalled to form an irresistible argument. Both are cries from the heart. Hudson Taylor depicts in detail each of the eleven inland provinces that had no Protestant missionary. His immediate call is for twenty-four fellow-workers, two for each unreached inland province and two for Mongolia. Why had Hudson Taylor taken this step? The answer is that he could do no other!

THE BIRTH OF THE CHINA INLAND MISSION

For months in 1865, Hudson Taylor went through a personal spiritual battle about all this. He could not sleep. His health was giving way. It all came to a head on Sunday, 25 June 1865, in Brighton, on the south coast of England. This momentous occasion for the history of the gospel in China must be put in his own words:

> Unable to bear the sight of a congregation of a thousand or more Christian people rejoicing in their own security, while millions [of Chinese] were perishing for lack of knowledge, I wandered out on the sands alone, in great spiritual agony; and there the Lord conquered my unbelief and I surrendered *myself* for this service. At Thy bidding, as Thy servant, I go forward, leaving all to Thee. I told Him that all the responsibility as to issues and consequences must rest with Him; that as His servant it was mine to obey and follow Him. Then and there, prayed for 24 men for inland China. Conflict all ended, how I did sleep that night! My dear wife thought that Brighton had done wonders for me, and so it had!

That night, Hudson Taylor wrote in the margin of his Bible against his Scripture portion for that day, 'Prayed for 24 willing, skilful labourers at Brighton, June 25 1865' — a clear reference to 1 Chronicles 28:20-21. The measure of the task and the magnitude of commitment can be seen in that at this time the total missionary force in China numbered only ninety!

Two days later, a bank account was opened in the name of the China Inland Mission with the sum of £10 and 'all the promises of God'. By October his missionary manifesto was published to the world, with its call: 'We do not hesitate to ask the great Lord of the harvest to call forth, to *thrust* forth, twenty-four European and twenty-four [Chinese] evangelists, to plant the standard of the Cross in the eleven unevangelized provinces of China proper and in Chinese Tartary.'

Hudson Taylor was taking up the vision of Robert Morrison for the conversion of all China, and most of the ideas of Charles Gutzlaff on how best to achieve it. What was new was his own unshakeable faith in the 'faithfulness of the covenant-keeping God to supply all need in answer to prayer alone'.

8. Hudson Taylor: establishing the China Inland Mission, 1865–75

The China Inland Mission (CIM), founded in England by Hudson Taylor in June 1865, was indeed a giant leap of faith for all involved. Yet it proved to be of God and prospered from the beginning. The foundations had been laid by six years' experience on the mission field in China, careful reflection and, above all, a single-minded burden to reach all the people of China for Christ. Within a year of publication of the manifesto *China's Spiritual Need and Claims*, Hudson Taylor and his family were on their way to China with the full number of twenty-four that he had prayed for either already sent on ahead or else accompanying them!

How this came about is a saga in itself. It is enough for us to know that it could only have happened because Hudson Taylor had worked tirelessly for the cause. He had trained recruits at his home in the east end of London, consulted an ever-widening circle of influential Christians and taken up every opportunity to speak on behalf of China. He had been invited to speak at churches, in private drawing rooms and at some of the most popular annual Christian conventions.

Significantly, recruits were chosen for their spiritual maturity, their call from God and their willingness to trust in God to supply their needs. Their social background and academic attainments were of secondary concern. This meant that Hudson Taylor was tapping into the vast resource of Christians from the artisan class for missionaries, rather than relying on the well-educated or on medically qualified personnel, as the traditional missionary societies did.

Even so, the success of the China Inland Mission was really due to the fact that the hand of God's blessing and protection was on the work. We need also to note the spiritual principles on which this mission was established and maintained. They were peculiarly adapted to survive the Communist onslaught in the mid-twentieth century after all foreign missionary agencies had been ejected, including the CIM. They have mainly been the means, in the providence of God, of producing the flourishing indigenous Chinese church that has emerged since. This fact alone warrants close attention to the history of the ministry and work of Hudson Taylor and the China Inland Mission.

THE PRINCIPLES OF THE CHINA INLAND MISSION

From the first it was decidedly a *'faith' mission*. There were to be no appeals for money, no collections at meetings, nor any personal solicitation for money: 'All who go out as missionaries shall go in dependence upon God for temporal supplies with the clear understanding that the Officers of the Mission do not guarantee any income whatsoever, and knowing that as no debt will be incurred, they can only be ministered to as the funds sent in from time to time will allow.' The motto was: 'Go and do the work, trusting in His sure word.' The mission was never to go into debt as a matter of principle, as this would be contrary to apostolic command in Scripture and also to the principle of faith.

Secondly, the mission was *evangelical*: 'Duly qualified candidates for missionary labour shall be accepted provided there be soundness in the faith on all fundamental truths.' Along with their application forms as candidates, they had to submit 'a written statement of their convictions as to the divine inspiration and authority of the Scriptures, the Trinity, the fall of man and his consequent moral depravity and the need of regeneration, the atonement, justification by faith, sanctification, the resurrection of the body, the eternal life of the saved, and the eternal punishment of the lost'.

Thirdly, the mission was *non-denominational*: 'Our work is evangelistic and unsectarian: we desire to win souls for Christ, and not to spread any particular views of Church government. Those of similar views are to be located near each other as far as can be arranged.' The fundamental purpose of the mission was to evangelize by pioneer preaching into the unreached provinces, constantly breaking new ground. The aim was also to plant self-supporting indigenous churches as soon as was practicable. From these, native evangelists would emerge to accompany the CIM missionaries and also to carry out pioneer work in their own right. God mightily blessed these efforts over the years.

Fourthly, *men and women, married or unmarried, from any background,* would be acceptable candidates, the requirement being the same for all — namely that they be spiritually equipped and called: 'The proposed field is so extensive and the need of labourers of every class is so great.' Of every qualified candidate, 'Each one has been qualified, we believe, for that sphere of service which the Lord intends him or her to occupy.' Women were needed to evangelize Chinese women, teach in schools and assist in medical work.

The plan adopted for the choice of personnel was as follows:

> After correspondence with and about them, personal acquaintance is sought, and every care is taken to ascertain that God has fitted them for the work. In order to know them more thoroughly they are invited to reside for a longer or shorter time with us. When satisfied of the fitness of one and another for the work in

China, the Lord is asked to open the way and provide the means for outfit and passage.

From a biblical point of view, a weakness was that there was no insistence on accepted candidates being sent out by a local church, though this was considered desirable.

Fifthly, *headquarters must be on the field,* under the leadership of a director. Hudson Taylor was immovable about this principle. The tail was not to wag the dog. It was not just a matter of logistics. For Hudson Taylor the heart of the matter was spiritual responsibility. Only those on the field, who had the ultimate responsibility of prayer and looking to God, could be in a position to direct affairs. Home directors were to be supporters, not masters. As the work expanded across China, the responsibility was delegated to field directors.

As a result of early experience on the field, it was soon required that *all new missionary recruits go out as probationers for two years* to learn the language and find their feet in the work. From the beginning it was required that all who were going inland should agree to dress in Chinese clothing and live like the people among whom they worked. This could not always be enforced as time went by, but the ideal remained. When churches had been organized, those who were subsequently appointed to succeed to the pastoral charge of a church were to continue the particular form of church government already established in that church. This allowed for different practices on matters such as baptism to coexist within the mission.

As for *the recruitment of missionaries,* Hudson Taylor says:

In the study of the Divine Word I learned that to obtain successful labourers what was needed was not elaborate appeals for help, but *first* earnest prayer to God to thrust forth labourers, and *second* the deepening of the spiritual life of the Church, so that men should be unable to stay at home. I saw the apostolic plan was not to raise ways and means, but to go and do the work, trusting in His sure word who has said, 'Seek ye first the kingdom of God and his righteousness; and all these things shall be added unto you.'

There can be no doubt that Hudson Taylor had read the times aright. The 1857–60 revival on both sides of the Atlantic had increased the membership of the churches in the United States and Canada by over a million, and it was the same in the United Kingdom. The spiritual power of the revival also created a depth of spiritual hunger and thirst for the continuing presence of God. This led to movements and conferences aimed at producing a deeper spiritual consecration and walk with God for the individual Christian. It was this tide of deep evangelical spirituality in the land that Hudson Taylor saw as an answer to his prayers. This upsurge of blessing continued for one generation and peaked in the late 1880s. After that the spiritual tide of blessing began to recede quickly and remorselessly in the United Kingdom, succumbing to the relentless rise of rationalistic liberal theology, which gained more and more the dominance in the ministerial training institutions and pulpits of the land. By the time liberalism had gained the ascendancy, the CIM had become international in its recruitment. It continued to expand at a remarkable rate, during and after the lifetime of its founder, without ever compromising its principles in any way.

THE CHALLENGE OF HUMAN RESPONSIBILITY

One of the driving spiritual concerns compelling the birth of the mission becomes clear right at the very beginning of the manifesto. Hudson Taylor quotes Proverbs 24:11-12, which he repeats again and again throughout his appeal:

If thou forbear to deliver them that are drawn unto death, and those that are ready to be slain; if thou

sayest, Behold, we knew it not; doth not he that pon-
dereth the heart consider it? and he that keepeth thy
soul doth he not know it? and shall not he render to
every man according to his works?

Hudson Taylor took seriously this concept of 'blood-
guiltiness'. Guilt comes on every believer who knows the
salvation of God and does nothing, or very little, to assist in
carrying out the command of the Great Commission. It is the
command of Christ. It is a duty. On behalf of China, he calls
for, at the very least, 'effectual, fervent prayer and strenuous
self-denying effort for the salvation of the benighted Chinese'.
Apathy and indifference concerning the eternal well-being of
the Chinese are a denial of the law of love. 400 million
Chinese, half of the world's unevangelized peoples, were
'perishing for lack of knowledge'!

To challenge the conscience, Hudson Taylor tells the story
of an incident in China. He was travelling along a canal in a
houseboat. A Chinese man in his party fell in the water and
did not come to the surface. Nearby were fishermen trawling
for fish. Hudson called for their help. They shouted back, 'It is
not convenient!' After he offered them money, they tried to
barter. In exasperation Hudson offered them all that he had
on him. They came over in their own good time, dragged the
river and found the body. Hudson tried artificial respiration
without success, as the man had been under water too long.
To Hudson Taylor, this speaks of the godless mind which is
indifferent to the value of human life, but it is also a picture
of the apathy of Christians who are content in their own
salvation and are reluctant and slow to raise a hand while
others die in sin and go to eternal damnation.

ESTABLISHING THE CIM IN CHINA

On 30 September 1866, a party of eighteen adults (which
included nine unmarried ladies) and the four Taylor children

The party that travelled to China on the Lammermuir

disembarked from the sailing ship *Lammermuir* at Shanghai. The journey had taken four months and they had survived two typhoons. Their arrival was at a time when there were only ninety-one Protestant missionaries in the whole of China. The party immediately adopted Chinese garb. They then moved as soon as possible to Hangchow (Hangzhou), 100 miles south-west of Shanghai. Hangchow was the capital of the coastal province of Chekiang (Zhejiang) and was strategic for establishing an initial base for the mission. Ningpo was a hundred miles to the east.

In Hangchow the missionary party were able to rent an old mansion with about thirty rooms, which were capable of being developed into sixty rooms. This was ideal for the mission headquarters. The house next door was procured for a boys' boarding school and put under the leadership of Mr Yu. A medical clinic was established, as was a printing press for literature in different dialects. On 16 July 1867 a Chinese church was formed, with Wang Lae-djung as pastor and with three other elders. There were eighteen members and fifteen applicants for baptism. Mr Tsiu was church evangelist and he was assisted by two exhorters. This was to be an independent Chinese church, responsible for its own affairs. A new and larger chapel site was purchased for them, but in the mission's name.

The first two years were of crucial importance. Hudson Taylor's many critics regarded the venture as foolhardy, ill-considered, presumptuous and doomed to failure. They were only too ready to let loose their criticisms at any opportunity. Hudson Taylor's friends held their breath. His leadership skills were indeed to be tested to the full, but he had counted the cost and held firm and resolute. The Ningpo church, left behind from his first visit to China, had matured. It now had fifty-nine Chinese members and had trained half a dozen excellent evangelists. These evangelists now helped Hudson Taylor in the vanguard of the advance. They, with other helpers, were a tower of strength. Without them there could have been no expansion.

By the end of 1867 six major prefecture cities, two county towns and three market towns were settled by a CIM missionary. Each missionary was accompanied by a Chinese evangelist. This was an amazing achievement in such short time. The large cities, governed by prefects, were Ningpo, Hangchow, Shaohsing (Shaoxing), Taichou (now Linhai), Wenchou (now Wenzhou) and Nanking. Nanking was also the second city of the empire, as well as capital of the province of Kiangsu (Jiangsu). It stood on the Yangtze River up from Shanghai. The Yangtze was also navigable for over a thousand miles further inland, deep into the heart of China. Here was the way forward for the CIM advance.

The beginning of gospel work in Wenchou in late November 1867, is worth mentioning. George Stott (d. 1889) was the missionary who settled there as his life's work. He was a one-legged Scottish schoolmaster. Wenchou was about 200 miles down the coast from Ningpo, in the same coastal province of Chekiang (Zhejiang). It was isolated by a ring of mountains on three sides and the ocean was the only natural outlet. Thus Wenchou had been spared the iconoclastic ravages of the Taipings. The Chinese dialect spoken there was incomprehensible to others. Its citizens were proud of its splendid temples and they thought their gods were of 'a superior kind'. The work of the gospel was slow but steady. The first Christian church there was built in 1878 in Chengxi Street. No one could possibly know then that Wenzhou was to become the area in China with the highest population of Christians. Up to 14% of its seven million inhabitants now profess to be of Christian persuasion.

In a letter to Grattan Guiness, Hudson Taylor writes, 'The difficulties of the work, intrinsic and extrinsic, are so great that, apart from the mighty power of God, we should indeed have a hopeless task before us.' In the first eighteen months the mission had to face much ill health, a death, major riots, unprincipled dissension from a small clique of their own missionaries and a sniping press in both China and Britain. Yet the annual day of prayer at the end of the year 1867 was full of praise to God for all that he had done and a joyful anticipation for the future. By the end of the year, there were thirty CIM missionaries on the field, with five more on the way. The largest Protestant mission in China up to that time was the LMS, which after sixty years had thirty missionaries on the field. The absolute conviction at the CIM day of prayer was that, in spite of all the difficulties, God was going to lead the mission deeper into China.

SLOW PROGRESS

The further the CIM pressed inland, the fiercer the opposition became. This was backed by the majority of the literati, the mandarin class, who were the scholar-gentry backbone of the Chinese culture. The literati saw that Western ways and modernization were being imposed upon China more and more by unscrupulous foreign powers. They regarded all this as being subversive both of the ancient order and of their own way of life, and therefore as deadly poison for China. They considered the twin evils of the barbarians to be the opium trade (forced on the Chinese by the gunboat) and the missionary. In the view of the literati, both brought disorder. Reactionary xenophobia struck back. Everything that went wrong in China could be blamed on the Christians. False rumours about them gained credence among the superstitious and the volatile, leading to riots and murder. A show of strength by the British navy became necessary to stabilize matters in 1868, though this was definitely *not* at the request of Hudson Taylor, whose settled policy was to trust in God alone. This was not just a matter of policy; it was a matter of principle for him and the CIM.

The common people were, by and large, willing to listen to the gospel. After all, their gods had failed to protect them in the calamities of the Taiping Rebellion of 1850–64, during which over twenty million had died as a result of war, famine and rapine. They were willing to listen, at least for a time. The China Inland Mission tried to rise to the occasion, though to begin with progress was painfully slow. There were obstructions at every turn, including fierce criticism of them back in Britain.

In July 1870 Mrs Taylor was ill with dysentery when she gave birth to Noel. They both were dead within weeks. Hudson Taylor too was suffering from dysentery, an illness which was to dog him to his dying day. By August 1871 he had to return to England for health reasons and to be with his children. Organization and deputation work were also pressing. In London, on 28 November 1871, he was married to Jennie Faulding, who was one of the original *Lammermuir* party. The Taylors set up home at a new CIM headquarters at 6 Pyrland Road in Newington Green, London. Hudson Taylor also organized a council for the management of the home affairs of the CIM.

It happened that the American evangelist Dwight L Moody was on his second visit to Britain at that time. They shared the platform at the Mildmay Conference on 26–28 June 1872. After the singing of the popular missionary hymn, 'Waft, waft, ye winds His story', Hudson arose and addressed the conference. 'My dear friends,' he said, 'the wind will never waft it! If the blessed story of His love is to be taken to the dark places of the earth it must be taken by men and women like ourselves ... who wish to obey His great missionary command.' This gesture won the friendship of Moody, who was to be a good and influential friend for the CIM in years to come.

Hudson Taylor and his new wife Jennie were back in China by the end of November 1872. The tremendous task that lay ahead can be seen by the fact that, on the day of their departure to China, there were only fifteen colleagues on station — nine missionary men, five wives and one single woman. Ill health and death had taken their grim toll! Without the invaluable help of the Chinese evangelists and other helpers, where would the CIM have been?

Hudson Taylor visited as many missionary stations as he could. However, he injured his spine in a fall and had to return to England in 1874. By that time, the CIM had entered three inland provinces. Firstly, they had proceeded west from Nanking along the mighty Yangtze River and settled in the city of Anking (Anqing) in the inland province of Anhwei (Anhui). Secondly, they then travelled further along the Yangtze and occupied the city of Kiukiang (Jiujiang) in the province of Kiangsi (Jiangxi). Thirdly, they then took residence further west in the triple city complex of Hankow (Hankou), Hanyang and Wuchan (now all united as the metropolis of Wuhan). These three were situated in the province of Hupeh (Hubei), where the rivers Yangtze and Han join, and they had a combined population of over a million. This city complex was a strategic place to settle, in order to reach into the farthest regions of China to the north, west and south.

Hankow was a treaty port, though 700 miles inland. The Yangtze River was a mile wide and thirty feet deep at that point and was navigable for sizeable ships all the way from the sea. Hankow had already been the residence since 1861 of the remarkable and intrepid LMS pioneer missionary Griffith John (1831–1912). His intense pioneering spirit had taken advantage of the new freedom to go inland. His was a unique ministry. He had been blessed to see a church established in the Hankow area with 353 baptized adult members by 1875. Here was a colleague after Hudson Taylor's own heart. When the LMS ordered Griffith John to return to the coast in accordance with their policy, he had refused, and had won the argument! Griffith John believed in the primacy of preaching in the missionary mandate and nearly every day he was out and about preaching in the open air or from house to house. No wonder his labours were richly blessed.

Nevertheless, in spite of the progress made by the CIM, pressing problems relating to the mission were weighing heavily on Hudson Taylor. In addition, British government policy had hardened against missionary activity away from the treaty ports. Hudson Taylor could not accept prohibition on inland work.

At the end of the year 1874, he was back in England, confined to bed, where he had to lie on his back, and suffering excruciating pain. He was almost completely paralysed in his back and leg, and had a map of China pinned to the end uprights of his bed. From this bed Hudson Taylor issued a public appeal in a written article. He made a request for 'prayer that God will raise up this [coming] year eighteen suitable men' to go into the nine still as yet unreached provinces in China. A. J. Broomhall says, 'The CIM was at its lowest ebb since its inception. It was a brave and defiant act, made from a paraplegic's bed.' It was also an act of total conviction and faith in the faithfulness of God, who had called and who would provide. The apostles did not wait for permission from the authorities before evangelizing and obeying the great missionary command of Christ, and nor must he!

Hudson Taylor's article was published early in 1875 in *The Christian*, in C. H. Spurgeon's *Sword and Trowel* and also in other Christian publications. The appeal was also included in the new CIM official magazine called *China's Millions*, which was first published in July 1875. The astonishing response to this article proved to be a crucial milestone in the history of the China Inland Mission. A. J. Broomhall justly describes it as 'the point at which the tide of all missions to China turned'.

The advance of the gospel throughout China during the last quarter of the nineteenth century can only be described as remarkable and decisive. We shall trace this signal work of God in the next chapter.

9. Hudson Taylor: the triumph of faith, 1875–1905

At the end of 1874, as we saw in the last chapter, Hudson Taylor was back in England, confined to bed, suffering excruciating pain and almost completely paralysed in his back and legs. He had a map of China pinned to the end uprights of his bed, and from this bed he had issued, in a written article, a public appeal for 'prayer that God will raise up this [coming] year eighteen suitable men' to go into the nine still as yet unreached provinces of China.

The responses to the published appeal turned out to be astonishing, with no less than sixty serious applications. Eventually more than eighteen persons were accepted and they were in China by early 1876. There had been a resurgence of missionary enthusiasm in Britain around this time. This was partly in response to the news of the death in Africa of David Livingstone in May 1873, followed by his burial at Westminster Abbey nearly a year later. That may well have been a catalyst, but the 1870s and 1880s also represented the crest of the final wave in the tide of spiritual blessing known to history as the Evangelical Awakening in Britain and Ireland. The revival had commenced as early as the 1730s. Now the final climax issued in widespread spiritual blessing. Evangelicalism was in the ascendancy in the nation. It was characterized by intense gospel evangelization within the nation and a great popularity for conferences aimed at deepening the spiritual life. There was also a leap forward in all missionary activity. The China Inland Mission played a prominent role in the expansion of this missionary effort.

Into the inland provinces

The good hand of God in providence became evident immediately. Hudson Taylor arrived back in China with the last of his team in 1876. The aim was to go into the nine unreached provinces. The Chefoo (Yantai) Convention had just been signed. This gave foreigners much-needed official imperial protection anywhere in China. The timing was impeccable! Hudson Taylor seized the moment as the answer to prayer and forged ahead. In the next four years the whole of China was criss-crossed and recrossed by the pioneer journeys of CIM missionaries. They also settled in strategic places in all but two of the target provinces. This explosion of activity took the foreign and missionary community in China by surprise, and accounts of it thrilled the Christian public back at home.

Once again the overruling hand of God was evident in the terrible famine of 1876–79 in north China. The CIM was there, on the spot, to report and assist. The combined efforts of all missionaries in China were then marshalled, and generous support was provided by Britain and other nations. About thirty missionaries distributed famine relief in the heart of the areas affected. Deep inland, the Chinese saw with their own eyes missionaries, who had nothing to gain personally, risking their lives time and time again for them. Indeed, about a dozen did lose their lives as a result of typhus, cholera, dysentery or smallpox. This went a long way towards winning respect, and even appreciation, for the missionaries by the Chinese people involved. Jennie Taylor and others in the CIM were allowed to set up an orphanage right in the heart of the famine area. Thus Shansi (Shanxi), one of the northern provinces, was settled by the CIM for the gospel. It is estimated that up to thirteen million perished during this famine.

PASTOR HSI

It was during this time that an opium addict was converted in the province of Shansi. Pastor Hsi (Xi Zizhi, 1835–96) was a scholar who had taken the first of the three literary degrees. David Hill (1840–96) of the Wesleyan Missionary Society was in Shansi, aiding in famine relief. He sought to awaken interest in the Christian faith among scholars by offering prizes for the best essays on Christianity. Hsi wrote winning essays and soon became Hill's teacher in Chinese. Hsi's conversion followed in 1879. Hsi was freed from his opium addiction through the power of Christ and started to preach the gospel to others. Ordained by Hudson Taylor in 1886, he was made superintendent of three CIM districts. This was the famous Pastor Hsi whose powerful ministry was widespread and effective in the southern part of Shansi. He took the

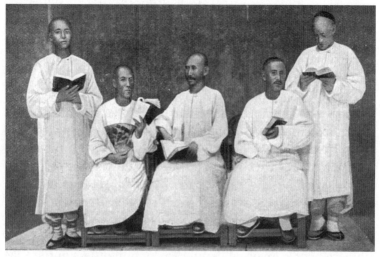

Pastor Hsi (centre), with a group of Christians from Shansi

name of Shengmo, or 'Conqueror of Demons' and gained a
reputation for the exorcism of evil spirits. He wrote many
hymns well suited to the Chinese. He also opened a total of
forty-five refuges for opium addicts, in four provinces. These
he called the 'Heavenly Invitation Office' (Tianzhaoju) and
used them to build self-supporting native congregations.
After his death there was a falling away in the refuges, due to
the loss of his strong leadership.

The case of Pastor Hsi highlighted the problem of the
traffic in opium, and this gave impetus to the movement to
ban this evil trade. It was so lucrative for Britain and the
Western powers. Indeed, Britain had at one time financed the
government of India, where the opium was grown, almost
entirely from this trade. The missionaries always resolutely
opposed the opium trade, but vested interests held sway until
it was eventually banned by Britain in 1911. This ban was
followed internationally in 1913. Benjamin Broomhall, husband to Hudson's beloved sister Amelia, had been the leader
of the struggle for abolition for many years. He died in 1911,
within days of having the satisfaction of knowing that an
irreversible victory had been won in the British Parliament.
To this day, the memory of the opium traffic and China's
consequent resentment towards the West, especially Britain,
constitute a running sore.

SEVENTY YEARS OF PROTESTANT MISSIONS TO CHINA

A general missionary conference was held in Shanghai in May
1877, commemorating seventy years since the coming to
China of Robert Morrison, the first Protestant missionary.
One of the highlights of the conference was the sermon given
by Griffith John on the theme, 'The Holy Spirit in connection
with mission work': 'The Holy Spirit is the source of all
spiritual illumination, the immediate source of all holiness,

Missionary Conference at Shanghai, 1877

the source of true spiritual unity, the fount of joy, the source of all power in dealing with souls, the inspirer of all true prayer.' John asked three questions: 'Are we and our converts filled with the Holy Spirit? Is a new revival [Pentecost] possible? How is the fulness of the Holy Spirit obtained?' He stated that one of the fundamental needs of the hour was for a genuine spiritual revival in China, not least among the missionaries themselves. The conference called for 'the Christian Church to evangelize China in the present gener-ation'. The evangelical principles that had been the bedrock of missions to China for the last seventy years, since the time of Robert Morrison, were still foundational.

However, it was at this conference that the first inroads of liberal theology into the mission field in China came to light. A small number of men, claiming to hold to orthodox evan-gelical theology, rejected the primacy of preaching the gospel for missionary work in China. They advocated that the primary place should be given to higher Western education and to reaching the most influential classes, on the grounds that this was 'more likely than preaching to the masses to overthrow superstition' and bring about moral improvement in China. W. A. P. Martin (1827–1916), Young J. Allen (1836–1907) and Timothy Richard (1845–1919) were proponents of this view. Hudson Taylor and Griffith John, both of whom were advocates of education in its place, nevertheless op-posed it as the main approach to mission. There was no breach of fellowship, but the conference did specifically endorse the primacy of preaching the gospel (biblical and evangelical) in the missionary mandate.

DOUBLING THE SIZE OF THE CIM

By 1881 Hudson Taylor saw the need for at least another seventy CIM missionaries. This was in addition to the ninety-six already in the field, in sixty-four locations. On 28 Novem-ber 1881, at a CIM missionary conference at Wuchan (Wuhan),

Hudson Taylor was led to pray specifically for 'other seventy' workers for China within three years, by the end of 1884: 'Within twelve months we could have forty-two [more] men and twenty-eight [more] women located and at work.'

By the time of Hudson Taylor's departure on another visit to England in February 1883, all but two of the targeted inland provinces of China had CIM missionaries resident in key cities, together with Chinese helpers. Yet such was the low state of CIM finances, and so stretched was the administration, that many questioned the wisdom of taking on such an immense commitment as that entailed in nearly doubling the size of the mission at a stroke. And it was not until February 1883 that the public call was made in *China's Millions* 'to unite with us in prayer ... for forty-two additional men and twenty-eight additional women, called and sent out by God'. Yet the date set was not altered; it was still to be by the end of the year 1884! Amazingly, all was fulfilled.

Three factors brought about success.

Firstly, on the trip to England, Hudson Taylor learned of a large donation for the specific task of expanding the work of the mission. This was seen as an answer to the prayer of faith. It settled the fears of the friends of the CIM who were concerned about the danger of overstretching resources. This gift turned out to be the first of a number of generous donations.

Secondly, as Hudson Taylor engaged in a round of speaking engagements, from large public conventions to small gatherings in private homes, it was a common testimony that he was 'a man filled with the Holy Spirit'. The fire and passion that he manifested for his Master and His cause melted many hearts to tears, and his personal counselling was equally effective. He was aware that he was riding a tide of deep spiritual blessing in the land, and he saw this as an answer to the prayers sent up to heaven for many years on behalf of China.

Thirdly, between 1881 and 1884, a series of evangelistic missions occurred in connection with the visits to Britain from the USA of Moody and Sankey. All classes of people

Five members of the Cambridge Band in 1900

were touched by the power of the gospel, not least university men. In November 1882 Moody was persuaded to take a week's mission to each of Cambridge and Oxford universities. Against all predictions, these turned out to be a triumph, and the spiritual effects had a direct bearing on the CIM. Over the next two years seven young men, known as 'the Cambridge Seven' or 'the Cambridge Band', yielded their lives to the service of Christ. They offered to serve on the mission field with the China Inland Mission. This caused a sensation in the media, especially as one of them was C. T. Studd, of Eton and Cambridge University, a well-known cricket player and a member of the team that had won back the 'Ashes' for England in Australia during the winter of 1882–83. Another of the seven was S. P. Smith, of Repton and Cambridge University, who had won his blue as stroke-oar for Cambridge in the

Varsity boat race of 1882 against Oxford University. He was a very able speaker and debater. One of the seven, Dixon Hoste, was to become, in due course, General Director of the CIM. Another, W. W. Cassels, was to become Anglican bishop to West China.

There was a large influx of recruits for the CIM. But the spiritual standards for acceptance of candidates were not lowered in any way. If anything, the opposite was the case. The number of candidates accepted and sent in 1882 was nine; in 1883 there were eighteen, and in 1884 there were forty-six, making a total of seventy-three. The original 'prayer of faith' uttered by Hudson Taylor on 28 November 1881 had been confirmed by its fulfilment.

REMARKABLE EXPANSION

Hudson Taylor returned to China in January 1885 to be ready to receive the Cambridge Seven. He took with him twelve more new missionaries. At the valedictory meeting for the Cambridge Seven, early in February 1885, forty undergraduates dedicated themselves to the foreign mission field, wherever God would lead them. The blessing was not for the CIM alone! By May 1886, the CIM personnel on the field were 188, with 114 Chinese colleagues. Hudson Taylor's leadership and administrative skills were tested to the full, but he was right. The mission was prepared and ready to harness this sudden influx of raw candidates effectively — so much so, that *another hundred* were prayed for *within one year*. And they duly arrived in 1887!

The number of communicant members of Protestant missions in China in 1854 had been around 350. By 1887, after eighty years of Protestant missions in China, the number of communicant members totalled around 32,000, mostly in the coastal provinces. Real and encouraging progress had been made. Yet nowhere near 1% of the population had been reached with the gospel in any way. The work of evangelizing the whole nation of up to 400 million had hardly begun. Hudson Taylor regarded this state of affairs as 'appalling'. The only response to it for a visionary like Hudson Taylor was to 'advance, always advance'. This he did with an iron will of faith, nurtured by his close walk with God in his daily meditation in and praying over the Scriptures. He saw Christ in all the Scriptures and drank deeply of the wells of salvation. The joy of communion with Christ was his joy and strength, and this saw him through the duties of the day, however trying. Many times he was literally driven to his knees in prayer, by grave and apparently intractable situations that had to be dealt with.

At the second Shanghai Missionary Conference, in May 1890, Hudson Taylor was called upon to preach the opening sermon. In it he made an appeal to the conference for no less than a *thousand* new evangelists for China within five years. One is left breathless just trying to keep up with this man! Not only was the appeal adopted, but it is a fact of history that, by 1895, 481 men and 672 women arrived in China, representing over forty missionary agencies. By then the CIM itself had 630 missionaries, including wives. By 1900 the total number of Chinese Protestant communicant members of churches and mission stations approached, and possibly even exceeded, 100,000. Viewed in perspective, the CIM build-up ran like this:

Year	Missionaries	
1866	26	
1875	40	
1881	96	
1886	188	
1890	383	
1895	630	
1900	811	before the Boxer Uprising
	745	after the Boxer Uprising
1905	849	

INTERNATIONAL MINISTRY

Back in England once more in the first part of 1887, Hudson Taylor met Henry Frost from the USA. The latter invited Taylor to visit North America and speak to various student groups who were very interested in foreign missions. They wanted, in particular, to join in and support the work of the CIM. This was backed up by an invitation from D. L. Moody. So Hudson Taylor decided to return to China via the United States. While in the USA he spoke at the influential North-field and Niagara Conventions. In all, he spent three months in North America and, on leaving their shores for China, he was accompanied by a band of fourteen North American workers. This was only the first of many contingents from the USA and Canada. This development was totally unexpected by Hudson Taylor and it turned out to be the beginning of a worldwide ministry for him. A further visit to North America

Hudson Taylor with a group of North American missionaries

followed in 1889, and he also travelled to Sweden and Norway. The next decade saw him visiting many countries, including Australia and New Zealand. By 1900 the CIM had 811 missionaries in China from over twenty countries worldwide.

In China, other missionary societies followed up the pioneer work of the CIM. To the great credit of the CIM, it 'always welcomed any group which would share in the missionary task'. From time to time, therefore, the CIM withdrew from centres where other societies were now operating, in order to concentrate its attention upon districts that were still unevangelized.

THE ENDING OF AN ERA

All this progress was achieved during a period of increasing turmoil in China, as the Qing (Ching) dynasty (which included all the emperors since 1644) was tottering towards chaos and dissolution. War had broken out between China and Japan in 1894. The Chinese were humiliated at the hands of a thoroughly modernized Japan. The shock wave throughout China led to the realization of the necessity to embrace Western educational curricula and modernization. The contributions of missionaries came to be recognized as crucial to this awakening and development. Timothy Richard, Young J. Allen, W. A. P. Martin and Gilbert Reid were honoured at the highest level and their services utilized. The Young Men's Christian Association (a thoroughly evangelical movement at its inception) took root among the student and working youth in a number of cities, including Shanghai. This was as a result of a visit to China by John R. Mott, one of the founders in North America of the Student Volunteer Movement.

However, the emperor's orders in 1898 for China to modernize led directly to the anti-foreign Boxer Uprising in 1900 and the final overthrow of the Qing dynasty in 1912. The death of Queen Victoria on 22 January 1901 also heralded the end of the great 'Victorian Era' in Britain. Within fifty years the British Empire would be no more.

THE BOXER UPRISING

The formidable Empress Cixi, who hated all things foreign, grabbed the reins of power in September 1898. By 1900 she let loose the well-trained band known as the Boxers (Yihe tuan), so called because the clenched fist was their emblem and because of their energetic military exercises. The empress gave a secret order to 'slay all foreigners wherever you find them; even though prepared to leave your province, they must be slain'. The Boxers' war cry was, 'Uphold the dynasty, exterminate foreigners,' and they had emblazoned on their banners: 'By imperial command exterminate the Christian religion.' The floodgates of violence were opened by them, together with elements of the imperial army, in June 1900 at Peking. The violence spread throughout its province of Zhili (Hebei) and the neighbouring province of Shansi, where the governor was the ruthlessly anti-foreign Yu-Hsien (Yuxian), 'the Butcher of Shansi'. The blood-letting was short in duration, but bloody in intensity.

In China as a whole, 135 Protestant missionaries were martyred, together with fifty-three of their children, from ten Protestant missions. Of the total of 188 who were killed, seventy-nine belonged to the CIM. Special hatred was poured out on Chinese Christians, nearly 2,000 of whom paid the price of torture and martyrdom. Often their homes were burned, with them and their families still inside. Equal anger was poured out on the Roman Catholics, of whom forty-one missionaries were martyred together with some thousands of Chinese Roman Catholics.

Swift action by a consortium of eight foreign powers led to the relief of Peking in August 1900. Then orders were sent out to stop the bloodshed. Mercifully, these orders were largely obeyed by the authorities. Bands of Boxers continued

Hudson Taylor (left) with Griffith John (centre) and W. A. P. Martin.
This is the last known photo of Hudson Taylor.

to be a menace to everyone for a time, until they were finally brought under control and disbanded. After a little more than a year from the outbreak of the Boxer Uprising, and five months after the last martyrdom in August 1900, the work of the CIM had been re-established in most of their stations in China. Heroically, 132 members returned from the coast, together with fifty-seven new recruits. The next years were to be fruitful for the gospel. 'The blood of the martyrs is the seed of the church.'

THE FINAL YEARS

News of the outbreak of the Boxer Uprising reached Hudson Taylor while he was recuperating from illness in Davos, Switzerland. His constitution was completely worn out by the labour of years. He officially retired on 1 January 1903, with D. E. Hoste (one of the Cambridge Band) succeeding him as General Director of the China Inland Mission. Hoste served in that capacity until 1935.

On 30 July 1904, Jennie Taylor died in Switzerland. Hudson Taylor then determined to return to China one last time. He sailed on 15 February 1905, with his heart set on visiting Changsha, the capital of Hunan province. Hunan had been the last province to yield to foreign missionaries settling in their midst. However, since the Boxer rising, this province actually welcomed the missionaries and by now there were thirteen missionary societies there, with 111 missionaries working in seventeen central stations. Hudson's arrival in Changsha on 1 June 1905 was one of the crowning moments of his life.

It was here that he died peacefully in the presence of Howard and Geraldine Taylor on 3 June 1905. His body was carried down the Yangtze River in a coffin lovingly supplied and furnished by the Chinese Christians of Changsha. He was laid to rest at Zhenjiang beside his first wife Maria and their children who had died in infancy. The cemetery is no longer there, but the monumental stones are in a museum in the former British Consulate.

So ceased the earthly labours of Hudson Taylor, one of a race of spiritual giants raised up by God during the nineteenth century in Protestant lands, when evangelicalism was in its ascendancy. Hudson Taylor's missionary vision was

Hudson Taylor's funeral

clear-headed and biblical, his determination single-minded and sacrificial, his spirituality warm and Christ-centred. Not the least of his achievements was welcoming and harnessing the energies of his North American brethren for the CIM, which led to the organization becoming a truly international missionary society during his lifetime.

Hudson Taylor would not want to be remembered except as one of a body of many, all raised up and called of God, to carry the good news of salvation to a lost world, in obedience to the command of Christ. He regarded himself as an unworthy servant of Christ. His motto, 'Advance, always advance', still stirs the heart today.

10. The beginnings of a new century, 1900–1910

THE TWENTIETH CENTURY

One of the lessons that we learn from the history of the gospel in China during the nineteenth century is that zealous, dedicated, consistent and prayerful witness for Christ had been blessed by God, whatever the political and social chaos prevailing in the nation. Indeed, by 1900 the gospel was well established in China, with about 100,000 communicant members of Protestant churches.

The next fifty years, up to 1950, saw a period of growth in the Protestant churches to about 1,000,000 communicant members and a number of gifted Chinese Christian leaders taking a leading role in the life of the local churches. This all occurred in a period of China's history just as turbulent as that of the nineteenth century.

For the following fifty years, to AD 2000, Chinese Christians lived under an atheist Communist regime and without any missionary presence in China. Yet Protestant evangelical believers multiplied towards 100 million in number. This constitutes one of the great stories in the history of the church.

EFFECTS OF THE BOXER UPRISING ON THE GOSPEL MISSIONS

Though the 1900 Boxer Uprising was put down speedily, the effects of the murderous hatred let loose on Christians had been traumatic for the missions. So, on 7 September 1900, 400 Protestant missionaries, from twenty societies, met in conference at Shanghai to take stock of their situation. It was recognized that the restraining hand of God had been clearly evidenced time and time again in the midst of the troubles and that the swift end to the uprising had prevented the troubles spreading to many more provinces. Many missionaries had chosen to stay and suffer with their Chinese brethren. There was also a determination on the part of surviving missionaries, who had been forced to flee to the coast, to return to their stations as soon as possible, accompanied by additional recruits.

The aftermath of the Boxer persecution in Shansi province, where persecution had been the bloodiest, led to a rallying of the churches there. Some fine Chinese Christian leaders had emerged in the midst of the furnace of affliction and many churches had learned to stand on their own feet to a greater extent. What followed was a fruitfulness in spiritual life and witness which led to a marked growth in membership. This fruitfulness was not confined to Shansi.

THE ISSUE CONCERNING REPARATIONS

The question of claims for compensation for loss of life or property, both by missions and by Chinese Christians, soon came under debate. Each society adopted its own individual policy. It was clear to the missions that there ought to be a clear-cut difference between the policies of the secular powers and those of the missionaries. A money-conscious nation like the Chinese would recognize the difference. The China Inland Mission and its associates, which had borne the brunt of the persecutions, set an admirable example. The CIM formally decided 'not to enter any claim against the Chinese government, but to refrain from accepting compensation even if offered to them'. This stand of principle was made in order to keep church and state, religion and politics separate, even though the cost of sustaining the refugees and re-establishing works from scratch was heavy, and fell on the mission. However, nearly all the denominational missionary societies decided to accept reparations for damaged property, for individual missionaries who suffered and for Chinese Christians, who likewise had suffered at the hands of the Boxers. For instance, the American societies made a united presentation of their claims through the US Department of State. America insisted that a large proportion of the reparations due should be used by China herself on educational projects.

An acid test concerning compensation came on the first anniversary of the date of the massacre at Taiyuan in the province of Shansi. Taiyuan was the scene of the bloodiest massacre of missionaries and Chinese Christians during the uprising. The massacre had been masterminded by the then governor, the ruthless anti-foreign Yuxian, 'the Butcher of Shansi'. Thirty-five Protestant British, twelve Roman Catholics and about thirty Chinese Christians had been beheaded on 9 July 1900 alone. The new governor, Cheng (Cheng Chunxuan), invited the missions for an official welcome back, and for direct face-to-face negotiations concerning reparations. The delegation was led by D. E. Hoste and A. Orr-Ewing of the CIM, and they had an official escort for the last thirty miles into Taiyuan. They were greeted on 9 July 1901 by an immense crowd waiting at the great south gate. Among them were many delighted Christians, 'their faces showing clear traces of their sufferings'. Rain fell shortly after their arrival and this was regarded as a propitious sign. After an official dinner, a memorial service was held at the site of execution. There were other elaborate Chinese ceremonies, and then formal discussions concerning reparations took place.

Memorial at Taiyuan to the martyrs killed in the Boxer Uprising

Claims from the missions were expected by the Chinese authorities to be exorbitant. Yet the CIM refused all compensation for itself. The basis of compensation for individual Chinese Christians was settled after careful consultation with Chinese Christian leaders. A letter addressed to all churches linked with the CIM set out the policy:

> Christians who have had relatives murdered and are willing that they should have laid down their lives for the Lord's sake, and do not wish to report the case to the official, will be following the best course... Those who have been wounded, and are maimed or disabled, but who have property and are able to support themselves, and are willing to forgive their enemies and therefore do not wish to report the matter to the Official, will do well. [Others should follow the normal process of law for compensation from the temporal government in vindication of law and order; this is also recognized as being of God.] ... There must be no carelessness or overstating, lest by your falseness the Lord's name be dishonoured.

All claims were to be truthful and were to be itemized carefully, then investigated locally by trustworthy men and confirmed by the elders before submission to the authorities. Xu Puyuan was recognized as the leading elder.

Dixon Hoste

The climax of this process was when Dixon Hoste submitted a statement of the CIM losses to Governor Cheng and his associates. Hoste added that no compensation would be claimed or accepted by the CIM and associate missions. The governor was incredulous. Hoste was then given liberty to explain the Christian thinking behind the policy. The governor responded generously with a proclamation of honour concerning the Christians' conduct. This remarkable proclamation was to be placarded permanently wherever the CIM had worked and suffered throughout the Shansi province.

THE ISSUE CONCERNING THOSE WHO HAD RECANTED THEIR FAITH

The other problem of common concern to the churches was the treatment of the members who had recanted their faith under duress and who now wanted readmission:

> The ground we have taken is that anyone recanting, places himself by his own act outside the church, and it

remains for those concerned [the local church] to consider the question of his readmission. We find that
there have been great varieties in the degree and manner of recantation. In many cases certificates have been
issued by the mandarin as a temporary expedient for
averting extreme penalties while the storm lasted. Many
local officials had shrunk from carrying into effect the
sanguinary orders of the governor [Yuxian] and hit
upon this device to tide over the difficulty. Other cases
[present] varying degrees of conformity to idolatry. You
can understand how extremely difficult our position is
... by any want of sympathy and love, nothing could be
easier than to quench the smoking flax, and simply
drive the poor, disheartened, suffering Christians to
despair. Yet, not to deal clearly and decidedly with the
matter would mean the end of all discipline and church
order in the future.

The poignancy of the situation was evidenced everywhere
as, in place after place, the grim details of torture, maiming,
terror and coercion, shame and bitter grief were revealed.
Dixon Hoste called it 'the most painful experience of my life'.
About 250 repentant former members were reinstated.

It was Dixon Hoste's conviction after his visit to Shansi
that 'The former basis of full independence of Chinese
churches, assisted by missionaries, led to a stronger Church
than those with joint leadership and responsibility shared by
Chinese and missionaries together.' Behind this statement
was the missionary strategy of seeking to establish self-
governing, self-supporting and self-propagating churches, but
the full implementation of this in China was in practice
illusive. Full independence only became a reality after the
Communist takeover of China, when the Chinese church was
thrown entirely upon God for survival.

PROTESTANTISM IN CHINA, 1900–1910

Protestant Christianity became considerably more diversified after 1900, as dozens of new missions, mostly small, established themselves in China. Also a large number of independent missionaries entered China. Between 1900 and 1919 the number of Protestant societies at work throughout China increased from sixty-one to 130. The theological menu became much more varied, including the advent of Pentecostal teachings. Modern Pentecostalism arrived in Hong Kong and Canton as early as 1907. This was an offshoot of the first wave of the Pentecostal movement that arose in California, USA, in 1906. By 1909 the Apostolic Faith Mission (Pentecostals) had a loose grouping of twenty-six missionaries 'sent to China by the Holy Spirit rather than by established mission boards'.

The Boxer Uprising shattered the sense of security that Chinese Christians felt under the protective wing of Western missions. Up till now there had been no urgency to separate. The new century brought change. Chinese Christians became more and more under pressure to shake off the foreignness of their religion and take control of their own churches.

Future indigenous Christian leadership arose from among the young people being educated in the rapidly growing number of mission schools, an increase which coincided with the abolition in 1905 of the straitjacket imposed by the imperial examination system. By the following year there were nearly 58,000 Protestant schools, compared with nearly 17,000 in 1890. Western education became all the rage.

INDIGENOUS CHURCHES

A new sector of Protestant Christianity came into being after 1900. This was the truly indigenous wing of the Protestant church. It was made up of a combination of organized church groups and individual independent congregations. Some of these churches interacted with the mission churches, and others went their own way. The forming of independent churches was actually banned by the imperial authorities, so the movement was slow to emerge.

In 1902, the Chinese Christian Union was formed in Shanghai by YMCA activists, with the express purpose of developing Chinese churches by the Chinese themselves. They produced a periodical, but failed to establish any churches. By 1927 the union had ceased to function.

In 1906 the congregation of the Presbyterian pastor Yu Guozhen (1852–1932) in Shanghai became independent, mainly for political reasons. It was renamed China Christian Independent Church. The congregation was drawn mainly from the emerging prosperous professional and commercial class in booming Shanghai. Most members retained their old denominational ties.

SHANGHAI CENTENARY MISSIONARY CONFERENCE 1907

How little progress had been made in giving leadership to the Chinese Christians can be seen by the fact that, after a hundred years of missionary activity in China, there were only seven Chinese delegates out of a total of 1,170 present at this centenary conference! Nevertheless, missions had made great gains numerically in the past twenty years of political confusion. By 1905 they had 3,445 Protestant missionaries and 178,000 communicant members. By 1910, within three years of the conference, the number of missionaries had increased to 5,144 and the number of communicant members had passed 200,000, double the number at the turn of the century.

The conference commemorated the arrival of Robert Morrison at Canton in September 1807. On his way to China, all alone and with no companion, Robert Morrison had been asked, 'Mr Morrison, do you really expect that you will make an impression on the idolatry of the great Chinese empire?' 'No, sir,' was his reply. 'I expect God will.'

The Shanghai Conference of 1907 brought to light some ominous signs for the future. Missionary work was becoming professionalized. The means of assisting the gospel were replacing the gospel itself. A liberal theology and a social gospel were making rapid advances among the missionary community. There was a strong ecumenical voice for church union on the basis of organization rather than doctrine. Western educational curricula marginalized the gospel. For an increasing number, Western education and medical work *were* the gospel. The ascendancy of evangelicalism was being challenged, but the largest missionary society in China by far, the China Inland Mission, remained true to the biblical gospel. It stood firm against all pressures and continued to pursue its proven ways. It also continued to develop its schools, medical clinics, hospitals and relief work.

THE YMCA AND YWCA

The Young Men's Christian Association in China had first been organized in mission colleges in 1885. By 1900 there were forty-seven associations in eight provinces. In 1901 a national convention brought together 170 delegates, over three-quarters of them Chinese. After this, the growth of the organization (originally founded on a thoroughly evangelical basis) was phenomenal and it developed a number of new and important types of work for young men. In addition to Bible classes and evangelistic services, programmes of educational lectures, debates, hostels, summer conferences, sports and social works were developed. Many of the revolutionary leaders and supporters came through the YMCA because the Chinese young men were hungry for Western knowledge. The YMCA set a new standard of turning Christian organizations over to the control and support of the local Chinese. Strong links were made with students going abroad to study, to aid them in the process of adjustment to their new environment.

In 1907 John R. Mott conducted the first organized meetings to reach government schools in the big cities with the gospel. So successful were these that by 1913 he was leading meetings, together with G. Sherwood Eddy, which had attendances averaging over 2,000 per night. Admission was by ticket only and was limited to teachers, students, officials and members of the local gentry. Many thousands enrolled to study Christianity. The emphases of both Mott and Eddy were on the renewal of China by social uplift. The liberal belief that social activity was itself the gospel began to dominate in the YMCA movement.

Ting Limei (Ding Limei, 1871–1936) became the first travelling secretary of the Chinese Student Volunteer Movement formed through the YMCA in China. Limei, a pastor in the province of Shantung (Shandong), had suffered for his faith in the Boxer Uprising. At Shantung Union College, under his leadership, over 100 boys decided to enrol for the Christian ministry. In 1910, the Chinese Student Volunteer Movement for the [Christian] Ministry was formed with the motto: 'The evangelization of our mother country and the world in this generation.' Ting was travelling secretary for twenty years. The breathtaking optimism of this type, so much the product of 'Western nineteenth-century optimism' at its height, was to be dashed to the ground by the searing experiences of the First World War of 1914–18.

The sister organization, the Young Women's Christian Association, followed the same programme as the YMCA, although on a smaller scale. In Shanghai, the YWCA started programmes for the women and girls employed in the factories that were beginning to make Shanghai the industrial centre of China. By 1913 there were three city associations and thirty-three student associations.

REVIVAL, 1908—11

A remarkable spiritual revival had broken out at Pyengyang in Korea during the Presbyterian new-year Bible class of 1907, a meeting with over 1,500 men. After the Shanghai Missionary Conference, a Canadian Presbyterian missionary named Jonathan Goforth (1859–1936), who had been almost hacked to death in the Boxer Rebellion, went to see for himself. He travelled back from Korea through the southern part of Manchuria, 'spreading the flame of revival' during 1908. His message was addressed as much to spiritually lethargic church members as to the unconverted. He revealed to the hearts of church members their 'unfaithfulness and ingratitude to the Lord who had redeemed them'. He exposed the sins of idolatry, superstition, jealousy, hatred, uncleanness, pride, falsehood, dishonesty, worldliness and avarice. The burden of his message was that while such sins remained unconfessed and undealt with, men and women bearing the name of Christ could obtain no such blessing as had come to the Korean church. This was an unprecedented revival for China, and gained nationwide and international publicity.

Jonathan Goforth was then given leave to pursue a ministry of 'revival meetings' throughout China. Often he would preach to crowds of up to 25,000 people. Thousands professed conversion and many Christians were awakened to a renewed repentance and a full recommitment to the Lord. Such an openness to listen to the gospel by so many Chinese was unprecedented in the history of the gospel in China. It was to usher in a period of spiritual blessing and growth. By 1920 the total Chinese Protestant community grew to more than 300,000 communicant members, from the 100,000 of 1900. After meetings, the spiritually awakened hurried home to their villages to encourage relatives and friends to go and experience God for themselves. Visitors who travelled in from the countryside were often deeply exercised by the Spirit of God, even before reaching the meeting. Falling on their faces or kneeling in the streets, oblivious to everything, they cried out for forgiveness of their sins by God.

In 1908–9, a revival came to Shansi under the preaching of Albert Lutley and a Chinese evangelist named Wang Qitai. Albert Lutley was no stranger to Shansi, as he and his family had been forced to flee from there during the Boxer Uprising and his two daughters had died during the escape. This revival came first to Shansi, then to the provinces of Shensi (Shaanxi) and Szechwan (Sichuan). It was remarkable for the depth of conviction of sin on believer and unbeliever alike. Whole congregations fell on their faces to the ground in prayer and confession, very quietly, without demonstration or excitement. The presence of God was real and profound.

This wave of revivals continued from province to province in China until 1911. Some of the later meetings were accompanied in places by extreme emotional and physical manifestations. These were similar to those in the early Methodist Revival in England in the eighteenth century and to those in the frontier districts of the United States in the early nineteenth century. Then during 1911 public meetings became impracticable, as China became convulsed by armed rebellion and lawlessness.

Edwin Orr records:

> The Christian and Missionary Alliance noted that 1908 was a year of glorious revival in South China. Into the year 1911 the revival seethed. The revival in China in these years proved to be the beginning of an indigenous spirit in the Chinese churches. In spite of opposition, a way was being prepared for the coming of greater awakening among the Chinese Christians *who were coming of age at last* (emphasis added).

In 1910 the total number of Chinese Protestant communicant members passed 200,000, a remarkable increase from about 100,000 in 1900. The revival was to maintain the momentum.

WORK AMONG THE TRIBES OF SOUTH-WEST CHINA

The minority tribes in south-west China were extremely poor and lived morally degraded lives in fear of evil spirits everywhere. Drunkenness and immorality were rife. The Chinese treated them as less than animals.

A notable work was begun in 1896 among the minority Miao people living in Kweichow (Guizhou) province. The work was born in suffering, as William S. Fleming of the CIM and the first Miao convert, Pan Sheoshan, were both murdered on 4 November 1898.

The next year, James R. Adam of the CIM opened a work among the Miao. He opened a chapel and a small school for boys in the village of Anshun. In preaching Christ, he confronted their idolatry aggressively. He demanded the burning of everything associated with idolatry and spiritism and the cutting down of their hallowed 'spirit trees'. In 1902 twenty Miao believers were baptized and by 1907 no less than 1,200 had been baptized. New converts had an eighteen-month programme of instruction and observation of their lives before being admitted to baptism. By the time of his death in 1917, when he was killed by lightning in his own home, Adam had baptized nearly 7,000 Miao.

Samuel Pollard, a Cornishman and Bible Christian Methodist, had worked in Kweichow since 1888. In 1904, at Chaotung (Zhaotong) in north-east Yunnan province, four Miao men appeared out of the blue on his doorstep, having travelled over 400 miles to hear the gospel. They had set out on a journey of 200 miles through the mountains to James Adam, who, finding that they lived near to Samuel Pollard, had then sent them all the way back to him! Pollard set up a new centre at Shimenkan (Stone Gateway) on the Yunnan-Kweichow border. By the end of that year, 4,000 Miao had come to visit him from the mountains all around. By 1910 he witnessed what was almost a mass movement into the church. New converts were given Christian names at baptism. The Miao had no personal names, so the gospel was giving them the dignity of personal identity. Pollard reduced the language to writing, devising a script for it, and translated the New Testament. He died of typhoid fever in 1915.

In 1906, Arthur Nicholls of the CIM pioneered a new work further west, in Yunnan province, not far from the capital Kunming. This was in response to a plea by two Miao who were suffering from leprosy to bring the gospel to them and their people. The work thrived and spread from the Miao to the Yi and Lisu communities nearby. By the time of the Communist takeover in 1950, there were over 200 churches and outstations, many health clinics, primary schools and a Bible college, just in the area around Sapushan alone.

Another notable work was among the minority Lisu people in the mountains of Yunnan in south-west China along the Burma border. James Fraser (CIM) was a graduate engineer and gifted musician. He worked among the Lisu people from 1913. Often working alone, among people bound by demon-worship and drunkenness, he became a prey to depression and illness. He set himself to prayer. By 1916 he began to see the Lisu turn from animism and demon-worship to Christ. By 1918 2,000 tested believers had been baptized and formed a strong indigenous church. The Bible, a catechism and a hymn book were printed in a script devised by Fraser. The Bible in their own language gave them a new sense of identity and helped lift them from the degraded culture of the past. Fraser became a superintendent on the China Council of the CIM. He died of malaria in 1938. Isobel Kuhn (1901–57) was to write many books about the Lisu church. By 1949 there were about 15,000 Lisu Christians. In the year 1993, the official Chinese government figures gave the number of Lisu Christians as 200,000 out of a total Lisu population of 575,000!

A page from the Lisu New Testament

One is reminded of the scripture: 'God has chosen the foolish things of the world to put to shame the wise, and God has chosen the weak things of the world to put to shame the things which are mighty; and the base things of the world and the things which are despised God has chosen, and the things which are not' (1 Corinthians 1:27-28).

11. Birth of the republic and World War, 1910–20

By 1920, the number of communicant members of the Protestant community had increased to more than 300,000 from 200,000 at the beginning of the decade. Also, Chinese Protestant Christians were being brought into local, provincial and national government. Altogether, this period was a fruitful time for the gospel in China, in spite of the World War of 1914–18.

THE END OF THE QING DYNASTY

The failure of reform, and that of the Boxer Uprising, convinced many that the only remedy for China's ills lay in outright revolution and modernization. The chief advocate for a republic was Sun Yat-sen (Sun Yixian, 1866–1925). His influence rapidly increased. A revolutionary military uprising broke out on 10 October 1911 at Wuchan, capital of Hupeh province. By late November 1911, fifteen of the twenty-four provinces had declared their independence from the Qing empire. The Republic of China was proclaimed in Nanking on 1 January 1912, with Sun Yat-sen as provisional president. The Qing dynasty collapsed. The child emperor Puyi abdicated the throne on 12 February 1912 along with the empress dowager. Imperial China had come to an end. The era of modern China begins.

THE REPUBLIC OF CHINA, 1912—16

Sun Yat-sen (1866–1925) was the popular political leader among the students and the overseas Chinese. He had received much of his education at the hands of Protestants in Honolulu. He was known to be a Christian and had been baptized in 1884 as a Congregationalist in Hong Kong. There he qualified as a doctor. Dr Sun Yat-sen's political philosophy was summed up in his 'Three Principles of the People'. These principles were: nationalism (overthrowing the Manchus and ending foreign hegemony over China); democracy (popular elected republicanism); and people's livelihood (social welfare). He liked to compare these three principles with Abraham Lincoln's 'Of the people, by the people, for the people'.

After a coup that he had plotted failed, he based himself abroad for sixteen years, in Europe, the United States, Canada

Memorial in Guangzhou (formerly Canton) to Dr Sun Yat-sen

and Japan. He lectured and raised funds for his party, which eventually was to emerge in 1912 as the Kuomintang (KMT, or Chinese Nationalist Party). Sun Yat-sen returned to China in December 1911. However, Yuan Shikai, who commanded the Northern Beiyang army, seized the power from Sun Yat-sen, who stood down to prevent civil war. Soon Yuan Shikai declared himself emperor, but was forced to abdicate in 1916. He died shortly afterwards, leaving a power vacuum.

With the end of the old dynastic imperial rule, there was a new beginning. It was a time of hope, free and unrestrained by the conventions of the past. Many students went to study overseas, to Japan, USA and Europe. In 1915 a new movement among intellectuals arose, with Peking University as its centre. This was the New Culture Movement. Intellectually it roamed freely, unrestricted by the narrow forms of the Confucian past. This movement did not accept Western values uncritically and was strongly patriotic, wanting distinctively Chinese answers to Chinese questions.

THE REPUBLIC OF CHINA, 1916—20

The power vacuum in China created by the abdication and death of Yuan Shikai in 1916 ushered in the era of the warlords. This was a period of complex chaos, during which China was ruled by shifting coalitions of competing provincial military leaders. During the First World War, Japan seized the German holdings in the province of Shantung. The weak warlord government in Peking accepted this, and also that Japan should have authority in southern Manchuria and eastern Inner Mongolia. At the end of the First World War, the Treaty of Versailles confirmed Japan's claims in Shantung. The sell-out became public knowledge and led to massive student demonstrations on 4 May 1919 in protest. This sparked the national awakening known as the May Fourth Movement which rekindled the cause of republican revolution and kindled anti-foreign agitation by students.

Many student debating clubs appeared, in which students advocated social and political theories ranging across the whole political spectrum, including the newly emerging Russian form of Communism. Three things were resented: infringement on freedom of thought and expression, curtailment of China's sovereignty and disparagement of Chinese culture by foreigners.

MISSIONS UP TO THE FIRST WORLD WAR

The period leading up to the outbreak of the First World War in 1914 was one of intense activity by Protestant missions. The American denominational missions had in their hands the larger part of the medical, social and higher educational work undertaken by Protestants. At this period, Protestants led the field in China for these institutions. Their standards were higher than those of the state institutions and they were very popular. However, the care of these institutions and overseeing the structures of denominational church activities absorbed much of the energies and resources of the denominational missions, including their new recruits. By 1911 it is calculated that less than half of all the missionary force was engaged in any direct evangelistic work. The proportion is considerably smaller if one were to omit the China Inland Mission and its associates, who were devoted to evangelism in one form or another, even in their social and educational programmes. The rapid advance of liberal theology, with its emphasis on a social gospel, accelerated this trend away from evangelistic activity which aimed at a personal conversion to Christ and a clear testimony to the experience of saving grace.

Up to this time, Chinese converts of the Protestant missions were mainly from the middle and lower classes. They were mostly men, rather than women. The majority of converts were farmers, shopkeepers, artisans, street-vendors and labourers. While fairly large churches came into being in the cities, converts were more numerous in the rural districts.

In general, it can be said that, up to this time, the converts were noticeable for a clear change for the better in their character. The fruit was good. Vices such as the opium habit, gambling, unchastity, lying, cheating, backbiting and filthy language were abandoned. Dread of evil spirits was cast out. Truthfulness in business, forgiveness of enemies, a healthy family life, patience in persecution and zeal in witness were commonplace. In society around, this was recognized and often secretly envied. Ancestor worship was firmly rejected, although family pressures for Christians to compromise in this area were often intense.

There was a massive increase in the number of foreign missionaries seen in China from the time of Hudson Taylor's appeal at the 1890 Shanghai Missionary Conference. As recorded in chapter 9, he had appealed for a thousand new evangelists to be in China within five years. The appeal had been very bold, because the total number of missionaries in China at the time was under 1,300. Not only was the number fulfilled, but the increase of missionary candidates accelerated all the more. By 1914 there were 5,462 missionaries in China, a remarkable figure and one that represented an increase of over fourfold in less than twenty-five years. However, the majority of the new recruits only had a social agenda. With them, evangelism was a distinct no-no. The Christianity of the new members in their churches was, more often than not, nominal rather than real, social rather than spiritual. The world came into the church. The inability to give a clear testimony to the saving power of Christ in their lives became almost commonplace in the churches under the influence of the liberal 'gospel' and, even more lamentably, in the Chinese pastors and teachers trained by them.

ECUMENISM AFTER THE EDINBURGH WORLD MISSIONARY CONFERENCE OF 1910

The Edinburgh World Missionary Conference of 1910 led to ambitious plans in China to unite missions organically under one umbrella, with a minimalistic confession of faith. There had always been some co-operation in common projects which were beyond the scope or resources of individual missions, such as Bible translation work. But now the idea was to unite all missions and all churches in China into one body. The vision was for the twentieth century to usher in an ecumenical age for the Christian church — one united church for the whole world.

In 1913, the International Missionary Council, the offshoot of the Edinburgh Conference, organized a conference in Shanghai under the energetic leadership of John R Mott. The agenda was to arrange a survey of all the missionary fields in China, settle a common procedure for entering new fields, encourage evangelism by the Chinese of their own people, and to bring all the churches under one umbrella which was to be called the 'Chinese Christian Church'. A 'China Continuation Committee' was formed to carry on the work of the conference. This committee was extremely active under very able full-time secretaries, E. C. Lobenstine of the American Presbyterian Mission (North) and Cheng Jingyi (C. Y. Cheng, 1881–1939), pastor of a Chinese independent church in Peking.

In 1914, the China Continuation Committee invited A. L. Warnshuis of the American (Dutch) Reformed Mission to be National Evangelistic Secretary. He formed the Forward Evangelistic Movement and launched a campaign which held fourteen special conferences in that year alone. Laymen and laywomen helped with the preaching and the secular press was utilized. The YMCA and YWCA participated enthusiastically. Sunday schools benefitted from a national organization, producing much literature and holding summer training conferences for teachers.

SUMMER RESORTS

Summer resorts were set up as refuges for the foreign missionaries and their families from the dangerous summer heat. This brought together missionary families and gave opportunity for sharing news and having spiritual fellowship. Many a prayer meeting cemented friendships and stimulated the lonely worker. These resorts became prominent in such places as Peitaiho, Kuling, Kuliang and other smaller places. Conferences for study and the deepening of the Christian life were organized for missionaries, pastors and other Chinese Christian workers. Overseas speakers were invited regularly.

INDIGENOUS CHURCHES

The China Christian Independent Church pastored by the Presbyterian Yu Guozhen formed a national network of independent churches, named National Free Christian Church of China. By 1920 they had over 100 member churches under the banner of the China Christian Independent Church. They were to be found in all the major cities. By 1948 hundreds of churches nationwide were affiliated, in total having more than 10,000 members.

A smaller but comparable federation called the North China Association of Chinese Christian Churches was founded, centred in the cities of Shantung and Zhili provinces. One of the leaders was Zhang Bolin (1876–1951) founder of Nankai University, Tientsin.

MISSIONS DURING THE FIRST WORLD WAR (1914–18)

There was no marked change in the attitude of the Chinese towards Christians until after the end of the war. Openmindedness towards the gospel was still on the increase.

Proscription of German missionaries as a result of the war was overcome by the American Lutherans stepping in to fill their place. Otherwise missionary work continued normally, except that missionary doctors were drafted by their respective countries for war duty. Even here, stability was maintained by replacement doctors from the USA. 200,000 Chinese labourers were recruited by the British and French armies in order to work behind the fighting lines in France. The YMCA in England and America undertook evangelistic, educational and recreational work among them. Missionaries were commissioned as officers to manage these Chinese.

The effectiveness of the Protestant missionary educational system in China became evident during this period when relations with the government and government schools were friendly. Only a third of the total number of the students came from Christian homes. Christian schools and colleges represented 5% of total schooling in China. Their influence was far beyond their numbers. At the peace conference in Paris four out of five of the Chinese delegates were former students in mission schools! However, there were criticisms. Complaints were made about the poor quality of the Chinese scholarship in the Christian higher colleges. Too often professing Christian graduates regarded themselves as elitist and felt out of place in their humble local churches; their Christianity was more nominal than real, and career-based rather than church-based.

The leading colleges were Canton Christian College, which became a university in 1916, and North China College in Peking. In 1915 the Union Theological College in Peking, where instruction was mainly in the English language, became part of Peking University. In all, by 1917 there were ten new or extended seats of higher education, mainly funded from America. There were sixty-four theological or Bible schools recognized by the China Continuation Committee in 1917. These had 1861 students, of which 128 were college graduates and 402 were of middle-school grade. Their constituency served mainly the liberal segment of Protestants, which made up a quarter of the whole by this time.

The range and extent of the social work of missionaries and churches (evangelicals included) brought credit to the name of Christ in the eyes of the Chinese. Examples were famine and plague relief, havens for the blind, deaf and dumb, orphanages, opium refuges, refuges for oppressed women, boys' clubs and free schools. Also social service leagues and clubs opposed the many evils in society such as the opium trade, foot-binding of infant girls, concubinage, slavery, infanticide, suicide, polygamy, bribery and all forms of vice. The Salvation Army arrived in China in 1916 and by 1919 had thirteen centres.

The war years saw fairly rapid progress in transferring responsibility to Chinese Christian leaders, especially in social work and higher educational establishments. The Chinese, especially in the main cities like Shanghai, also took a larger share of responsibility in financing them.

THE 'TRUE JESUS CHURCH' SECT

The sect calling itself the True Jesus Church was founded in Peking in 1917 through the vision of Paul Wei (Wei Enbo, 1876?–1919). This movement was Pentecostal, millenarian and exclusivist. It rejected the doctrine of the Trinity and taught the unitary and undivided 'True God'. It also observed Saturday as the Sabbath and regarded 'foot-washing' (see John 13:6-10) as a sacrament and essential for salvation. Baptism had to be by face-down immersion. Also it called itself the 'Universal Correction Church', as it regarded all other churches as corrupt and heretical. It believed that the war in Europe between Christian nations was final proof that we are in the final years leading to the Second Coming of Jesus. Salvation was to be found only with the True Jesus Church. They drew their numbers from the Seventh Day Adventists and by poaching from established churches.

Within two years they had sixty churches, in five provinces, and over a thousand followers. After the death of Paul Wei in 1919, the sect spread rapidly through the ministry of the evangelist Barnabas Zhang (Zhang Dianju).

THE AFTERMATH OF THE FIRST WORLD WAR

The end of the First World War saw the prestige of the Westerner sharply reduced in the eyes of the Chinaman. Also, the refusal by the powers to grant China equal nation status at the peace talks in Paris caused extremely bitter anti-foreign feeling to erupt in China, especially among the young students. Worldwide there was a rising tide of nationalism. China was included in this. China refused the benefits of the 'unequal treaties' to the new government of Russia and also the newly founded country-states of Europe. Indeed, abolition of the 'unequal treaties' imposed on China by foreign powers, from the Opium Wars onward, became a major platform of the Nationalist Party. From now on, the Christian missions could not be supported by the unquestioned prestige and power of the West. This was not a bad thing, as this was a step towards freeing the gospel from a perceived association with politics and hated Western imperialism. Of course all this did not happen overnight, nor was it welcomed by some missionaries, but the process had begun.

REACTION AGAINST LIBERAL THEOLOGY

Between 1910 and 1915 a series of booklets was published in the USA called *The Fundamentals*, which made a stand for the tenets of biblical Christianity which we now know as evangelicalism. It was a stand against the infidelity of liberal, rationalistic theology, which was taking over the denominations. Free distribution was organized so that all leaders in the Christian world, such as pastors, theological professors, theological students and missionaries, received copies. Over three million free individual copies were distributed. The ensuing controversy was very sharp. The significance for China of this stand for the historical gospel in America was that, after the First World War, the Americans took over leadership in world missions in terms of numbers of personnel and resources. So it was inevitable that this controversy should come to China. Evangelicalism was represented in China by the China Inland Mission and its associates, nearly all the smaller missions and a number of missionaries in the main Protestant denominational missions.

In 1920, the Bible Union was formed in China with a clear evangelical statement of faith. Its object was to resist the tide of liberalism in the missionary agencies of China. It lobbied the home boards of management, urging them to accept only candidates faithful to the biblical gospel. It also campaigned for the requirement of fidelity to the Scriptures in the religious teaching in the Christian schools and colleges of China. This action was resented. The conflict was a bitter one. By 1923, the Bible Union had over 2,000 members.

It was in 1912 that the CIM, with associates, passed the 1,000 mark for the number of missionaries in China. The CIM was a critic of sending Chinese students abroad for advanced theological training, especially to America. Too many students chose not to return, or were not able to adapt to the conditions they found in the churches when they did return. All too often they preached too academically, lacked the inward experience and power of the gospel and had been ruined by liberal theology. The CIM's chosen path to training Chinese Christian leaders was systematic Bible teaching, familiarity with the Bible background, priority of preaching, active evangelism and on-the-job training in local churches. Further training was given at evangelical Bible colleges and seminaries in China.

EVANGELISTIC CAMPAIGN TO THE SOLDIERS

It was in this chaotic situation that Jonathan Goforth was given the opportunity in 1919 in Hunan to have a ten-day evangelistic campaign among the soldiers under the command of the 'Christian General' Feng Yu-Hsiang (Feng Yuxian, 1882–1948). As a young soldier, Feng had been deeply impressed by the calmness of the American missionary martyr Mary Morrill at her execution by the Boxers in 1900. Later he came to faith under John Mott, and was baptized into the American Methodist Episcopal Church. The evangelistic campaign was by his invitation. Two meetings were held each day and Goforth baptized 507 officers and men. A Chinese Methodist pastor had a follow-up campaign with another 1,165 conversions. The chairman of the mission commented concerning the follow-up work that it was impossible to doubt the sincerity of the converted men. General Feng's men became known for their discipline and lack of ordinary camp vices. The men were taught to read and write and were instructed in useful trades.

Another opportunity to evangelize Feng's soldiers was extended to Goforth in Henan. Each meeting was attended by a thousand soldiers with their officers. During the thirteen-day campaign, 960 men were baptized. The final meeting had an attendance of 4,600. At that meeting, General Feng Yuxian prayed publicly, with tears rolling down his face as he knelt on the platform. Officers and men were sobbing and confessing their sins. In the words of Jonathan Goforth, 'It was a never-to-be-forgotten scene as the Holy Spirit came down and swept over that great gathering of officers and men, cleansing and purging, and purifying and reviving.'

12. Emergence of Chinese Christian leaders, 1920–30

The 1920s were to see major setbacks to the missionary movement, as a result of violent political moves against it. The Protestant church nevertheless saw consolidation and the emergence of indigenous Christian leaders of high quality. By the end of the decade, the number of communicant members of the Protestant community had increased to more than 350,000 from 300,000 at the beginning of this period. This was after the most severe test to membership in the mid-1920s.

THE REPUBLIC OF CHINA, 1920–30

In 1921 Sun Yat-sen headed a government in the south and sought to unify China. He was allied with the newly formed China Communist Party (CCP). The tiny CCP brought funding and co-operation from Russia. The 'Christian General' Feng Yu-Hsiang occupied Peking in 1924 and, with associates, invited Sun Yat-sen to re-establish the republic as president. Sun Yat-sen died of cancer while in Peking in 1925.

Sun Yat-sen was succeeded by General Chiang Kai-shek (Jiang Jieshi, 1887–1975). This was the era of regional warlords and the rise of the Communists. Natural disasters, civil war

and banditry made life almost impossibly difficult in rural
areas of China. Chiang Kai-shek turned against the rapidly
increasing influence and power of the Communists. The
irreparable breach occurred in April 1927. Chiang set up his
Nationalist (KMT) government at Nanking. By the end of
1928 all of China was nominally under Chiang Kai-shek's
control and his government received prompt international
recognition as the sole legitimate government of China. A
decade of substantial national consolidation and modernization by Chiang Kai-shek followed. But these efforts to
rebuild China were undermined by insubordinate warlords
and the implacable opposition and rising power of the China
Communist party. The result was that Chiang Kai-shek had to
be constantly on the field of battle. He had married into a
Christian family and he himself was converted in 1930.

THE EFFECTS OF CIVIL STRIFE IN THE TWENTIES ON THE CHURCH IN CHINA

Life under the warlords was an increasingly hazardous
matter. Kidnapping for ransom, murder and pillage occurred
all too often and, after 1920, missionaries and Chinese Christians were more and more sharing the sufferings of their
neighbours. In 1920 students in Peking, and elsewhere,
formed the Young China Association, which limited its
membership to those who had no religious faith. It was
virulently anti-Christian and was fuelled by rampant nationalism. In March 1922 a conference of the World's Student
Christian Federation was held in Peking. Delegates from all
five continents and most provinces of China attended. This
attracted much attention in China. In reaction to this Christian conference on Chinese soil, the Anti-Christian Movement was formed in Shanghai. They believed that science and
religion were incompatible. They also believed that Christianity was an ally of capitalism and imperialism, which were

oppressing weaker nations. Christian education became a target of the Anti-Christian Movement's demonstrations.

Since the May Fourth Movement of 1919, Chinese Christian students naturally discussed the national and international issues of the day, as seen from their point of view. They began distancing themselves from the foreigner, in order to escape the jibes of their fellow countrymen that they were traitors. At grassroots level, future independent Chinese Christian evangelists were being prepared.

On 30 May 1925, the police of the British and American Shanghai International Settlement opened fire on striking factory workers. This sparked off nationwide anti-foreign demonstrations and boycotts. British and American missionaries and their works became particular targets of agitation. These troubles also revived the 1922 Anti-Christian Movement. Students, especially those in government schools, colleges and universities, were the chief agitators. 'China for the Chinese!' was the cry of the students in their demonstrations and riots. Christian schooling came under severe criticism. Students in Christian schools felt their loyalties divided and increasingly sided with the 'China for the Chinese' bandwagon.

With the Nationalist army forces moving northwards from Canton in a campaign in 1926, the radicals took advantage to harass Christians. The right-wing KMT were allied to the left-wing CCP at that time. This led to loss of Christian life and destruction of property, notably in Hunan, Foochow and Nanking. It became a major time of crisis for the gospel in China, more threatening than even the Boxer Uprising of 1900. Nine out of ten foreign missionaries had to leave the interior on orders from their consuls. About 5,000 missionaries, more than half of the total missionary force of 8,235, left China on furlough in 1927. 2,000 of these never returned.

When Chiang Kai-shek gained national control and international recognition in 1928, the crisis and tensions eased somewhat and evacuee missionaries began to return inland. But Christian lives were still being taken.

A TOUCH OF REVIVAL

When the troubles in Shanghai erupted on 30 May 1925, Mr Paget Wilkes (1871–1934), founder of the Japan Evangelistic Band, had already been invited to lead a mission at Kuling, the largest summer resort and conference centre in all China. This became impracticable now. But, rather than cancel the invitation, Dr and Mrs Wood (Southern Presbyterian Mission and members of the World Wide Revival Prayer Movement) were convinced, after two weeks in prayer, that a valuable ministry could be carried out among the missionaries now coming into Shanghai. The team would be joined by Rev. and Mrs Russell Howden of England, on the invitation of the Stewart Evangelistic Committee. They all became convinced that the mission should also be extended to include evangelistic meetings for the Chinese.

A large hall at the Union Church in Shanghai was secured for the meetings. This was a step of faith, because the Union Church was a British one, and the Chinese wrath and intense hatred were particularly directed against the British at that very time. Leland Wang (Wang Zai), the young Chinese evangelist, was invited to share in the preaching ministry.

An all-day meeting commenced on 18 July, devoted to prayer, fasting and praise. The Chinese came in numbers. The whole church was then opened for the following meetings. It was filled with 700 daily, for six and a half weeks from 19 July to 4 September 1925. The agenda consisted of preaching morning and evening and a prayer meeting in the afternoon. Many were converted, and the prayer meetings were remarkable for the spirit of repentance and confession. A number of missionaries were revived. The Union Church recorded their gladness at the success of the event. They noted how all bitterness, and even national feeling, had been swallowed up in the tide of spiritual blessing. A veteran missionary declared that a foreign church crowded with Chinese was something that had never before been witnessed in Shanghai.

ECUMENISM

A national Christian conference had been convened at Shanghai in 1922 and had formed the National Christian Council as its crowning act. The agenda was ecumenical, to foster a united Church of China. The NCC sought to represent the various Protestant groups in China and co-ordinate their actions. It set itself to study the development of the church in China towards self-support, self-government and self-propagation. The statement of faith was minimalist. The majority of the council membership of 100 were Chinese, with a Chinese chairman, David Yu (Yu Rizhang, 1882–1936), the general secretary of the national committee of the YMCA. The American Southern Baptists did not join the council, and the China Inland Mission and the Christian Missionary Alliance both withdrew within four years.

By 1927, the breach between evangelicals and liberals was complete. Both pursued their separate paths and agenda and both continued to prosper in China. The liberals prospered in numbers and with their educational and social programmes. They also sought political influence. The evangelicals prospered in numbers and in spiritual fruitfulness and with their educational and compassionate ministries. For most missionary societies, the economic crisis following the Wall Street crash of 1929 had a major adverse affect on the recruitment of new workers.

THE 'JESUS FAMILY' COMMUNITY

The northern Shantung province, through which the lower reaches of the Yellow River flowed, suffered from regular floods and droughts. Intensifying natural calamities and economic hardships led to four million peasants migrating to Manchuria during the 1920s. Its relatively flat terrain easily lent itself to the scourge of banditry. Armies fought their battles there. Accordingly, the common people often sought to form themselves into communities of self-help, not only for defence, but also for economic mutual aid. The Jesus Family was an indigenous Pentecostal community of this type which attracted the impoverished Chinese peasants in Shantung.

The founder of the Jesus Family was Ching Tien-ying (Jing Dianying, 1890–1957). After the death of his parents when he was in his teens, he was educated in a Methodist school. In 1924, when he received his 'baptism of fire' at a Pentecostal (Assemblies of God) revival meeting, he was expelled from his membership of the Methodist Episcopal Church. In 1926 Ching founded the communal 'Jesus Family' in his home village of Mazhuang, in rural Shantung. His emphasis was on simplicity of life and sharing, imitating the example of the apostolic church in Jerusalem, as recorded in Acts 2 and 4. The rural communities of the Jesus Family were akin to the modern Israeli kibbutzim. However, not only was there no private ownership, there was segregation of the sexes, even for the married. All marriages were arranged by Ching. Children were brought up separately in nurseries, to ensure that parents did not develop a special love for them (something seen as being incompatible with love for Jesus). They validated this approach by citing the words of Jesus: 'Who is my mother and who are my brothers?' Jesus' answer to His own question was: 'Here are my mother and my brothers! For whoever does the will of my Father in heaven is my brother and sister and mother' (Matthew 12:48-50). They saw their commune as an end-time ark, to save them for the imminent coming of Jesus and as a pattern for the millennial reign of Jesus.

Also around that time, and in the same province, appeared the Pentecostal 'Spiritual Grace Society' and the 'Holy Spirit Society'.

THE 'TRUE JESUS CHURCH' SECT

The sect known as the True Jesus Church spread rapidly under the ministry of evangelist Barnabas Zhang (Zhang Dianju). By 1922 it had a membership exceeding ten thousand in a number of provinces. Fukien (Fujian) province became its centre of gravity and from there the sect spread to Formosa (Taiwan) and Hawaii by 1930. It had global claims and ambition (after all, it believed itself to be the Universal Correction Church, and that salvation was to be found nowhere else). According to its scheme of things, the TJC was fulfilling the 'Last Day' prophecy of Jesus that 'The lightning that comes from the east is visible in the west.' The TJC saw itself as destined to spread the message westward to the rest of the world. In the 1930s it became the largest indigenous Christian sect in China. In 1947, on its thirtieth anniversary, it reported 40,000 members in 570 churches, in eighteen provinces. Double that number were to be found overseas in south-east Asia, Taiwan, Hawaii, India and Japan.

CHINESE EVANGELICAL CHRISTIAN LEADERS AND MINISTRIES EMERGE

The 1920s saw the emergence of some outstanding Chinese Christian preachers and evangelists, whose ministries made a significant contribution to the total life of the Christian church in China. They were well suited to declare the gospel to their generation in a relevant manner. They could preach about revival, both the blessings and the dangers, from first-hand experience. Six such men gain our attention.

Andrew Gih

Andrew Gih (Ji Zhiwen, 1901–85) was one of fifty young Chinese men and women who consecrated their lives for full-time evangelistic ministry at the remarkable meetings in Shanghai of 19 July to 4 September 1925. He was moved in particular by the preaching of Paget Wilkes. Andrew Gih had been converted at the age of twenty-three while he was studying English at Bethel Mission Secondary School. Now he was baptized by Leland Wang and chose to take upon himself the name of Andrew. Immediately afterwards he formed the Bethel Evangelism Team, to spread the gospel in Shanghai and nearby cities. He was ordained in 1926 at Bethel Church, a part of an independent holiness mission in Shanghai.

The Bethel Mission had been founded by Jennie Hughes and Mary Stone (Shi Meiyu, 1873–1954). Mary Stone was the first Chinese woman to gain a medical degree in the USA (in 1896). She ran the hospital and nursing school.

Andrew Gih was to become a joint founder of the Bethel Worldwide Evangelistic Band with John Sung (see below and chapter 13).

Mary Stone

John Sung

Dr John Sung (Song Shangjie, 1901–44) was brought up in a Christian home. His father was an American Wesleyan Methodist pastor in Hinghwa (now Putian) in Fukien province. In 1920 he was sent to America to the Wesleyan University of Ohio and Ohio State University, where he was a brilliant student and earned a doctorate in chemistry within five years. Turning his back on lucrative career opportunities, he went to Union Theological Seminary in 1926 for theological studies. He was convinced of a call to Christian service.

John Sung and his father preaching in the open air

On 10 February 1927, in prayer, 'the love of God was poured out into his heart by the Holy Spirit given him' (see Romans 5:5). 'This is my spiritual birthday,' he says. 'The Holy Spirit poured onto me, just like water on top of my head. The Holy Spirit continuously poured onto me wave after wave.' The theologically liberal seminary authorities were not impressed, and when he stood up to them they confined him to an asylum for the insane for a period of six months! During this enforced confinement, John Sung read through the Bible many times. His whole experience in America was surely the best training he could possibly have had for his future ministry.

The Chinese Consulate eventually obtained his release and he returned to China. On his return, he immediately began his preaching ministry in the churches. His main topics were 'the blood of Jesus' and 'the cross of Christ'; his recurring themes were the need of repentance, saving faith and bearing a cross for Jesus. He also saw a place for faith healing. In 1931 he joined with Andrew Gih in founding the Bethel Worldwide Evangelistic Band, and together they commenced a nationwide evangelistic ministry.

Leland Wang

Leland Wang (Wang Zai, 1898–1975) has already been mentioned as the evangelist invited to minister at the Shanghai meetings of 1925. He was converted to Christ in 1920 at Nanking when he was a young naval officer. In 1921 he went ashore at his home city of Foochow and was attracted by hearing Christians sing at one of the meetings of the evangelist Miss Dora Yu (Yu Cidu, 1873–1931). She was a medical graduate turned evangelist, and since 1919 had been holding a series of evangelistic meetings for the Chinese at the Congregational church. Watchman Nee and his mother were among the converts there in 1920. Leland Wang joined fellowship with them and soon resigned his commission in the navy.

Leland Wang

It was in Leland's home in 1922 that the first informal meeting was held at which all were encouraged to minister. Watchman Nee was there, as was his mother. This insignificant gathering was indeed the original Brethren assembly of 'the Little Flock'. They were soon to be joined by Leland's brother Wilson Wang and two others. Watchman Nee and both his mother and brother were baptized in the river Min at Pagoda Anchorage. Faithful Luke and four others followed their example in the summer of 1923, and before the end of the year another eighteen people, mostly students, had been baptized into the fellowship. Nee worked for three years under Leland Wang; then in 1924 Nee went his own way.

In 1928 Leland Wang became the joint founder of the Chinese Overseas Mission, which was committed to the task of mission to the Chinese diaspora in south-east Asia. The mission board consisted of only Chinese nationals. The mission was the first of its kind and worked in as many as thirteen countries within his lifetime.

Watchman Nee and the Little Flock

Watchman Nee (Ni Shuzu, 1903–72) was the third of nine children born to a family in Foochow in the province of Fukien. His grandfather was a Congregationalist pastor. Nee, who was the eldest boy, later adopted the name Ni Tuosheng (Tuosheng means 'sound of a bell', hence 'Watchman').

Watchman Nee

He had exceptional intelligence and memory and was always top of his class at his Anglican school, Trinity College. He was converted at the age of sixteen. As a result, he became convicted of the sin of cheating at a past Scripture examination. He had to put the matter right, even if it meant expulsion. When he confessed, the missionary headmaster wisely took the matter no further. This act of obedience and self-humbling was rewarded when many of his classmates were converted through his testimony and the example he set of a changed life.

Nee's life work really began in 1927, when he set up in Shanghai an independent Chinese work on Brethren lines. It was called the 'Little Flock' after the hymn book which he published. Nee contended that there could only be 'one body

of Christ' in any geographic area, and a church planted on
any other basis was not a true church. The Little Flock
embedded the principles of self-support, self-governance and
self-propagation. Nee never ceased to regard missionary
societies and denominational churches as sectarian and in
need of repentance. His advice to Chinese Christians was:
'Walk out of your denominations.' An 'open' communion
table was maintained and no formal membership, along
Open Brethren lines. It is not surprising that he and his
ministry were seen as a threat by many established works.
Students were warned off him and much bitter opposition
came his way. Entire congregations broke away from their
affiliations and joined the new movement, especially in
Chekiang province. Ironically, the CIM was hit hard in this
way. Nee's base continued to be in Shanghai.

Nee was a voracious reader. He also had the ability to
digest what he was reading and memorize it. He read as
many as 3,000 Christian books, reaching back to the early
Church Fathers of the second century AD. It was his practice
to apportion his income — a third for personal needs, a third
for helping others and a third for books to add to his library.
He issued many publications, including a magazine, *The
Christian*, a hymn book and a newspaper. His holiness, or
'higher life', teaching was mystical and extreme. It bordered
on sinless perfection. By making his understanding of the
doctrine of the church to be a matter of prime importance
and a basis for fellowship with others, he himself fell into the
trap of becoming schismatic. Nevertheless the Little Flock
movement became a bulwark of evangelicalism, and went on
from strength to strength.

Wang Mingdao

Wang Mingdao (1900–91) was born in Peking in the year of
the Boxer Rebellion. His father took his own life during the
siege, just before Wang was born. His mother had to struggle

to raise both him and his elder sister. Wang was educated at a LMS primary school. He was top, both in his class and in examinations, so he gained a scholarship for further education. He was converted at the age of fourteen while in middle school.

In 1920 he surrendered his life to the will of God and changed his name from Tie-zi (iron son) to Mingdao (witness to the truth). He lived up to both names magnificently. When he declared for believer's baptism he lost his job at the Presbyterian school where he was a teacher. He was baptized in a stream with five of his students, his clothes freezing with solid ice as he emerged from the water.

In 1923, Wang Mingdao spent eighteen months privately waiting upon God and in Bible study, during which he read the whole Bible six times in a period of sixty-two days.

He was invited to speak at an eight-day CIM conference at Zan Huang. It was greatly blessed and opened up many doors for ministry. A public clash at a Congregational leaders' conference with a speaker who disparaged the Scriptures met with this riposte from him: 'I am unwilling to accept the reasonings that are not found in the Scriptures.' This episode opened his eyes to the extent to which heterodox views were emanating from foreign missionary and denominational sources. It sharpened his awareness of the need for clarity in his own views. He also saw the need to take nothing for granted, as he found so many nominal Christians in the churches.

It was in 1924 that Wang started Bible studies in his home. These developed into a strong independent evangelical church in Peking. In 1925 Wang began his twenty years of travel throughout China. In both 1926 and 1927 he was away from his Peking home for more than six months each year, in order to respond to over forty invitations to speak at conferences and churches.

Wang was not hampered by the political turmoil of these years. He early published booklets of a polemical nature: *A*

Cry amid the Evil World; Christians and Idols; A Most Important Matter; Who is Jesus? and *The Cross of Christ.* Also, from the spring of 1927, Wang Mingdao started a periodical called *Spiritual Food Quarterly* which eventually gained nationwide circulation. Over the years this magazine reproduced his sermons and Bible expositions. This constitutes a valuable resource for Chinese Christians to tap into today.

He waged a lifelong crusade against the spread of liberal theology in China. He did not mince his words in denouncing prominent liberal Christian leaders, yet he was also meticulous and detailed in exposing the lack of holiness and spirituality of many professing Christians. He called on all such to repent. He did not hold any Pentecostal views. Wang Mingdao became the most complete and influential of all the Christian preachers.

David Yang

David Yang (Yang Shaotang, 1900–1981) was a Christian farmer's son from Yang village, Quwo, in the south of Shansi province. He was born in the midst of the bloody 1900 Boxer Uprising. In this area of Quwo, Mr and Mrs Duncan Kay of the CIM and their little daughter, together with a number of Chinese Christians, were killed and homes were looted and burned. The Yangs, however, were spared and little Yang had a happy childhood. He went to the local Christian primary school where he took the name Shaotang (though later he adopted his Christian name of David). He loved the Bible.

When he was twelve, he moved away from home to the provincial Christian middle school at Hongdong, where he received a solid grounding in the Christian life. The D. E. Hoste School gave an excellent, all-round education and Yang excelled. He felt called to the Christian ministry and, with the blessing and help of his parents and the churches, he was sent in 1923 to the best evangelical theological college in

North China. This was the Presbyterian Seminary at Tengxian, in the coastal province of Shantung.

He did not find his feet spiritually until, in 1924, he went to a convention for the deepening of the spiritual life, held in the summer resort of Kuling. There he came under a deep conviction of sin. He continued in prayer until 'early on the morning of

Wang Mindao and David Yang

the 7 July, He [Christ] found this lost sheep. The blood of the cross flowed into my heart and the burden of sin fell away. For the first time, I enjoyed a true relationship with Jesus Christ. And, from that day until now, the Lord has continued to do His marvellous work in my life.'

After graduation in 1925, David Yang returned home to oversee thirteen churches in thirteen counties, of which Quwo was the base. There he worked away happily in his constituency of farmers and local merchants. He was being prepared for great usefulness in the revival coming to Shansi in the 1930s.

ASSESSMENT OF THESE SIX MINISTRIES

There can be no doubt that these were all leading evangelical gospel ministries, attempting to do justice to Scripture teaching. These leaders all experienced and preached an evangelical conversion of personal repentance for sin and a simple saving faith in Christ. This was to be evidenced by a holy walk with Christ and a holy life. They sought to grapple biblically with contemporary problems in the existing churches and in society. Their works each complemented that of the others. They all wanted purity in personal and church life. It is also true to say that some of them embraced certain Pentecostal experiences in moderation, yet with them 'speaking in tongues' was never regarded as the necessary evidence of being 'filled with the Spirit', or even as evidence of conversion itself.

These indigenous church ministries emerged when the spirit of Chinese nationalism was rife in the land. God was providentially preparing the ground for a strong evangelical indigenous church that would be ready to meet an even greater challenge to its existence in China in the not-far-distant future.

13. Revivals,
1930—37

Though the Protestant church in China had grown rapidly to over 350,000 communicant members by 1930 (from 100,000 in 1900), the spiritual quality was all too often not of the stuff from which the martyrs of the 1900 Boxer Rebellion were made. Worldliness had invaded much of the church, which had already been weakened by liberal theology and lower moral standards. The grossest sins were not uncommon among church members and the staff of Christian schools. Among the leadership, both foreign and Chinese, were many spiritually blind men leading spiritually blind followers. There was need of a deep, convicting and regenerating work of the Holy Spirit. The period from 1930 to 1937 was marked by some powerful revival movements that to a large extent met that need.

THE RISE OF COMMUNISM IN CHINA

Mao Tse Tung (Mao Zedong, 1893–1976) was the son of a prosperous farmer in Hunan. He was introduced to Marxism while working as an assistant librarian at Peking University at the time of the 1919 student May Fourth Movement. By 1920 he had become a committed Marxist and was present in July

1921 at the first congress of the Chinese Communist Party held in secret in Shanghai. Mao came to believe in the revolutionary potential of the peasantry rather than the orthodox Marxist-Leninist's faith in the urban proletariat. He organized a peasants' politicized guerrilla force in his native Hunan province and across the border in Kiangsi province. By 1928 Mao had a peasants' and workers' army of about 4,000 in the mountains. Yet he was not a member of the ruling Politbureau of the China Communist Party, which was Soviet Russia-orientated and which opposed his ideas.

The Communist insurgents, including those led by Mao, lived off the land as guerrilla fighters and were greatly feared. 'It is necessary to create terror in every rural area,' said Mao. The Communists executed the landlord class and those whom they considered 'bad elements', and redistributed land to the peasants. Forced indoctrination through political cadres was introduced. For Mao Tse Tung, 'terror' also included ruthless purges within the Communists' own ranks.

In November 1931 what was called the Chinese Soviet Republic was established by Mao. Its headquarters was in South Kiangsi province. This soon had tentacles reaching out into the neighbouring provinces of Fukien and Anhwei.

THE LONG MARCH

When in 1934 Generalissimo Chiang Kai-shek had the Communist forces in Central China surrounded, they managed to slip away. The result was the year-long epic 'Long March' of the Red Army, begun on 15 October 1934. 100,000 people embarked on a year-long trek which has been stated as being 6,000 miles (actually it was nearer 3,700 miles) through eleven provinces, eighteen mountain ranges and across twenty-four rivers. Guerrilla tactics of rapid hit-and-run attacks and keeping to the mountains proved to be a highly successful strategy of survival in the face of the continual pursuance by republican forces. The Chinese churches and foreign missionaries were singled out by the Communists for physical attack and many lives were lost. Demanding a ransom for captured foreigners could also be a means of raising much-needed funds or materials. The Communists finally arrived in the province of Shensi (Shaanxi) in the north in October 1935. The immense hardships endured during the Long March can be seen in the fact that the number of survivors who arrived in Shensi under Mao's leadership was only 8,000. However, the ranks soon increased to 30,000. The Red Army headquarters were set up there at Yenan (Yan'an) in 1936. It was during this march that Mao gained unchallenged control of the China Communist Party.

In 1935, Chiang Kai-shek and his wife (both of whom were Christians) launched the New Life Movement, an attempt to renew the nation morally. The campaign had limited success, though their personal example of doing good gained much admiration at home and abroad. In 1936, Chiang Kai-shek was forced to agree to a united front with the China Communist Party against the Japanese, the common enemy. The power of the Nationalist government was slowly but surely crumbling.

CAUGHT UP IN THE LONG MARCH

John and Betty Stam, two China Inland Mission missionaries from the USA, were taken prisoner at Tsingteh (Jingde) in the south of Anhwei province on 6 December 1934, as a result of the sudden advance of some Communist forces. A Chinese who pleaded for the life of Helen Priscilla Stam, their two-month-old baby girl, was summarily executed on the spot in her place. 'Your life for hers', he was told. The next morning John and Betty Stam were beheaded in nearby Miaosheo, together with a Chinese Christian who pleaded for them on his knees and consequently shared their fate.

The faithful evangelist Lo found baby Helen alive after almost thirty hours, safe in her sleeping bag! To him fell the

Helen Priscilla Stam

task both of burying the dead and of preaching the gospel to the crowd. The Communists had moved on.

Mr and Mrs Lo then took on the perilous task of a journey of about a hundred miles through mountainous country to deliver Helen Priscilla Stam, safely and in perfect health, to the Methodist hospital in Wuhu which is on the Yangtze River upstream from Nanking. The full story of the Stams is found in the book aptly titled *The Triumph of John and Betty Stam* by Geraldine Taylor, published by the Overseas Missionary Fellowship.

Another vivid account of what it was like to be caught up in this epic historic march has come to us in the eyewitness account of the Swiss missionary Alfred Bosshardt, in his timeless classic, and best-selling missionary book, *The Restraining Hand*. Alfred and Rose Bosshardt were returning to their mission station from a ten-day prayer conference of twenty-four missionaries. They had been praying for their province of Kweichow (Guizhou) because, after decades of gospel witness, there were only a few hundred Chinese Christians in the entire province. They were captured by the Communists who were fleeing westward in the Long March.

In all, five members of the CIM, together with two children, were taken on 1 and 2 October 1934. They were 'tried' as spies and government agents and a huge ransom was demanded. The women and children were released as encumbrances, but Alfred Bosshardt (Swiss) and Arnolis Hayman (from New Zealand) were made to accompany the forced marches. In the case of Arnolis Hayman (who was eventually released on 18 November 1935) this was for 413 days, and in that of Alfred Bosshardt (released on Easter Day, 1936) it lasted for 560 days. The account gives us a fascinating insight into the historic Long March from the point of view of two men caught up in it. And it also gives us a testimony to the power of Christ in love and patience as we see it displayed in His servants in very trying circumstances.

THE 'INTREPID TRIO' IN THE NORTH-WEST

In the far north-west province of Sinkiang (Xinjiang) the Russian influence and intrusion were strong. The Russians acted as a strong rearguard buffer for Mao Tse Tung in Shensi. The itinerant missionary pioneers of the Gobi Desert oases were an 'intrepid trio' of CIM missionaries. These were

The 'intrepid trio' (Mildred Cable is in the centre)

Eva French (1871–1961), her younger sister Francesca French (1873–1961) and Mildred Cable (1877–1952). Mildred Cable was a gifted and prolific author. Her books about their work in the Gobi and the biographies of CIM missionaries George Hunter and Percy Mather of Urumqi are classics of exploration and pioneering in Central Asia. The books were best sellers.

An inn in the Gobi Desert in the early twentieth century

In 1932 seven missionaries of the CIM crossed the Gobi Desert by Ford truck with George Hunter to join Percy Mather at Urumqi, capital of Sinkiang province. They arrived just in time for the Muslim uprising of 10,000 Kazakhs in January 1933. The nine were overwhelmed with the care of the wounded and typhus-ridden. Worn out, Percy Mather succumbed and died of typhus. When the Russians took control, all except George Hunter were expelled from the province. Hunter was held prisoner for eighteen months, during which time he was tortured by the NKVD (the secret police) then finally deported with his health shattered. In 1946 he died while seeking to re-enter the province to resume work there.

GLADYS AYLWARD

It was in the context of troubled and dangerous times in China that Gladys Aylward (1902–70) spent her life savings in 1930 on a passage from England to Yangcheng (Yungcheng) in the south of Shansi province.

Gladys Aylward (the 'Cockney Sparrow') was a domestic servant from London who had been turned down by the China Inland Mission because her academic background was inadequate. Gladys was put in touch with an elderly independent missionary lady in China, Jeannie Lawson, who invited her to join her. This Gladys did, travelling all alone by train across Russia, then by ship to China via Japan and lastly by train and mule to Yangcheng.

Jeannie and Gladys together founded the Inn of the Eight Happinesses to evangelize the muleteers by telling Bible stories. Gladys became employed by the authorities as a 'foot inspector'. She had the task of travelling the area to enforce the new law against the foot-binding of infant Chinese girls, a barbaric old Manchu custom. She came to be known as Ai-wei-de (Virtuous One) and became a naturalized Chinese in 1936.

Gladys Aylward

Her bravery in facing down a desperate mob in a Chinese prison won her many admirers.

In 1938 the region was invaded by the Japanese and Gladys Aylward led ninety-four children to safety over the mountains and across the Yellow River to Sian (Xian). The full story of this remarkable missionary is told in the book *The Small Woman* by Alan Burgess.

THE MINISTRY OF MARIE MONSEN

Marie Monsen (1878–1962) was a catalyst for the revival in Shantung, north China, in the early 1930s. Marie Monsen went to China in 1901 with the Norwegian Lutheran Mission as a teacher and worker among women. She suffered both from a bad accident and from acute illnesses. After suffering continual headaches for six years she was healed through anointing with oil and prayer (see James 5:14). She was moved to a pioneering work at Nanyang in Honan (Henan) province. The work was hard and discouraging. When she heard of the revival of 1907 in Korea which had been born through a prayer-revival among missionaries, Marie wanted to visit, but was arrested by the thought: 'What you want through that journey may be given you here, where you are, in answer to prayer.' This was accompanied by such a profound experience in prayer that she was enabled to pray constantly for revival amid all her work over the next twenty, apparently barren, years.

In the countryside, the political and social upheavals of the late 1920s forced many Chinese women to come out of the traditional place of staying at home. The congregation at Marie Monsen's station increased at that time by up to five times, and, of those, three out of every five persons attending were women. It was among these women in 1927 that Marie saw the first touches of a revival.

Previous to a women's Bible course, the same burden of prayer which she had known years before came upon Marie Monsen again so strongly that she was convinced that 'something was going to happen'. On the fourth day of a group meeting of sixteen heathen women, one after another confessed to the sin of infanticide. Marie Monsen had never heard any woman confess to this before. This was followed by the lamentation that they had been unable to sleep since these meetings had begun. They then queued up one by one for a talk with Marie in another room. One stood at the door with her hand on the door-handle, saying, 'I must come first. I have such pain, I cannot wait!' This woman fell down in anguish of spirit and confession of sin to God. She arose transformed, with light shining from her eyes and the peace of God radiating from her face. In a similar way, almost all the women found the Saviour. During all this time Marie had been overwhelmed with a spirit of helplessness and God-given compassion. A number of these women became members of a little church among the mountains known as the 'widows' church' because bandits had so ravaged the area that there were forty widows in its membership.

This first experience of revival power marked Marie Monsen's soul so deeply that she never forgot it. She became known as the 'soft-spoken' evangelist and her ministry was marked by an ability to expose personal sins with compassion. Her particular forte and love was exhorting at prayer meetings. She was a passionate believer in the necessity of prayer meetings and in their potential power. She held that the original biblical intention 'to give themselves continually to prayer and the ministry of the Word' (Acts 6:4) had so often been reversed in the churches into 'to give themselves to the ministry of the Word and [desultory] prayer'. Her burden to seek to rectify the situation in practice was to bear magnificent fruit. It was said of her that in personal exhortations at prayer meetings she had the surgical skill to expose the sins hidden behind the smiling exteriors of many a trusted Christian worker. Her quiet insistence on a clear-cut experience of the new birth set the pattern for others to follow. She was also ideally suited by her long experience in the mission field to be an encourager of dispirited missionaries.

REVIVAL IN THE NORTH

A burden to pray for revival spread widely from missionaries who were at the Summer Conference season of 1929 at Peitaiho (Beidaihe), where Marie Monsen was one of the leading speakers. Peitaiho is in the north of China by the sea, near the Great Wall. She was then invited by the American Southern Baptists at Chefoo (Yantai) in Shantung province to share her testimony and her message. The revival started there, from interdenominational prayer meetings led by Marie. College faculty members, pastors, evangelists, Christian workers and students in mission schools attended. At the end of each prayer meeting, Marie Monsen stood at the door and asked each and every one the same question: 'Are you born again?' The Holy Spirit worked deeply and widely in those meetings. The revival then spread throughout that province by the returning missionaries and was subsequently taken up by the Chinese preachers and elders at grassroots level. The revival spread into the neighbouring provinces of Hopeh (Hebei), Honan and Shansi, further to the west. It was particularly strong in Manchuria, to the north. This revival was by and large confined to the north of China.

In Tsinan (Jinan), capital of Shantung province, was Cheloo University, a Union university known for its liberal theology and 'advanced thinking'. A small group of evangelical staff met weekly in the home of Dr Thornton Stearns and his wife Carol to pray for a revival in the university. Dr Stearns was professor of orthopaedics in the medical school. He had the responsibility of arranging the annual special meetings, when it was the custom to invite an evangelist or Bible teacher to speak.

In December 1931, John Sung happened to pass through Tsinan and was invited to the home of Thornton Stearns, where he preached to some students. Within days forty or fifty students had become professed converts to Christ. The work of conviction of sin spread among the student body and seekers after salvation went to the Stearns for counselling. Much prayer was made as to whom to invite as speaker at the next spring retreat. Leland Wang was unavailable and the then little-known Shanghai preacher Watchman Nee was invited. Over a weekend, the medical school auditorium was exceptionally crowded. In the words of Angus Kinnear:

> The longed-for revival spread, as more and more students found the Saviour. Among many of them the experience was to become a legend, for heaven itself seemed to open to their hearts. Afterwards, a group of more than a hundred students gathered at a mountain beauty spot, the traditional site of Confucius' grave. They studied the Bible and a large group of them were baptized in the cold pool of a mountain torrent, publicly confessing Jesus as Lord.

The general revival in the northern provinces continued until it moderated by late 1935, well after Marie Monsen's return home to Norway in 1933. The Pentecostalism in the Shantung countryside spread considerably in this revival, through the agency of the Spiritual Gifts Society. Pentecostalism was no part of Marie Monsen's ministry, apart from her belief in divine healing in answer to prayer. Nor was it part of the beliefs of the vast majority of the churches. In the latter stages, after 1933, there were many cases of Pentecostal excess which ended the genuine revival. In 1936 Watchman Nee observed that 'Looking back over this period [the last three years], the gain has been rather trivial, the loss quite large.' He and the Little Flock opposed Pentecostalism from 1936 onwards.

THE BETHEL BANDS REVIVAL

1931 was a year of calamity for China. Widespread misery resulted from two failed military campaigns by Chiang Kai-shek against the Communists, and the Yangtze River flood was one of the worst of the century. Manchuria was occupied by the Japanese and a flood of refugees came from there, adding to the woes.

It was in 1931, in Shanghai, that Andrew Gih organized and led the Bethel Worldwide Evangelistic Band. He teamed up with John Sung. The evangelistic team was well organized, after the style of a contemporary American campaign. The ministry was very fruitful and brought new life to many moribund churches and Christians. The team were actually in Mukden (Shenyang) in Manchuria on 18 September 1931. They left the city only hours before the Japanese attack on the city, which heralded the occupation of Manchuria.

Within four years, the team visited 133 cities and preached to over half a million people. They saw 50,000 make professions of faith, among them people drawn from all walks of life. The group established ten regional teams across the country, for the purpose of evangelism and revival meetings. These were to be held in both town and countryside, in buildings, tents and the open air. Many local churches were inspired to form their own evangelistic groups. It was the opinion of Edwin Orr that Andrew Gih and the Bethel Bands he founded did more to extend the revival in China than any other agency.

The *China Christian Year Book* took notice:

> The churches were swept by the spirit of revival. Bloodthirsty bandits, rapacious officials, overbearing soldiers, anarchistic students, dishonest servants, communists, polygamists, sedate scholars, hard-headers, businessmen, rickshaw coolies, beggars, men and women, young and old, city dwellers and country folk

The Bethel Band.
Back row (from left to right): John Sung, Philip Lee, Frank Ling.
Seated (from left to right): Lincoln Niels, Andrew Gih

were moved to confess and forsake sin and to make reparation and restitution.

Generally, the conversions were lasting.

Edwin Orr regarded John Sung as one of China's greatest evangelists of all time, if not the greatest. Sung has been called 'China's apostle of revival' and 'China's John the Baptist'. John Sung had been chief editor of the Bethel Mission magazine, *Guide to Holiness*. He came to disagree with their doctrine of eradication of sin, believing instead in the believer putting to death sinful deeds himself, in the power of the Holy Spirit. In 1935 he became an independent evangelist.

In addition to exercising an influential ministry in China, John Sung made visits to Chinese churches overseas. Between June 1935 and December 1939 he visited the Philippines, Formosa (Taiwan), Malaysia, Indonesia, Vietnam and Thailand, and went seven times to Singapore. It is calculated that fifteen million Chinese lived in south-east Asia and Formosa at that time, most of whom came from South China. Sung was from the southern province of Fukien. Thousands were converted in these overseas visits. Everywhere he went, he formed evangelistic bands and groups for prayer and Bible study. In 1937 the Chin Lien Bible School was founded in Singapore to train converts from his ministry.

John Sung proved to be a unique and compelling preacher. He believed that formulaic conversions were insufficient. Repentance for sins had to be real, deep and detailed, followed by determination to correct sinful habits in the life. Sung listed twenty categories of sin, and he would go through them in detail. His hearers would then often be moved to tears by his message of Christ's love in saving repentant sinners. His illustrations were famously graphic and pungent and he was not afraid to use visual aids and theatricals. Yet he was intensely serious and his abrasiveness could cause offence. He was a good singer and would often break out into a hymn in the middle of his preaching. He was not Pentecostal, though he believed in and practised a healing ministry. From 1940 until his death in 1944, John Sung suffered intensely from intestinal tuberculosis and cancer.

REVIVAL IN THE SOUTH-WEST

The revival visited Yunnan province. The mass of the Lisu tribe had turned from animism to Christianity. Inevitably, many had only made an outward profession of faith. They had not experienced the transforming power of the new birth. The revival came to Yunnan under the ministry of the Danish lady evangelist Anna Christensen and others. The distinctive message of heart repentance and the new birth was so blessed by God as to consolidate the work among the Lisu. This work was to endure in spite of the severe persecution that was to come under the Communists.

EFFECTS OF REVIVAL

As a result of revival, the Chinese Christians became more conscious of their spiritual responsibilities. Their churches came to see that the goal of self-support was attainable. With this gain in confidence, the Chinese Christian leaders showed a new gratitude towards missionaries for their work in laying the foundations of a vital church in China. Happy co-operation in the gospel effort was widespread wherever the biblical gospel was upheld, with the exception of decidedly independent works such as Watchman Nee and his Little Flock assemblies. The latter continued to flourish. By 1933 there were over 100 Little Flock assemblies and by 1938 over 200. A significant development during this period was the impetus of taking the gospel by the Chinese evangelists to their kinsfolk in neighbouring countries. This in itself was the beginning of what has turned out to be a worldwide missionary movement of its own.

1935 CONSERVATIVE EVANGELICAL CONFERENCE

As a result of the continuing influence in China of liberal theology among the denominational churches, in May 1935 the Conservative Evangelical Conference was convened at Kaifeng in Honan province. The speakers were Dr Chia Yuming, Marcus Cheng, Calvin Chao, Leland Wang, Wang Mingdao and Pastor Li of Nanking. The purpose was to show a united front against doctrinal infidelity by the emerging indigenous Chinese church. The influence of these men and their ministries was of immense importance for the future development of the Protestant churches in China.

14. Awakening among university students, 1937—45

In July 1937 the Japanese invaded China. The 1937–45 Chinese war with Japan took place within China. This invasion caused major disruption to many aspects of life in China. Millions were evacuated to the comparative safety of west China. After 1941 this included missionaries and societies whose countries were at war with Japan. Chinese churches in Japanese-held areas had to rely solely on their own resources and were marshalled under the umbrella of a single church by the Japanese, who sought to maintain a close control over them. In the area controlled by the government of Chiang Kai-shek, West China — known as Free China — there was a spiritual awakening and revival among university students. Starting in 1939, the revival lasted throughout the period and beyond.

THE WAR WITH JAPAN, 1937—45

On 7 July 1937 there was a clash between Chinese and Japanese troops at the Marco Polo Bridge (Lugou Bridge) outside Peking. This began the full-scale Japanese invasion of China from Manchuria. In that same month of July 1937, there in Peking, the building of the Christian Tabernacle was completed and it was dedicated on 1 August 1937. Wang Mingdao was the pastor, though he regarded himself as only one of the deacons. The Tabernacle had a membership of about 570. A week later the Japanese troops entered Peking.

The Nationalist government of Chiang Kai-shek was forced to move westward and set up its capital in Chungking (Chongqing) behind the safety of the Yangtze rapids and gorges. War provisions for China then had to come all the way overland from Russia, or else from French Indo-China by railway to Kunming in Yunnan province, or by road from Burma along the 'Burma Road' to Kunming. By 1942 allied supplies were forced to come by air from India over the 'Hump' to Kunming.

During the war up to eighty million people became refugees, many thousands of them Christians. They fled westward to comparative safety behind the Chinese lines of defence. Providentially in this way the gospel was spread to many places in the north-west, west and south-west of China, and reached many people unacquainted with the good news of salvation in Christ. Universities, their staff and students, packed their libraries and scientific instruments and fled before the advancing invaders to the safety of the mountains in the west in Free China. The Japanese bombed everywhere they could with little opposition. J. Edwin Orr was in south-west China between October and December 1938 and in his book *Through Blood and Fire in China* he gives a graphic account of the bombings in which he and Andrew Gih were caught up.

After Japan's attack on Pearl Harbour in December 1941, almost all the remaining Western missionaries in occupied China were interned in camps, such as at Weihsien (Wei-fang). This was the camp where the famous Olympic athlete Eric Liddell was interred and where he died in 1945. He was a missionary serving with the London Missionary Society. The Oscar-winning film *Chariots of Fire* portrays incidents from the life of Liddell. His biography *Running the Race, Eric Liddell — Olympic Champion and Missionary* by John W.

Keddie gives a graphic account of conditions in an internment camp.

Chiang Kai-shek's policy of consolidation and unification was thrown into reverse gear. Wartime conditions encouraged corruption, racketeering and hyperinflation. By contrast the disciplined Communists, avoiding pitched battles, found themselves able to consolidate, and even expand, their hold on parts of northern China. Nationalists and Communists were united in their determination to fight and defeat the Japanese. The war came to an end with the swift and unconditional surrender of Japan on 15 August 1945 after atomic bombs had been dropped on Hiroshima and Nagasaki.

WANG MINGDAO AND THE JAPANESE IN PEKING

At the Christian Tabernacle in Peking, Wang Mingdao was able to continue his ministry right through the war years, in spite of all the difficulties he faced.

The first of these concerned the continued publication of his magazine *The Spiritual Food Quarterly*. The Japanese issued a directive commanding all future publications in Peking to insert four slogans drawn up by the Japanese Army Bureau. Disobedience would be severely punished. Rather than publish political slogans that were dishonouring to God in his widely distributed Christian magazine, Wang Mingdao, on advice, chose not to publish at all. He was subsequently convicted of the sin of disobedience to God and of cowardice. His wife asked him, 'Are you prepared to be arrested, examined and be jailed?' He replied, 'I am prepared.' She said, 'Then you must go and act as God has shown you.' He published without the slogans and sent copies to the bureau as required. They did not reply and it was his happy testimony that, in the eight years of Japanese occupation, at no time was the *Spiritual Food Quarterly* 'adulterated with political matter'.

Wang Mindao

A second major diffi-culty arose for Wang Mingdao when the leaders of all the churches in Peking met to set up a committee called The Peking Christian Preserv-ation Committee. They were to meet at the hall of the Ministry of Home Affairs. Wang Mingdao refused to go. He believed that, as the church leaders were going to seek advice from the Japanese, instead of looking to God alone for direction, the churches could not avoid accepting the conditions the Japan-ese would impose. This indeed proved to be the case. Wang saw this as a breach of the biblical principle of separation of church and state, an attack on the only headship and lordship of Christ in His church. The scripture that convinced him was clear: 'What part has a believer with an unbeliever?' (2 Cor-inthians 6:14-16). Also the same scripture passage applied to the many false teachers in the churches which were unfaith-ful to the biblical gospel and who were taking the lead in what was to become the North China Christian Federation Promotion Committee.

Attempts to persuade the Christian Tabernacle to join the puppet organization gave way to threats as participation became compulsory. After a funeral, Wang Mingdao met a Japanese pastor from Peking, Rev. Odakamo, who also tried to persuade him to join. Then, finally, on 30 April 1942 an official letter came from the committee, who demanded participation and a formal response. Wang Mingdao entered his personal 'Gethsemane'. He knew the Japanese could order the church to be closed and have him and others arrested, imprisoned, or even killed by the Japanese military. All the arguments for and against, with their practical implications, tossed and turned in Wang's mind that night. After a severe inner struggle, his answer by letter was 'no' to participation.

Wang Mingdao was kept waiting in suspense by the Japanese until he was summoned to the Japanese Cultural Investigation Bureau on 10 October 1942, Chinese National Day. Riding on his bicycle, singing the hymn 'Stand up, stand up for Jesus', he attended. Wang was actually invited to participate in the leadership of the North China Christian Federation, which was about to be inaugurated. He explained that 'On principle, the Tabernacle cannot associate with any organization or establishment.' When he was told that the Japanese had decided on the unification of all the churches and that this must be achieved, Wang replied, 'As I obey the Lord whom I have served, and as I keep the truth which I have believed, I will not obey any man's command that goes against the will of God. I have already prepared myself to pay any price and make any sacrifice, but I will not change the decision I have made.' He politely but firmly refused to discuss the matter further. Marvellously (for the Japanese were brutal towards any sign of defiance), the Japanese authorities left him and the Tabernacle alone for the duration, except that they managed to install a spy as gatekeeper, to report on activities at the Tabernacle. Those 'activities' led to the gatekeeper's conversion!

The experience of Wang Mingdao is worth recording at length because the principles for which he stood have caused a division among evangelical Protestant Christians in China during the Communist era. To conform or not to conform to state control of the church and its agenda is the question. This is at the heart of the difference in China today between the non-conforming 'house churches' and the conforming state-registered church (known as the Three-Self Patriotic

Church). Under the Communists, Wang Mingdao was once again called upon to stand firm for these same principles, and he suffered imprisonment for nearly twenty-three years.

During the whole of the Second World War, Wang Mingdao continued, uninterrupted, his powerful ministry in Peking. Even though travel was severely restricted, he managed to visit some churches in occupied north China. His magazine continued publication and was widely distributed, as ways and means allowed. It was appreciated more than ever, in view of the dislocation of many ministries during those years. Neutral foreigners in Peking took the opportunity to attend his biblical ministry, though none were invited to share in the leadership of the church, or even to preach.

One of the very few persons to be invited to preach at the Christian Tabernacle was David Yang from Shansi province. Earlier, in Shansi, he had had the vision to form the Spiritual Action Team in 1934. The team lived a communal life. Half the year was spent in Bible study and the other half in going out in small teams to evangelize. The young missionary David Adeney was one of the team for a short time. He regarded David Yang as a radiant, skilful expositor and a man of intense prayer. The team was forced to disband in 1939 when the Japanese burned their premises to the ground. David Yang took his family to Peking, where he remained for the duration.

Wang Mingdao took the funeral service of the great evangelist John Sung on the latter's death in 1944. Sung had suffered intensely from cancer. When he died in pain at his retreat in the hills outside Peking he was humming, 'In the cross, in the cross, be my glory, ever.' His funeral was attended by about 300 people. John Sung had seen only fifteen years of active service, yet his influence for the gospel among Chinese, both inside and outside China, had been incalculable.

TIMOTHY CHAO AND THE JAPANESE IN SHANGHAI

Timothy Chao (Zhao Shiguang, 1908–73) was a direct descendant of a Song emperor. He was one of the fifty young people who, with Andrew Gih, gave their lives for full-time evangelistic ministry at the remarkable meetings at Shanghai in 1925. He changed his name to Shiguang, meaning 'world light'. In due course he was ordained pastor of a Christian and Missionary Alliance church in Shanghai. When the Japanese seized the International Settlement in December 1941, Chao went independent, and soon built up a remarkable ministry under wartime conditions. In August 1943 the Spiritual Food Church (Ling Liang) was founded and began to develop its own network of schools, orphanages and nursing homes. By 1947, five other churches had been founded, together with a seminary.

THE LITTLE FLOCK EXPANDS UNDER THE JAPANESE

The strength of the Little Flock, the group of Christian Brethren assemblies founded by Watchman Nee, lay in the spiritual quality of its people. Educated Chinese Christians, such as doctors, university staff, army officers and businessmen, were attracted to, and joined, the fellowship. In 1936 an assembly was opened in Peking, where the congregation was predominantly made up of students who had gained top honours from the universities. In Chefoo, on the Shantung coast, the Little Flock was led by Witness Lee (Li Changshou). In 1943 many of the fellowship gave up all their possessions to enable some 100 families to migrate north beyond the Great Wall, as 'instant congregations' and bases for evangelism. The results were mixed, yet by 1944 there were forty new assemblies as a result of this initiative. There was little trouble from the Japanese.

It was different in Shanghai, where the Japanese insisted on the Little Flock joining a united church. They refused and were shut down. They had to meet in private homes. Watchman Nee came under the displeasure of his fellow elders, who suspended him from preaching in 1942 for about five years. This was because he went into business in order to meet his commitments to support a number of workers personally. A large drop in church income, combined with runaway inflation, had brought about this situation.

THE GOSPEL IN FREE CHINA

Providentially the migration of Christians to Free China carried the gospel to many places in the north-west, west and south-west of China. Naturally, many Christians sought the haven of Chiang Kai-shek's wartime capital at Chungking and it became a centre for much Christian activity.

MARCUS CHENG FOUNDS THE CHUNGKING THEOLOGICAL SEMINARY

Marcus Cheng

Marcus Cheng (Chen Chonggui, 1884–1963) was the co-founder and president of the Chungking (Chongqing) Theological Seminary in 1944. Brought up in poverty near Wuchan in Hupeh province, he was given some schooling by the Swedish Covenant Church Mission. He excelled at languages and soon spoke good Swedish and English. He took a post as part-time English teacher with the small mission school. He did this as a dutiful son, in order to help support his parents. In the spring of 1906 he married, but his wife died within six months. This precipitated a spiritual crisis in which he entered into a deep experience of Christ, under the preaching of the gospel by a Chinese evangelist, Pastor Li Shuqing, a doctor from Suzhou.

Between 1921 and 1923 Cheng visited Sweden and the USA. Speaking fluent Swedish, he was popular both in Sweden and in the USA. He was sponsored by the mission to enter Wheaton College and he graduated with a B.A. at the age of thirty-eight. On his return to China, Marcus Cheng began to accept more and more invitations to preach on the emerging 'revival circuit', where he was welcomed by most denominations. He taught at the mission's seminary, but clashed with the authorities in 1925 over foreign control. This was when anti-foreign feeling ran high. He was dismissed.

In 1927, Marcus Cheng took his family to Shanghai. He became the managing editor for a new Christian magazine called *Evangelism* (*Budao zazhi*). This magazine became the most widely read Protestant evangelical periodical in China, with up to 5,000 copies per issue at its peak in the late 1930s. After disruption as a result of the war, the magazine was relaunched in 1943 and continued to be published right through the decade.

In 1929, Marcus Cheng joined the faculty of the evangelical Hunan Bible Institute in Changsha, where he remained until 1937. With the outbreak of war with Japan, Marcus Cheng went on preaching tours in Free China. But on a visit abroad in Singapore, he was caught up in the surprise attack and capture of Singapore by the Japanese in February 1942. He managed to escape from Singapore and make his way to Chungking (Chongqing), the wartime capital of Free China. There he met up with Bishop Frank Houghton, General Director of the CIM, who raised with him the idea of starting a theological seminary. This would not be under the control of any missionary organization.

*Marcus Cheng (third from left, back row) in 1941. Calvin Chao
(see below) is standing at the extreme right (middle row).*

The challenge and the desire to teach again made Marcus
Cheng receptive to the idea and in March 1944 the Chungking
Theological Seminary was formed. Marcus Cheng was president and principal, at the age of sixty. The purpose of the
seminary was to train pastors and evangelists up to university
graduate level. Already there was evidence of a spiritual
awakening among university students, so hopes were high.

CHIA YUMING IN CHUNGKING

Another who found refuge in Chungking was Chia Yuming
(Jia Yuming, 1880-1964). He had been ordained as a pastor in
1904, after graduation from Tengchow Presbyterian seminary. He pastored in Shantung (Shandong) province. Then in
1915 he moved on, to teach in mission-run seminaries. He
established a national reputation as a conservative systematic
theologian. In 1936 Chia started the Chinese Christian Bible
Institute in Nanking and became its principal. Following the
Japanese invasion, the college had to move to the safety of
Chungking. Chia was the author of *Study of Theology, Basic
Bible Truth* and a hymn book with the title *Saint's Heart Song.*

SPIRITUAL AWAKENING AMONG UNIVERSITY STUDENTS

Paul Contento was an Italian American and missionary in Ningxia, Inner Mongolia, from 1929 to 1936. He had just returned to China after having been abroad to undertake studies in preparation for work among Muslims. By necessity, the route into China was by the south-west into the province of Yunnan, where there happened to be about a million Muslims. He arrived at the capital Kunming with his gifted Scottish wife Maida in 1939. They contemplated staying there to work among the Muslims.

However, they had been there only a very short time when they had visitors. At the door stood some Chinese university students wanting to learn English. The Contentos were astonished, for they knew that students had up till this time been so nationalistic and anti-foreign that nothing could be done with them. The war with Japan was having unexpected effects. Thousands of university students had fled with their faculties westward for safety from the Japanese, especially from the great cities like Peking, Tientsin, Shanghai and Nanking. Many from these elite universities had come to this area. In the face of this expressed desire to learn English, Paul Contento replied that he had no textbooks. The students suggested, 'Use your English Bible. We know that it is better [for the purpose] than Shakespeare.' Paul Contento states: 'So that's what we did. We never did get started among the Muslims there.'

The Gospels in English were mimeographed and used. The pattern for teaching was set. Both Paul and Maida would teach for one hour each:

> ... forty-five minutes pure English, fifteen minutes gospel. There were forty or fifty in each class, four classes each, every morning. They would wait in a line, you know. One class out, one class in ... one class out ...

*Paul and Maida Contento (first and second left, front row standing)
with university students*

it was unbelievable, unbelievable. That was the beginning of the student work in China. A very remarkable
thing ... we found the parables and the metaphors of
the Gospels wonderful material to teach both English
and the Gospel to the Chinese students ... the rich
young ruler, the story of Lazarus, the rich man who
went to hell and above all the Prodigal Son because of
the high value placed on loyalty to parents in China.

Maida Contento, as Maida Bolster, had been one of the
founding members of the Inter-Varsity Fellowship in Edinburgh University. Inter-Varsity Fellowship organized student
Christian groups in universities and colleges to meet for Bible
study, prayer, training in principles of Bible interpretation,
discipleship and evangelism among students. 'So we started
an Inter-Varsity group right then and there in Kunming, the
first China Inter-Varsity Christian Student Fellowship. We
were very fortunate to find a very keen and able Christian
medical student who became the first chairman.'

Paul Contento goes on to say:

And from there on, the students kept moving. They came to Kunming, then they'd go to Guiyang in Guizhou province and then they'd go to Chengdu in western Sichuan province. You see, the government moved them to where there was plenty of rice available. And Sichuan was a real rice country. And so they settled at half a dozen universities there.

Thus the gospel spread.

The Inter-Varsity Christian Student Fellowship (IVF) took root and spread rapidly. The Contentos were sent north by their mission and became members of staff at North-West University, teaching English. This was at Hanzhong in Shensi province, south of Xian, where there was a cluster of exiled universities. Inter-Varsity took root there too, as it did at Chengdu in western Sichuan, where Paul Contento taught for a year, and which was home to two great universities and the refuge for five others. It was there, he writes, that:

I hooked up with an old friend of mine, Calvin Chao. And, oh, he had great power, he had great power. I remember in one service there in Chungking, he was preaching. There were over a thousand students and there was hardly a dry eye in the audience ... two hundred came to the front, not only to be saved, but to dedicate their lives to the Lord ... you know that revival was genuine because students began to confess their sins publicly, and then do something about it. Students who had stolen books out of the library, took the books back and told the director of the university. It's not like Chinese to ... confess their sin publicly, you see.

CALVIN CHAO AND THE CHINA INTER-VARSITY FELLOWSHIP

Calvin Chao (Zhao Junying, 1906–96) had been educated at mission schools. When at college he had been afflicted seriously with tuberculosis and had to go to the Southern Presbyterian Mission Love and Mercy hospital at Tsing-kiangpu (Lianyungang) on the coast of Kiangsu, north of Shanghai. Dr Nelson Bell (whose daughter Ruth was to marry Dr Billy Graham) was his physician. After recovery, Chao was converted in 1931, at one of the early series of revival meetings held by Andrew Gih and the Bethel Band. He soon became an evangelist in the team.

In 1943, the China Native Evangelistic Crusade (later Partners International) was formed by a group of Christian businessmen in Seattle USA, meeting in the living room of a dentist, Dr N. A. Jepson. They sent a cablegram to Calvin Chao asking him if he would prayerfully consider leading a Chinese evangelistic movement in China. They would provide the resources. Calvin Chao saw this was an answer to prayer. By February 1945, Calvin Chao had twenty-two national workers and twenty-two students in training. The workers were well trained in theology. At least seven churches were established in Sinkiang among the Han Chinese by the end of 1950. These churches have survived and are still flourishing today.

The IVF movement had spread to such an extent that, as Contento says, 'In [July] 1945 we had a great convention in Chungking. And I was there. There were representatives from fifty Chinese colleges and universities already. That was when Inter-varsity went national... Calvin Chao was the first executive secretary of the All-China Inter-Varsity Committee [CIVF].' A large number of non-Christians attended as well. Many were converted and many dedicated their lives to the service of Christ. It was a wonderful time of continuing revival. Many Chinese Christian student groups and Chinese churches around the world today can trace their roots to the spiritual movement birthed by this convention.

Such were the stirring events for the furtherance of the gospel in China, even while the nation was being subjected to the horrors of war. With the opening of the hearts of the students to the gospel, China could not be the same. Either it would issue in great renewal and blessing for the nation after the war, or it would be the preparation for great suffering and human tragedy. Only time would tell which it was to be.

15. The gospel in China, 1945–49

The number of communicant Protestant Christians in China rose from about 350,000 in 1930 to at least 834,000 in 1949, when the Communists came to power. Some estimate a more realistic number of believers as a million. This was a remarkable increase. Much of the increase was due to the faithful labours of Chinese evangelical preachers. Even so, the Protestant Christian community must be seen in the context of a country of over 500 million people. At the end of World War II, for the space of four years, there were reports from all quarters of unusual responsiveness to the gospel.

CHINA AFTER WORLD WAR II

After World War II, civil war broke out in China between the official Nationalist (Kuomintang) government of Chiang Kai-shek and the Communists. The government of Chiang Kai-shek collapsed, depleted in resources and morale. It was given no time to recover from the shock, weariness and disruption caused by the war. In October 1948 Mukden (Shenyang) in Manchuria was taken by the Communists. This gave them access to the Trans-Siberian railway and supplies

The Tiananmen, Beijing

from Russia. The effect on China was shattering. The currency fell, and rich people rushed to get out of China.

In January 1949 the Communists took Peking (now renamed Beijing) and Tientsin (which they called Tianjin) and on 1 October 1949 Mao Zedong proclaimed the birth of the People's Republic of China from the Tiananmen (the gate of heavenly peace) in Beijing.

From 1 October 1949, the atheist People's Republic of China sought the destruction of all religion in China. Already, between 1945 and 1949, in areas under the control of the Communists hundreds of pastors had been killed and thousands of Christians mercilessly driven from their homes, to fend for themselves as best they could. In rural areas in the north, covering about a quarter of China, the church was already being driven underground.

CONTINUING REVIVAL AMONG THE UNIVERSITY AND COLLEGE STUDENTS

When the students and their universities returned home after the war, the revival continued to reap a harvest for the gospel.

This continued unabated right up to the time when the Communists came to power.

Something of the flavour of what actually happened among the students in the awakening and revival that took place around this time can be seen by what Paul Contento observed among students in an engineering college in the north-west. It took him by surprise. Some of his students began holding an early-morning prayer meeting, which meant meeting at four o'clock in the morning. Paul Contento went along:

> Those guys really meant business, they were really serious. They'd believe that sin was sin. You'd got to get rid of it ... this guy was holding a candle in this dark room, reading some Scripture. They'd start to pray one after another, the whole circle round, and no matter [that] your feet were freezing, you just stood there... One girl said to me 'I heard about this meeting and I ... I ... I laughed at it.' She said, 'I'll go and see what they do... As they were praying I suddenly realized I was a sinner.' And so, she said, she prayed in her turn, 'Lord I know that *I'm* a sinner now. Please forgive *me* and cleanse *my* sins.'... And so it went on ... it was really the work of the Spirit of God.

From before the founding of the China Inter-Varsity (Christian) Fellowship (China IVF) in July 1945, a good friend and confidante to the emerging evangelical student Christian movement was Bishop Frank Houghton. He was general director of the China Inland Mission. He encouraged Paul Contento in his work among university students. So did Calvin Chao. It was Calvin Chao who took leadership in founding the China IVF (see the previous chapter), which was fundamentally an indigenous Chinese movement among students. Calvin Chao approached Bishop Houghton in late 1945, asking if the mission could loan a worker to help the work along. The CIM headquarters was in Chungking at that time.

Houghton suggested David Adeney (1911–94). He was contacted and asked to fly out immediately from London to Chungking. He did so, leaving his family to follow. He became a very able staff worker for Calvin Chao and worked tirelessly right up to the disbanding of the organization. China IVF went into voluntary dissolution when it saw that it was in danger of being taken over by a Communist regime, which would only use it for its own ends.

David Adeney arrived by aeroplane in late 1945, just in time to sleep on the floor at the packed winter China IVF Conference at Chungking. He recalls that at the conference:

> ... everyday there were students coming to know Christ. Between meetings, there were prayer meetings everywhere. The ferry people knew something was going on by the number of students who came to pay for the false tickets with which the students had defrauded them. There was a great stir when one student had gone to the authorities and confessed he had entered university with a false graduation certificate. There was just a great sense of the working of the Spirit of God in the midst of the students.

Many students who found Christ went on to teach in schools. There they would witness for Christ and start a Students' Christian Fellowship.

Paul Contento was on the national committee of the China IVF, as an adviser. He was authorized to contact the British and American IVFs, with a view to starting an international fellowship. So it was that in 1946 China IVF joined with nine other Inter-Varsity Fellowships (from Australia, Britain, Canada, France, Holland, New Zealand, Norway, Switzerland and the USA) to form the International Fellowship of Evangelical Students (IFES). For a time, China IVF was the largest

David Adeney (right) with John Chang

movement affiliated. Calvin Chao and Paul Contento were the delegates representing China at the formation meeting held at Harvard University in the USA.

For the next four years David Adeney plunged into tireless ministry with China IVF. He encouraged both personal and small-group times for Bible study and prayer. He led by example. He saw the need, at that time, of fostering deep spiritual foundations and discipline in the lives of young Chinese Christians. That would sustain them in the difficult years to come. David Adeney also worked with such Chinese Christian leaders as David Yang, Moses Yu, John Chang and Timothy Lin, and he had admiration for Wang Mingdao in Peking.

David and Ruth Adeney left China in 1950 with their children, when it became clear that their continued presence there would cause acute trouble for their Chinese friends. David Adeney continued his work among students on a wider stage. He was highly respected by Chinese Christians around the world. He was one of only two foreigners to deliver plenary addresses to the 1986 Chinese Congress on World Evangelism held in Taiwan. The other was James Hudson Taylor III.

STUDENT CONFERENCES

In July and August 1946, a memorable China IVF conference was held in Peking. It commenced with a prayer conference for students held at the Christian Tabernacle, the church of Wang Mingdao in Peking. The conference was followed by an evangelistic campaign for students, which was held in the Salvation Army Citadel. Wang Mingdao was the main preacher. There were many conversions. Small groups, representing the fifteen colleges and universities returning from west China at that time, hardly knew each other. There were, however, several outstanding student Christian leaders, who were well organized. On Sunday mornings at 8 a.m, a

Second China IVF student conference at Madame Chiang's Orphanage, Nanking, July 1947

fellowship meeting at the tabernacle attracted about 150 students. A wall-newspaper recorded the multiplying activities of the unions and those of the newly formed Peking Fellowship of Christian Students.

In July 1947, 350 students from every Chinese university gathered for the Second China IVF National Conference of Evangelical Students, held at Nanking. Students came by land, sea and air. The speakers were Calvin Chao, David Yang, Andrew Gih and the venerable Dr Chia Yuming. Calvin Chao opened the conference with a reminder that Christians must expect, and be prepared for, persecution and suffering in the name of Jesus. Testimonies at the closing meeting sparked a revival among the students.

Communist students were always trying to infiltrate the organization. They did not realize that they stood out like sore thumbs! One strategy used to prevent this was to hold two-hour prayer sessions at the meetings where elections were held, immediately before the voting. Even so, by the time the revolution came, most of the groups had been infiltrated.

In August 1947 the Peking Fellowship of Christian Students had its own local summer conference. It was held in the ramshackle buildings that were once the emperor's stables, outside the walls of the Summer Palace. The facilities were of the simplest kind, but it was a spiritually glorious week. The preaching of David Yang had a profound effect, as did that of Wang Mingdao, who preached on 'sin', 'the virgin birth', 'the resurrection of Christ' and 'the Second Coming'. Already, as if in anticipation of a deluge of suffering to be endured in the near future, the prayer times were overwhelming. There was a profound spiritual renewal going on in the souls of the students. The final testimony meeting went on for hours, as the students poured out their hearts with thanksgiving for what God had done in their lives. Truck-loads of students returned to Peking, singing hymns of praise. This annual student conference continued to meet, as best it could, until 1955.

In late January 1948 a student conference was held for ten days in Peking. It was crowded. By this time the left-wing students in Peking were militantly active against the Christian students. Wang Mingdao warned against 'false prophets'. In the words of eyewitness Leslie Lyall, it was 'Another memorable conference, characterized by the almost incessant sound of prayer between the meetings, from every available room in the house. Here were young people, knowing that the future held only great trials, who were determined to get to know God in a real and deep way.' The Peking Youth for Christ Committee then arranged what was the largest evangelistic campaign ever to be held in Peking.

Later in 1948, the Second Summer Conference of the Peking Fellowship of Christian Students was held. The chief speaker was Calvin Chao of China IVF, who came from Nanking, where the headquarters of China IVF was then based. Pastor Xu Hungdao gave a series on the Song of Songs and Wang Mingdao highlighted lessons from his twenty years of married life. The spiritual zeal and courage displayed by

Peking IVF Conference, summer 1948

the students was tremendously impressive. Peking was to fall into Communist hands within months, in January 1949.

ASSESSMENT OF THE STUDENT CHRISTIAN WORK

Marcus Cheng was in a position to evaluate the student Christian movement from the viewpoint of a theological seminary principal. He noted that the movement did have its weaknesses. Christian students were too easily taken up with their own fellowships and activity among fellow students. They often lacked church-consciousness and a sense of the importance of the oneness of all believers. Some never attended a church at all. When they graduated and left to work in other places, they too often did not join a church, and even lost touch with meaningful Christian fellowship.

Another weakness was the lack of willingness to consider studying theology even when there was a shortage of jobs and they were unemployed. Among those who consecrated them-selves for Christian service, there was too often the notion that studying and training were not necessary for it. It was low on their priorities. It was the custom in China to marry young, and the new marital responsibilities hindered, if not actually prevented, many from considering training at a seminary. The result was that there was a shortage of appli-cants, even in such stirring spiritual times as those in which Marcus Cheng was living. Likewise, there were still too few churches willing to welcome trained men, or those which did would too easily cast them off.

MARCUS CHENG IN CHUNGKING

The experience of Marcus Cheng in Chungking during the period after World War II in some ways encapsulates the situation for the gospel generally in China at that time. There was an unusual responsiveness to the efforts to evangelize. In

Chungking Theological Seminary staff and students, 1948

March 1944, the Chungking Theological Seminary had been formed, with fifteen students. Marcus Cheng was president and principal. By the summer of 1948, there were eighty students in residence and ten staff. There were five churches where students could assist during term time. During the winter and summer vacations, the seminary sent out students to work further afield, assisting many congregations. The students were also to engage in evangelism in all the areas they visited. The reports and the testimonies of the students themselves evidenced a general receptiveness towards the gospel. There was manifest fruitfulness in response to the gospel and numbers professed conversion. All this was an encouragement. The feedback from the distribution of tracts and booklets confirmed this picture of a general openness to hear and believe the gospel.

A PRISON WORK IN CHUNGKING

It was not many years in the past that conditions in the prisons had been appalling. The National Government under Chiang Kai-shek had, however, taken action to improve things. There were three prisons in Chungking, two for short-term, and one for long-term prisoners. The seminary had permission to visit all of them on a regular basis. Remarkably, the governor of the long-term prison welcomed the students

Prisoners attending a service

to preach the gospel. There were about a thousand prisoners, about a hundred of whom were women. The women students ministered among the female prisoners. A hall had been constructed, called the 'Hall of Instruction', which could seat about 500. This was used for meetings.

Over a period of time, more than a hundred 'definitely accepted the Lord Jesus as their Saviour'. These organized themselves into a church inside the prison and had six elected deacons! Marcus Cheng taught candidates for baptism, and a baptismal service was held on the Sunday before Christmas 1947. There were forty-three baptized, of whom thirteen were murderers and one was a warder! The head warder also desired baptism. He said that the changed lives of the saved prisoners had led him to seek and find the Saviour for himself. A generous gift made possible a copy of the New Testament, not only for those who were baptized, but for any person within the prison who desired a copy.

There were no medical facilities or doctors in the prison. Also there was much undernourishment and the death rate was high among the prisoners. The spiritual awakening within the prison led to practical measures. The prisoners and their families decided to do something about the conditions.

Elders and leaders of the church in prison

The governor encouraged this and contributed to the fund. The result was a hospital ward fully equipped with twenty beds. On 24 January 1948 the dedication service was attended by the prison governor and a High Court judge.

Easter Day 1948 was a memorable day in the prison. Baptismal services were held in different parts of the prison for twenty women and no less than 199 men. Of those baptized, two women and thirteen men were members of staff. The governor went on record as saying:

> From the time your students began coming here to preach the gospel, many lives have been changed. As a result, the whole atmosphere of the prison has improved. Formerly, these prisoners were talking about their rights and making democratic demands. There were constant disturbances and frequent riots. They would not even allow us to lock the cell doors. We had to call in the local militia to keep them in order. Now, the whole prison is peaceful and easy to govern; we no longer require the assistance of the militia and have dismissed them. I especially send the worst characters,

the troublemakers, to listen to the gospel message, and it changes them.

A WORK IN THE FACTORIES AROUND CHUNGKING

More than 80% of the population of China were peasant farmers. The industrialization of China took place in earnest only after 1900 and was mainly located in the eastern cities. Many factories moved west during the Second World War. They went back after the war, but a number stayed. These factories were located out of town. There were many evils within these factory communities.

A remarkable work developed at a cotton mill. A doctor and his wife, who was a nurse, were Christians. They were too far away to attend Sunday worship in the city. They invited two of the students from Chungking Theological Seminary to come and start prayer meetings in their home. Hearing of this, other Christians joined them. The students noted that there were a large number of women working in the mill who had nothing to do in their leisure hours. They gathered some of these women together and preached the gospel to them, and found them responsive. During the winter vacation four students, two men and two women, were sent to preach the gospel to the factory workers. The manager was co-operative and allowed the use of a large hall.

One of the executive staff of the mill had been very im-moral and an earnest idolater. He became extremely ill with tuberculosis and day and night he burned incense to the image of the goddess by his bedside. He lay dying. A Christian nurse introduced Jesus Christ to him and he repented. Not only was he truly converted, but he did not die and was com-pletely healed. He led his wife and three grown-up sons to Christ and, back at work, though only a Christian of two years' standing, he was enthusiastic in the work and chaired the meetings in the large hall. Some time later, the owner of the factory came to Chungking and, as a result of this man's witness to him and his wife, a large factory building was set apart for a church. All expenses, including those for the support of a full-time preacher, were to be met by the factory. A number of factories followed suit and several fully indigenous churches were planted.

THE FIRST MISSIONARY ATTEMPT FROM CHINA

During the war with Japan, the newly formed North-west Bible Institute was among the relocated missionary works in the west of China. It was situated in Fengxiang, Shensi province. It was run by James Hudson Taylor II, with his vice-principal Mark Ma.

Mark Ma was from Kaifeng in Henan province. He was a government teacher, converted in 1937. In November 1942, Ma felt a call from God to take the gospel west into the Sinkiang region, also known then as Eastern Turkestan. On the Easter morning of 25 April 1943 he revealed this call and found that eight others confessed that they too had received such a call.

A weekly prayer meeting was set up. They formed a small evangelistic band called the Preach Everywhere Gospel Band (literally, Pinzhuan Fuyin Tuan). This initial call developed into a larger vision for evangelism westward, all the way back to Jerusalem, the place from where the gospel had originated. Ma put it this way in May 1943:

> Since Pentecost, the pathway of the gospel has been for the greater part in a westward direction from Jerusalem; to Antioch, then to all of Europe; from Europe to America, and from there to the East [to China]; then, from the south-east of China to the north-west. However, westward from Gansu [province] it can be said there is no firmly established church. We can go westward, preaching the gospel all the way back

to Jerusalem, causing the light of the gospel to complete the circle around this dark world.

Attempts to take the gospel into Sinkiang were made by the Preach Everywhere Gospel Band after the war. The team was known in the English-speaking world outside China as the 'Back to Jerusalem Band', but not so in the Chinese church. The stirring vision was to carry the gospel to Sinkiang, Tibet, Afghanistan, Iran, Saudi Arabia, Iraq, Turkey, Syria and back to Jerusalem. This programme was halted by closed borders and the Communist victory in China in 1949. Mecca Zhao was one of this band, and was given that name as a result of a particular vision he had.

By 1949, independently of the Back to Jerusalem Band, there were reports of at least five small Chinese Christian groups leaving home in east China and travelling to west China to take the gospel there and to regions beyond. These were all unconnected with each other. Among them were the Central Asia Spiritual Work Team and the Chinese Christian Mission. Another of these bands was called the North-west Spiritual Movement (NSM). The founder was Zheng Guquan. The background of this movement was the Jesus Family of Ching Tien-ying, which by then had 20,000 followers in more than a hundred groups throughout China. The strategy of the NSM was simply to preach the gospel, believing that Christ would return very soon. In this mission they did not seek to establish congregations or communities.

Towards the end of 1948, one of their leaders, Simon Zhao (Zhao Haizhen, 1918–2001) arrived in Sinkiang and reached Kashgar by January 1950. He was one of about twenty in all from this mission to reach Kashgar. Kashgar became a centre, as the North-west Spiritual Band, the Preach Everywhere Band and the Chinese Christian Mission met up. They cooperated together in the work, and the needs of the Islamic nations to the west were discussed. The 'Back to Jerusalem' vision was caught by all the agencies. However, they came face to face with the difficulties of work among Muslims, and it was found expedient to evangelize the minority Han Chinese first. Only the Chinese Christian Mission engaged in systematic planning to reach the Muslim Uighur people.

Soon the Communists controlled the area and sealed the border. The workers who did not return east were imprisoned. Several of these died in prison, including Zhao's wife. In Kashgar, Simon Zhao languished in a labour-camp prison for thirty-one years, all the while nurturing the vision of 'Back to Jerusalem'.

THE LITTLE FLOCK

In 1947 Watchman Nee was joyfully restored to his senior position, from which he had been suspended in 1942 for going into business. In May 1948, Witness Lee (Li Changshou, 1905–97) organized a grand welcoming conference for him at the Hardoon Road premises in Shanghai. Watchman Nee had already assigned all his business assets to the Shanghai local church, and in the euphoria others also gave their assets to the church. They cited the example of the early Christians in Acts chapter 4. This was to have an unforeseen consequence. When the Communists came to power, they charged the Little Flock with being a 'capitalist' organization!

The Little Flock planned to evangelize China by means of mass migration of Christian groups. These were to settle inland in unevangelized places and earn their living by practising their trades. So the congregation in Shanghai, of about 5,000, would become a seedbed from which small but mature church groups would be planted. The emphasis would not be on communal living, but on communal worship. Witness Lee was the driving force behind this project.

By 1949 the Little Flock had about 700 assemblies around the country, with a total attendance of more than 70,000. These figures are a conservative minimum because, on principle, there was no systematic effort made to count their people. Even so, the Little Flock had developed from being a movement with local church autonomy to being, in practice, an organization run by a strict internal hierarchy, with tight control by the top leaders. In April 1949 it was agreed that Witness Lee should emigrate to Formosa (Taiwan). There a flourishing work was established.

STATE OF THE PROTESTANT CHURCHES IN CHINA

The differences of thought and agenda between evangelicals and liberals within the Protestant Church in China remained as wide apart as ever. Yet there can be no doubt of the depth and power of the spiritual awakening and revival among the students and among the converts in the Protestant Chinese churches and fellowships. This gave evangelicalism the ascendancy in the Protestant church. The spiritual roots were strong enough and deep enough and widespread enough for the biblical faith to survive the fiery trial of the persecution which was about to burst upon the whole church. The solid spiritual groundwork left by the missionaries could not be fully uprooted and destroyed. The Chinese Protestant churches were ready to become entirely indigenous, upheld by the grace of God and the power of the Holy Spirit. Christ had prepared His church for the ordeal about to burst upon it.

16. The Communists take over China, 1949–53

On 1 October 1949 Mao Zedong proclaimed the birth of the People's Republic of China. By the end of 1949 the Communist army had established virtual control of China. There was a widespread welcome for the peace. It turned out to be the calm before the storm. The new civic Communist officials were taking careful stock. A reign of terror was being deliberately organized.

Then they launched into a programme of widespread arrests and public trials. The victims were landowners, businessmen with interests abroad and supporters of the old 'imperialistic' government of Chiang Kai-shek. University faculty members, professionals, artists and writers were also the objects of hatred. These trials were held in public. When the charges were read out, the people were asked to pass the sentence — whether it was confiscation of property, being sent to a labour camp, or execution. Executions were carried out without any delay. House searches were made by day or night. Suspects were taken away for interrogation, some of them never to be seen alive again.

Meetings for indoctrination by Communist cadres were compulsory. Accusation meetings, including a call for self-accusation, abounded. Self-accusation meant criticism of one's past thinking and actions. The group, led by a well-trained cadre, would demand a change to toeing the party line. Any resistance or reluctance was met by intimidation. It was blatant brainwashing.

By the end of 1951 up to five million people had been executed or perished in other ways (Mao admitted to 800,000). Many Christians were killed. Christians had served in the government of Chiang Kai-shek and there were many Christians occupying senior positions in commerce and education.

THE IMMEDIATE COMMUNIST DOMESTIC POLICY WITHIN CHINA

The Communists set about giving China the strongest government that the country had ever had. To achieve this they set about complete domination in three areas of life:

1. In the area of *politics* — to maintain absolute domination of all China by a one-party state backed up by ruthless power. Tibet, regarded as part of China, was invaded and annexed by May 1951.

2. In the area of *society* — to introduce and maintain a programme of social engineering so as to thoroughly remould the Chinese people and their culture. This would be achieved by a programme of re-education. Communist ideology would be imposed, with its view of the universe, man, history, ethics and all the structures of society. Resistance would be summarily dealt with. Class enemies were to be regarded as irredeemable and eliminated.

3. In the area of *religion* — to introduce a policy of strict state control until religion died a natural death and became history. As atheists and humanists, they believed that all religion was mere superstition and

would vanish away through the process of re-education.

Confucianism was regarded as the major enemy because it was an indigenous philosophy and religion. It was deeply rooted in Chinese culture and life. To break its hold on the people there needed to be the break-up of the traditional family, the destruction of Confucian ethics and the reinterpretation of history along the lines of a class struggle.

Buddhism and Taoism were regarded almost as indigenous faiths and could be dealt with by closing down most of the temples and monasteries, expropriating their land and sending the 'parasitic' priests to tasks of productive labour and re-education.

Christianity was viewed as a foreign religion used to impose foreign ways and foreign powers on a weak China. The first task was to expel all foreign missionaries. All mission assets, such as properties, hospitals and institutions of education would be taken over. Expulsion would be achieved as quickly as possible and without offending world opinion too much. Any residual Christianity would be controlled by the state until it had withered away.

Islam was a minority foreign religion by and large confined to the western provinces. It was to be strictly kept down because of the history of perennial armed revolts.

THE IMMEDIATE COMMUNIST POLICY TOWARDS THE PROTESTANT CHURCH

As noted in the previous chapter, in January 1950 a directory published by the National Christian Council indicated that there were 834,000 Protestant communicant members in China. A more realistic assessment estimated the number of believers as at least one million. There were 19,000 churches, chapels or evangelistic stations, over 2,000 ordained Chinese pastors and 10,500 evangelists and Christian workers. Forty-eight theological colleges and twenty-one Bible schools were training thousands of students. In addition there were eighteen Christian universities and over seventy Christian hospitals, as well as 270 Christian upper schools and 262 small mission hospitals.

At the beginning of 1948 there were 110 Protestant mission groups with over 6,000 missionaries in China. At the end of 1949 the number of missionaries was down to 4,062. By the end of 1951 all remaining missionaries had either left or were in the process of leaving China for good. Thereafter, for a long time, the only direct missionary input into China was from Christian radio ministry. The Far Eastern Broadcasting Corporation began to beam programmes into China from 1949.

In May 1950 the new premier, Zhou Enlai, invited four liberal Protestant leaders to a conference in Beijing. At three late-night sessions, they worked out a manifesto with the title *Direction of Endeavour for Chinese Christianity in the Construction of New China,* but which is more popularly known as *The Christian Manifesto.* It was first published on 10 August 1950. This required an admission from Protestant Christians that the church had been a tool of imperialism. Now they were to give their first and foremost loyalty and obedience to the Communist Party and to purge themselves of all imperialistic influences. In return they could hope for freedom of religious belief according to the constitution. The manifesto embodied the threefold principle of self-government, self-support and self-propagation for the church. Implementation of this policy would be through the Three-Self Reform Movement, which was to be controlled by the Religious Affairs Bureau.

The TSRM (later to become the Three-Self Patriotic Movement) was launched in April 1951 with its slogan of 'Love Country; Love Church'. Chinese Christians of all persuasions were to cut off completely any connection with their brethren in the West and to ensure the removal of all missionaries out

of China. Within two years the authorities claimed that
400,000 Protestant Christians had endorsed the manifesto.
Even that figure was only about 40% of Protestant membership. Actually, approximately 40,000 had signed up. Clearly,
there were going to be problems.

Communists had places of influence and authority within
the Chinese church and in organizations such as the YMCA,
YWCA, denominational bodies and some theological colleges. The person mainly responsible for drafting the manifesto, and chairman of the newly formed TSRM, was Y. T. Wu
(Wu Yaozong, 1893–1979), a long-time-serving secretary of
the YMCA. He was a radical liberal in his theology and had
been a secret Communist party member for many years. Wu
was also trusted by the Communist leaders. He had an
unbridled animosity against fundamentalism and evangelicalism. He opposed the biblical gospel on principle. The principal organ of propaganda for the Three-Self Movement became the *Tianfeng* ('Heavenly Wind'), the main magazine of
the Protestant church and founded by Y. T. Wu in 1945. *The
Christian Manifesto* was first published in it.

ACCUSATION MEETINGS IN THE CHURCHES

Accusation meetings in the Protestant churches were organized by the TSRM. The first accusation campaign was
launched in Beijing, at the inauguration conference of the
TSRM in April 1951. Then, on 2 May 1951, the *Tianfeng* published a summons to the whole Protestant church in China to
take part in accusation meetings. Accusations and self-
criticisms of all 'imperialist associations', past and present,
were to be made. The slogan was: 'Propagandize well, accuse
minutely.' Elaborate preparations were made and every detail
rehearsed. Betrayals were deliberately planned. Only participation by churches and by all their members in these accusation meetings would qualify them to join the new ecumenical Protestant church body being set up, called the Three-Self

Reform Church. The accusation meetings became extraordinarily intense because many churches in some way had links with the USA through the missions. The USA and China had troops on opposite sides in the Korean War, which had broken out in June 1950. The USA was now the number one imperialist enemy. Chinese Christian was made to accuse Chinese Christian, and congregations had to accuse their pastors. In this way, the spirit of love in the Christian fellowships was deliberately destroyed by the spreading of lies, suspicion and fear.

Accounts of the meetings were published by national and local newspapers. Thousands of Christian pastors and church workers were imprisoned or sent for productive labour on farms or in factories. Many were only to be released in 1979. Many Christians withdrew from the organized church altogether and met in the private homes of trusted friends for fellowship and worship. This was the origin of the housechurch movement. This practice of Christians meeting only in private homes for fellowship and worship was to accelerate dramatically during the 1950s. It was a matter of survival.

LAST DAYS IN CHINA FOR FOREIGN MISSIONARIES

In 1950 it became clear that missionaries were vulnerable. They were told that they were not welcome, since they were foreigners and agents of imperialism. The Chinese Christians began to tell the missionaries that it was dangerous for them to stay and that their presence constituted a danger for the indigenous church. The China Inland Mission was the last mission to withdraw from China. At the beginning of 1951 the CIM had 637 missionaries in China, together with over 200 children.

About twenty church leaders from the provinces of Shanxi, Hubei and Henan arrived at the headquarters of the China Inland Mission in Shanghai. They had come to bring news of churches that had not been heard from for at least ten years

Chinese pastor and his family, 1951

and to thank the CIM for all it had done for them. Phyllis
Thompson records:

> Divested of status and income, preachers and church
> leaders had taken to peddling cloth and vegetables, or
> going with a bag of tools to do odd jobs as a carpenter.
> They visited scattered believers in the course of earning
> their livelihood. 'Suffering is never welcomed by man,
> but suffering can cause a man to know God better' was
> a constant theme in the testimonies they gave. Chris-
> tians in name alone are winnowed away. Churches
> merely concerned with external appearances disappear
> altogether.

Evacuation of the CIM missionaries was to take place
through Hong Kong. Kaifeng Hospital in Henan province had
already been handed over to the Chinese Christian staff. Four
other hospitals would have to be handed over to the local
authorities. At a time when church and mission premises
were being confiscated, or requisitioned by the army, a providential sale of a three-year lease of the CIM headquarters

property was negotiated. Amazingly, it was agreed to by the authorities. It was calculated that this would provide the needed funds to evacuate and repatriate all the CIM missionaries from all over China.

Evacuation was not a straightforward task. The situation inland was complicated. Missionaries were held under virtual house arrest, with no work possible, while exit visas were obtained. These were only granted after advertisements had been placed in local newspapers urging anyone to whom they owed debts, or with any other grievances against the missionaries, to come forward. Doctors could be charged with murder just because patients had died! A Chinese citizen must also be found to act as surety for debts, crimes and all future behaviour towards the People's Republic of China. Even then permission could be withheld. However, in spite of everything, by the end of 1951 there were only thirty-three CIM missionaries, with five children, still remaining in inland China, mainly in the north-west and south-west regions.

On New Year's Day 1953 four German CIM missionaries were released. This left only four to be evacuated, and this was completed on 20 July 1953. It was the joyful testimony of the CIM that 'Since the decision to withdraw was taken, not a life nor a limb was lost. To God be the glory.'

The 'open century' of freedom to evangelize throughout China by foreign missionaries was over. It was not quite 100 years since Hudson Taylor first set foot on mainland China on 1 March 1854. The withdrawal of the last CIM missionary also brought to a close the 146 years of direct Protestant missionary endeavour in mainland China dating from Robert Morrison's arrival in 1807.

ASSESSMENT OF 146 YEARS OF PROTESTANT FOREIGN MISSION INPUT TO CHINA

How much had been achieved for the gospel in China since Robert Morrison's arrival in China on 7 September 1807? The answer would become clear within the next quarter of a century. The spiritual foundation of the Chinese Protestant church turned out to be sound and strong. And, from that foundation, the Protestant church would not only survive, but would multiply numerically. It also maintained its essential evangelicalism. This has been the legacy of all the sacrificial missionary service in China, together with the supporting prayers and sacrificial giving of the worldwide church for the cause of Christ. The gospel of free salvation to be found by saving faith in Jesus Christ is still the power of God unto salvation, wherever it is declared.

CHRISTIAN STUDENTS AND THE COMMUNISTS

The Communists gave a high priority to gaining control of students' minds and actions. Though Christian fellowships were able to meet on campus to start with, it was not long before this became impossible. Political pressures on the students were tremendous. Every student was placed in a political group with endless indoctrination meetings and parades. The difficulty was that the Christian could not accept the Marxist atheistic view of life. These were really tough times for Christian students. Most were strong enough to stand up to the pressure, but some were not. Christians could get into trouble just for saying grace at meals. There was always the threat of losing their scholarships hanging over them. Application forms of all description, including those for jobs, would ask the question: 'Do you have any religion?' Christians knew perfectly well that any answer in the affirmative would mean rejection of the application. The shouting of blasphemous slogans such as, 'Our eternal liberator, Mao Zedong, our Saviour,' was expected. Students had to write out their life story time and time again. It had to include criticisms of the individual's past thinking, and then the others in the group would criticize in turn. If the Christian stood firm he would be subjected to *douzheng*, which is 'struggle'. This is when the group would accuse and struggle against him, to change his thinking and attitudes to that which was 'correct' — that is to say, to the party line.

We can see the importance of the powerful outpouring of the Holy Spirit in revival among the students in the period leading up to the Communist People's Republic of China coming into being. A special strength from God was needed to be faithful to Christ.

DILEMMAS AND THEIR RESOLUTION

Great determination and skill were exercised by the Three-Self Reform Movement in order to unite all the churches under the banner of patriotism and firm central control. The individual church leaders were given special attention and every effort was made to win them to the cause. Co-operation with authorities was rationalized and attempts were made to justify submission on biblical grounds. Some succumbed to blandishments, fair promises, threats and specious arguments in the hope of preserving the continued existence of their church. Some of those who held liberal theological views, or those with no firm views at all, could acquiesce quite happily. Others just made the best of the situation. Those who were won over, one way or another, were placed in positions of authority and influence. At the end of the day it came down to the individual's conscience before God.

Leaders with evangelical convictions differed among themselves in their response. There is nothing new about that. Church history clearly has many similar examples where the preciousness of the biblical truth of the 'priesthood of all believers' comes into sharp focus. Each believer has the right to stand before God in the light of his or her prayerful under-standing of Scripture. Some good men just could not go along with what they saw as fundamental compromise and dis-obedience to Scripture. For them the path would be a path of suffering. Other good men — very few — stayed with the

Scene in China, 1951

Three-Self movement to the end, convinced it was the will of
God for them. Then there were those who were at first convinced it was the will of God for them to submit but, as time
went on, came to see it as an error and confessed it to be so.
To such, no mercy was shown by their Communist masters.

The Communist press conducted a remorseless campaign
of abuse and hatred against the church and against individual
Christians. Also the *Tianfeng* was unsparing with its abusive
criticisms. Liu Liangmo, the national secretary of the YMCA
in succession to Y. T. Wu, justified these vilifications. They
were, he claimed, only like Jesus' rebuke of the scribes and
Pharisees. The main targets of the campaigns were naturally
the most influential theologians and the most charismatic
leaders. Three early arrests were those of, firstly, Bishop Chen
Wenyuan, a prestigious Methodist leader ('China's No.1
Protestant') in 1951; then, in 1952, T. C. Chao, (Zhao Zichen)
professor of theology and Dean of the School of Religion at
Yanjing University, Beijing; and, thirdly, Ching Tien-ying,
founder of the Pentecostal organization the Jesus Family. The
Jesus Family was dissolved the following year. The next major
leader to suffer was Watchman Nee.

WATCHMAN NEE AND THE LITTLE FLOCK

Early in 1951 Watchman Nee and some of his colleagues visited the CIM at Shanghai. Time had been when they had kept strictly apart from all Western missionary societies. This gesture of friendship was greatly appreciated and helped to heal the breaches of the past.

Watchman Nee expressed the view that he believed Communism would not take root in China, and the day would come when missionaries could return, but, he warned, 'Only come then as guest Bible teachers; meanwhile prepare translations of Bible commentaries, Bible handbooks, and the spiritual treasures of the centuries that are available to you in the West. Be ready to share them with us when you come back.'

Watchman Nee refused to move to safety from Shanghai. He was arrested and imprisoned for his faith in May 1952. He was sentenced to twenty years' imprisonment. He died on 1 June 1972, a few weeks after being released from prison. *The Collected Works of Watchman Nee* have been published in English in sixty-two volumes. His most influential books were *The Spiritual Man, The Normal Christian Life* and *The Normal Christian Church Life*. These were also popular in the English-speaking world. In them, Nee embraced the Keswick, or 'victorious Christian life', teaching to such an extent as to lay him open, at times, to the charge of teaching a form of automatic sanctification akin to sinless perfection.

The Little Flock (Christian Assembly) had always been free from foreign connections and independent of foreign financial support. So it had been expected that they would be regarded with favour by the new regime, yet they too were required to sign up to *The Christian Manifesto*. They did so, but any favour was not lasting. In 1954 the Little Flock pulled out of the Three-Self Movement. In 1956, the authorities rounded up most of their leaders throughout China, and appointed their own men instead. By then the Little Flock had over 80,000 members in 870 assemblies.

MINISTRY TO CHINESE OUTSIDE OF CHINA

Some influential evangelical leaders saw their future ministry as being outside China. Five such men were Calvin Chao, Andrew Gih, Witness Lee, Leland Wang and Timothy Chao.

Calvin Chao moved to Hong Kong. He visited Singapore in 1950 to hold revival meetings there and was asked to return in order to start the Singapore Theological Seminary with Paul Contento. He also started the Chinese Youth Gospel Centre in Manila, Philippines. In 1956 the Chao family moved to the USA.

Andrew Gih held evangelistic meetings from 1949 in the Kuai Le ('Happiness') Theatre in Hong Kong on Sunday mornings with congregations each week of more than 1,200. The scale of the need and opportunity for the gospel at that time in Hong Kong can be gauged from the fact that the population of Hong Kong, as a result of refugees from mainland China, multiplied from 500,000 before World War II to more than three million by 1955. A Gospel Hall was formally established.

Andrew and Dorcas Gih

Gih's influence upon Chinese churches in south-east Asia was to be profound.

Witness Lee had emigrated in 1949 to Formosa (Taiwan) and there a flourishing Little Flock work was established. He then emigrated to the USA in 1962. His leadership was authoritarian. His branch of the Christian Brethren was called 'The Local Church Movement'. It has expanded around the globe, including into China. It now has over 2,300 assemblies with a worldwide membership of 250,000. In 1965, Living Stream Ministry was founded in Anaheim, California, and published the works of both Witness Lee and Watchman Nee.

Leland Wang had co-founded the Chinese Missionary Union in 1928 to reach overseas Chinese with the gospel. He was the first Chinese from within China to engage in this field of work. He was known as the 'Moody of China'. His ministry extended to the USA, Canada, Europe and the Middle East. He also received a DD degree from Wheaton College.

Timothy Chao moved his ministry to Hong Kong on New Year's Day 1950. Overseas works in India and Indonesia were developed. Timothy Chao was a prolific writer, producing, among other things, thirty-five exegetical works on biblical books. A lasting testament to him is provided by the Faith Theological Seminary, Indonesia, and the International Theological College in Hong Kong.

For the church of Christ still in China it was the beginning of sorrows, but God was with them.

17. The church fighting for survival, 1953–66

In 1953 the first modern census taken in China showed there to be a population of 583 million. By 1980 the number had passed one billion.

By the end of 1953 China was a united country where the will of the government was enforced. Advances were being made with ambitious infrastructure projects. These included flood control of the Yellow River, irrigation projects, bridges built over the Yangtze River, new roads and railways constructed, factories booming and improvement of public utilities in towns. Much of this, to be sure, could only be achieved by contingents of forced labour, swelled by many who had fallen foul of the 'Five-Anti Campaign' of 1952 (opposed to bribery, tax evasion, fraud, the theft of state assets and the leaking of state economic secrets). Inflation was in check; taxes were collected; there was no famine; gangsters and vice were largely eliminated; cities were cleaned, education vastly extended and widespread efforts made to improve public health. Land reform had redistributed land to peasants. Laws were introduced abolishing child marriage, polygamy and concubinage. Equal rights for women were also party policy. Yet there was widespread disillusionment setting in. The Chinese Communist Party

(CCP) ruled over all aspects of the people's lives, including their minds.

THE PROTESTANT CHURCH, 1953–58

By the end of 1958 all denominational structures and organizations had been destroyed by the Three-Self Reform Movement, or as it came to be known from 1954 onwards, the Three-Self Patriotic Movement (TSPM). This was all done in the name of unity and patriotism. All foreign financing had been cut off. The goal of the 'Three-Self' movement was self-governance, self-support and self-propagation of a united Protestant church. The Protestant missionaries had failed to achieve self-governance, self-support and self-propagation for the churches in 146 years of work. Now it was achieved by the force of the state. Yet freedom to exercise these liberties was severely curtailed in practice. The TSPM was controlled and directed by the CCP. For the Christians in China the loss of fellowship with the body of Christ overseas would also be a grievous loss. But by being thrown on the grace of God and His resources there would be spiritual gain and greater usefulness to God. A qualitatively different church would emerge after twenty years.

In October 1955, the TSPM issued a decree declaring all Christian activities outside its own jurisdiction to be illegal. The government Religious Affairs Bureau conducted a house-to-house search of every Christian home for Christian literature to confiscate. The Little Flock was forced into the TSPM. In spite of all this, reports showed growth in church membership and baptisms in many places. Christian university students had managed to continue meeting in conferences until 1955. These were stopped, but as late as 1957 a delegate conference from nine universities was held in Shantou (Swatow).

By the end of 1958, city churches had all been brought under the firm control of the government and their numbers drastically reduced, as was their membership. In Shanghai, over 200 churches were reduced to fifteen; in Beijing, sixty-five to four; in other cities there remained between one and four churches. In Taiyuan, capital of Shanxi province, there was only one church left open, with a staff of four. Already, during the land-reform campaign, rural churches had been closed down. The sect known as the True Jesus Church had conformed, but was now closed down. 20,000 Protestant churches were closed, leaving less than 100 show churches open in all China.

Chinese pastoral leadership over congregations was for all practical purposes removed. Those pastors and leaders who remained were only those who agreed to toe the party line and submit to its control. Hymns and sermons were all vigilantly vetted by CCP office-holders known as cadres. Various subjects were banned, such as the Second Coming of Christ, the book of Revelation and the vanity of this world. Teaching about the duty of absolute obedience to Christ came into conflict with government policy. Belief in miraculous healing and also in exorcism was distinctly frowned upon by Religious Affairs cadres. Books were censored. No one under the age of eighteen was to be allowed in a church. Evangelism was strictly forbidden.

The consequence of state domination in the affairs of the formal churches was that the great majority of Christians had to withdraw from them in order to worship and pray in their own homes and in those of fellow believers. The house fellowships were spontaneous and informal, but very determined in the defence of their faith. These Christians were very fervent in their praying for each other and they supported the persecuted Christians and their families in whatever way they could.

The Little Flock, with its emphasis on the church being the company of believing people, and not a building or ecclesiastical organization, came into its own. The loss of church buildings meant that they could fall back on the flexibility of their numerous fellowship groups in homes. Many house churches today are directly derived from the Little Flock. Many other groups owe a substantial debt to Little Flock doctrine and practice, both for their survival and for their beliefs. The Little Flock was non-Pentecostal, yet believed in the possibility of divine healing in answer to prayer. It also was tolerant of glossolalia, or speaking in tongues, though it did not believe in this as an article of faith.

Y. T. WU PRESIDENT OF THE THREE-SELF MOVEMENT

Y. T. Wu was born on 4 November 1893 to a non-Christian family in Guangdong province. He came to faith at a mass rally conducted by Sherwood Eddy in 1918 and was baptized as a Congregationalist. By the end of 1920 Y. T. Wu had become a secretary of the student department of the Peking YMCA. At that time Y. T. Wu opposed the Communists. In 1924 he went to the USA to receive a theological education at Union Theological Seminary and Columbia University. His M.A. was awarded in 1927 for a dissertation on 'William James' doctrine of religious belief'. Wu returned to the YMCA at Shanghai. From 1932 he was in charge of the publications of the Association Press of the YMCA. In 1945, as noted in the previous chapter, he started the magazine *Tianfeng*, which has been the main magazine of the Protestant church on mainland China ever since. He was a liberal in his theology.

Y. T. Wu's thinking evolved in three stages. The first phase was between 1920 and 1930, when he was a *Christian pacifist*. He believed the essence of the gospel to be in the power of love, 'the way' of love as exemplified by Christ. In 1927 he organized the China Christian Student Movement. He still opposed Communism. He said, 'The advocacy of the class struggle, the use of brutal force, terrorism, the breaking down of all moral virtues, were their [the Communists'] ideal methods and these were to be abhorred. The Chinese people hold an entirely different philosophy of life.' Wu admired Mahatma Gandhi and translated Gandhi's autobiography for publication.

The second stage of Y. T. Wu's thinking developed between 1931 and 1940, when he embraced *the social gospel*. In 1931 Japan occupied Manchuria. For Wu, the principle of love became no more than a 'beautiful dream'. In 1934 a series of articles he had written were collected into a book with the title *The Social Gospel*. He showed an interest in social revolution. In 1937 Wu went to the USA again to study at Union Theological Seminary for a further six months. There he was influenced by the theories of Henry Frederick Ward (1873–1966), who has been called the 'leftist prophet of labour', and the popular liberal theologian Reinhold Niebuhr (1892–1971). Wu's definite leanings towards Communism can be dated from this period.

The third stage of Y. T. Wu's thinking developed between 1941 and 1949. Wu now became a *Christian Socialist* and pro-Communist. In his treatise *No Man has Seen God*, he wrote, 'Belief in God is not contradictory to materialism, just as it is not contradictory to evolutionism. For what we know, the two seemingly contradictory systems of thought [atheism and theism] will achieve a new synthesis.' On 27 May 1943 Wu had an in-depth talk with Zhou Enlai in Chungking. He became a secret member of the Communist Party. In April 1948 Wu published his article *The Present-Day Tragedy of Christianity*. This was his declaration of war against the foreign missions in China.

After the 1949 revolution, Y. T. Wu emerged as the recognized leader of the Chinese Protestants as far as the Communists were concerned. He was president of the official Three-Self Reform Movement from 1951 until his death in 1979. Wu saw his task as 'saving the church' by finding a way to coexist with the totalitarian atheistic state. In this task he was single-minded. For him it was the church, the structure, that needed to be saved, even if this meant complete subservience to the

China Communist Party. Wu had no time for dogmatic doctrinal Christianity. He bore an unbridled animosity towards evangelicals and their teachers. He regarded them as a threat to everything he believed.

WANG MINGDAO AND THE THREE-SELF MOVEMENT

Wang Mingdao had stood firm against the Japanese attempts to impose a political agenda on the church. He would now have to stand firm against the Communists for the same reasons. He could not be involved with the TSM. Their muzzling of the freedom of the pulpit and their following a secular political agenda was a direct challenge to the only headship of Christ in His church. Another reason for not joining the movement was its theological liberalism, which Wang regarded as a departure from the biblical gospel and therefore heretical. Thus his reasons for not joining the TSM were theological, not political. Wang declared from the pulpit the biblical principle of separation of church and state and that a church which had become the servant of an atheist government had ceased to function as the true church of Jesus Christ.

Wang Mindao

Such criticism of the TSM by a Christian leader of national importance could not be tolerated. The irony was that, if ever a man and his church had been consistently true to the principles of self-governance, self-support and self-propagation, it was Wang Mingdao and the Christian Tabernacle church in Beijing. Likewise his moral integrity and life were of the highest order.

In the spring of 1954 the Three-Self Patriotic Movement, as it was now called, required all the churches and Christian organizations in Beijing to appoint delegates to attend a meeting in July at which Wang Mingdao was to be publicly accused. Leslie Lyall says:

> At that meeting there was great excitement as many people raised their voices at the same time. Mr Wang, the accused, for his part, sat quietly on the platform, his eyes fixed on the ceiling, never uttering a word. Following the accusations, the chairman asked the delegates whether they recommended death or prison. But only a quarter of those present assented to either. The rest sat silent, some weeping, and no punishment was decreed.

When Wang Mingdao resumed preaching it was to larger crowds than ever. Many conversions resulted from the best-attended evangelistic meetings he had ever held. Such are the ways of God.

In May 1955 the TSPM made one last effort to win him over. This failed, so it was ordered that accusation meetings against him were to take place all over China. The TSPM organ *Tianfeng* listed all the charges against him. Wang held another two weeks of evangelistic meetings in July and then went on two weeks' holiday with his wife to the seaside resort of Beidaihe.

On his return he published an issue of his magazine *Spiritual Food Quarterly* and two important pamphlets, which were typical of his writings. The first pamphlet, *Truth or Poison*, was an analysis of the Communist claim that the teaching of missionaries was 'imperialist poison'. Wang demonstrated that the 'poisonous doctrines' complained of are actually the fundamental doctrines of Christianity in Scripture, the truth of God for which one must be willing to die. Wang was defending fundamental Christianity (evangelicalism) and at the same time challenging the liberal theology of the TSPM leaders such as Y. T. Wu and K. H. Ting (Bishop Ding Guangxun, b. 1915). The second pamphlet, *Loyalty to God without Respect of Persons*, was a challenge to faithfulness to Christ.

Wang Mingdao's last sermon was on 7 August 1955. That night, after midnight, he and Mrs Wang were arrested at gunpoint, bound with ropes and led to prison. He was sentenced to fifteen years' imprisonment. The Christian Tabernacle was closed down and sealed.

In prison, every effort was made to extract a confession of guilt. Wang Mingdao cracked under intense brainwashing and signed a confession. He was released from prison on 30 September 1956 and forced to make a public confession before a large meeting of TSPM delegates. As a result of all this, his conscience was in torment and his mind in turmoil. He was heard to mutter, 'I am Judas', or 'I am Peter'.

He was delivered from this torment by the power of the Holy Spirit applying Micah 7:7-9 to his soul. Christ was his deliverer. Wang's sin of betrayal had been covered by the Son of God who had died for his sins. The gospel truths were applied afresh to Wang's tortured heart and he found peace with God afresh. Wang had been a 'Peter', not a 'Judas'. Peter was a true-hearted servant of Christ who, in weakness, fell into sin. Judas was a false-hearted servant of Christ who apostatized. Peter was regenerate; Judas was unregenerate. Peter had been truly saved; Judas had never been saved. Peter repented; Judas only had remorse. Wang Mingdao would not change places with his enemies for anything. He prayed for them.

Wang Mingdao was rearrested in April 1958 and had his sentence increased to life imprisonment. His wife was released from prison in 1973, blind in one eye as a result of the mistreatment she had received. Wang Mingdao himself was released from prison labour camp in January 1980, old, toothless and nearly blind and deaf. He became involved in the house-church movement in Beijing and wrote several books. Finally Mr and Mrs Wang Mingdao lived quietly at their son's home in Shanghai until his death on 28 July 1991, followed by hers on 18 April 1992. They had both witnessed a good confession in their lives and had entered into their everlasting rest in the presence of their Saviour

THE HUNDRED FLOWERS CAMPAIGN, 1956–57

In May 1956, Mao Zedong allowed some freedom of expression under the banner of 'Let 100 flowers bloom; let 100 schools of thought contend.' As can be imagined, this campaign led to a chorus of criticisms and complaints against the China Communist Party and CCP officials. Also inland, some religious groups came out in the open during this brief period of respite. Around this time a pastor from an inland region was obliged to sell vegetables for his living. He managed to sell all his vegetables during the daytime and at the same time visit the homes of the Christians to pray with them. Many of his congregation were in prison. However, revival broke out in his church up there in the mountains, and the number of believers increased from 300 to 3,000 before he himself was imprisoned.

Angus Kinnear also states that 'In the summer of 1956 there was a widespread awakening among students throughout China, fed by carefully preserved writings of Wang Mingdao and Watchman Nee. Many Christian students were taking seriously the question of committing large sections of the Chinese Bible to memory, against a day of trial.' These Christians were being equipped to be future spiritual leaders for believers.

THE ANTI-RIGHTIST CAMPAIGN, 1957—58

The Hundred Flowers campaign was quickly put into reverse by another campaign by Mao Zedong called the 'Anti-Rightist Campaign'. This was a 'rectification' programme against 'stinking intellectuals', in which many people were made to regret that they had ever spoken out. Several million intellectuals — scientists, professionals, teachers, students, writers, and many Christians, were sent to labour camps. The Anti-Rightist campaign led to the loss for the nation of much-needed skills over a period of twenty years.

It was under the Anti-Rightist campaign run by the TSPM leadership that Marcus Cheng suffered, as did Dr Chia Yuming and forty of his graduates. They were among 700 Christians who were imprisoned round about Christmas time in 1957. The Episcopal Bishop Stephen Chang and fourteen other Christian leaders were denounced. David Yang was sent away for a period of 'reform by labour'. What distressed him most was that it was his own students at the Spiritual Life Seminary who were foremost in accusing him.

EVANGELICAL LEADERS AND THE TSPM

Chia Yuming (see chapter 14) had his own Bible school, entirely free from foreign support or direction. He continued to run it until 1954, when he was chosen as a vice-chairman of the TSPM. A quiet Confucian-type man, he was a book-loving scholar. His focus was always on gaining knowledge and maintaining a daily quiet time of Bible meditation and prayer in order to be Christlike in character. For him, the presence of evil within the church was no ground to leave it. In 1956 his fifteen-volume *Commentary on the Bible* began to appear. His Bible college, the Spiritual Life Seminary, was reopened in October 1956. But not for long. He fell foul of the Anti-Rightist Campaign and was stripped of his licence to preach and imprisoned. He died in 1964 still in fellowship with the TSPM.

David Yang of Shanxi (see chapter 14) owed much personally to the work of foreign missions. To them he owed his Christian home, education and conversion, as also his theological and church training and early ministry. He was always close to the China Inland Mission and it was to him that they entrusted the premises of the Free Christian Church in Shanghai. With such connections David Yang, as an evangelical theologian and leader, was always in line as a prime target for an accusation meeting. He was ejected from his pastorate at his old Nanjing Church. Great pressure was brought to bear on him to work with the TSM, a pressure to which he yielded with a certain amount of reluctance. It did not help that he was used for propaganda purposes by the TSM and then the TSPM, as it was renamed. Finally the TSPM's patience ran out with him for being 'two-faced' and he spent time being 'reformed by labour'. After that, he was denied the freedom to carry out any ministry at all. He returned to his ancestral home at Quwo in the province of Shanxi in 1964. He died of a heart attack while doing hard labour in freezing weather on Chinese New Year Day 1969. His tombstone in Quwo reads, 'God's Servant Pastor Yang Shaotang.'

Marcus Cheng of Chonqing Theological Seminary surprised many by throwing in his lot with the TSM 'hook, line and sinker'. He joined the Communist Party and was one of the six vice-chairmen of the TSM. He also wrote extensively for *Tianfeng*. Like David Yang, he was very useful to the TSM, and later the TSPM, for propaganda purposes. Nevertheless he was regarded by the leaders of the TSPM as a wolf in sheep's clothing and was accepted on sufferance.

In March 1957 a speech that Cheng made was reported in the *People's Daily*. In it he defended the church against abusive acts by Communist Party officials. For this action he was hauled before an accusation meeting. There his comments were condemned by Y. T. Wu as 'the greatest defamation ever made against the Communist Party, the People's Government and the vast people of our nation'. Cheng was severely punished and was forced to live in unbearable and humiliating circumstances until his death in March 1963. His funeral service was taken by Y. T. Wu.

Allen Yuan (Yuan Xiangchen, 1914–2005) of Beijing was converted in 1933 and then trained at the evangelical Far East Theological Seminary in that city. He attended the Christian Tabernacle and his ministry paralleled that of Wang Mingdao as to beliefs and practices. After the war with the Japanese he opened a prayer room for his ministry. Every year saw him baptize between twenty and thirty people. Yuan refused to join the TSPM and was imprisoned in 1958 until 1979. During those years his wife and six children suffered very much and he himself was subjected to torture, especially during the Cultural Revolution. Up north in the region of the Russian border, conditions in the labour camp were very hard, 'but,' as he later said, 'I came back alive; many did not. I also had no Bible for twenty-two years, nor met any other Protestant Christian, though I met four Roman Catholic priests who had refused to join the Chinese Catholic Patriotic Association.' On his release he refused to join the TSPM and continued to do so till his dying day.

Samuel Lamb (Lin Xiangao, b. 1924), the son of a Baptist pastor, was born in Macau. He pastored a church congregation with a membership of 400 in the Dongshan District of Guangzhou (Canton). Though he half-heartedly joined the TSPM at one stage, he was a marked man. Lamb was first arrested in September 1955 and then again in May 1958 when he began a twenty-year prison term. This was largely spent in a coalmine in Shanxi province. Since his release in 1978 he has gained international fame for maintaining a prominent unregistered house church in Guangzhou.

Moses Xie (Xie Moshan, b. 1918) became a Christian at the age of fourteen. Born in Jiangsu province, he has spent much of his life there and in Shanghai. As director of the Chinese

Mission in Shanghai, he refused to join the TSPM and so was arrested in May 1956 and was cruelly tortured. He remained in prison until 1979 and has been imprisoned again twice since then.

Li Tianen (b. 1928) was to become one of the most influential leaders of the house-church movement. He was born in the Fangcheng County of Henan province into a Christian family (his grandfather was converted under the preaching of Hudson Taylor). Li was converted in the 1940s and had a theological training at the Huazhong Baptist Theological Institute. During the 1950s he was an independent house-church evangelist and pastor in the Pudong area of Shanghai. Arrested at the height of the Great Leap Forward campaign in 1960, he served a ten-year sentence in a labour camp in Anhui province. Bizarrely, two prisoners in the beds next to him had the duty of reporting any movements of his lips in prayer while he was in his bed at night. The punishment was for him to stand up against a wall out in the open for hours on end with arms and legs outstretched and without wearing a shirt, even in winter.

The Pudong (waterfront), Shanghai, today

Surviving Christian leaders of this generation have been given the honorary title of 'patriarchs' within the house-church movement. Their principled stand not to compromise the gospel, as well as their willingness to suffer for the sake of Christ, has been profoundly influential on the younger generations of Christians.

THE GREAT LEAP FORWARD, 1958–60

Mao Zedong was dissatisfied with the economic progress that had been made, so in May 1958 he introduced a radical programme. This was the second five-year plan, covering 1958–62, termed the 'Great Leap Forward'. It was Mao's commitment to a permanent revolution. Everything was nationalized. The people in the countryside were marshalled into communes, work brigades and production units. By 1960 over 95% of the peasants in the countryside lived in about 25,000 communes, each of which consisted on average of 5,000 households. Organized along paramilitary lines as self-sufficient communities, these communes had communal kitchens, dining rooms and nurseries. Apart from anything else, this programme was a determined effort to destroy the institution of the family on ideological grounds. All organized Christian life in the countryside was now impossible. Christians were forced to carry on their Christian worship at irregular intervals and in secret. Deprived of institutional church and pastoral leadership, they were on their own.

In 1958 the Communists boasted that Wenzhou, on the coast in Zhejiang province, was a 'religion-free' zone. Wenzhou thus became China's first officially atheist city. Henan province was another area declared to be an achieved 'atheist zone'. Ironically, now Wenzhou has the greatest number of Christians of any city in China and Henan has the greatest number of Christians of all the provinces of China! Behold the power of Christ to save!

The Great Leap Forward produced economic breakdown and was abandoned after two years. Disruption to agriculture led to the death by starvation of between twenty and thirty million people. Despite the domestic setback, China flexed her muscles in the foreign field. This was a sign of growing self-confidence. A Tibetan revolt in 1958–59 was crushed and the Dalai Lama fled to India. An aggressive propaganda campaign declared the intention of liberating Taiwan and was backed by a massive artillery bombardment of offshore islands. In 1959 the alliance with Russia cracked under the pressure of mutual suspicion. Under Khrushchev, the Russians reduced economic aid and withdrew technicians and advisers from China.

A PARTIAL ECONOMIC RECOVERY, 1961–66

As a result of the disasters of the Great Leap Forward, Mao Zedong stepped down from his position as chairman of the People's Republic but he retained his position as chairman of the CCP. A more moderate leadership, headed by Deng Xiaoping, set about corrective economic measures. Policies of the Central Committee's Secretariat met with some success, yet by the end of 1965 forty million 'intellectuals' and students had become farm labourers.

Mao Zedong began a fightback to regain absolute power. The Socialist Education Movement of 1962–65 was his campaign to restore ideological purity, reinfuse revolutionary fervour and intensify class struggle. He called on the CCP and the People's Liberation Army (PLA) to unite behind his call to make 'Maoist Thought' (later encapsulated in the *Little Red Book*) the guiding principle of thought for the future. A thorough reform of the school system along the lines of 'Maoist thought' tightened control for Mao. In a further move against the moderates in 1964, he abolished the United Fronts Works Department and everything under it, including the Religious Affairs Bureau and the TSPM. By the end of 1965, Mao was ready to strike, and strike hard.

OUTBREAK OF THE CULTURAL REVOLUTION IN 1966

In June 1966 Mao Zedong let loose the Cultural Revolution. Religion, in any and every form, was banned and attacked viciously by the iconoclastic youthful Red Guards. All remaining churches were closed down and their buildings secularized. Bibles were burned. All Christian literature was banned and destroyed. Searches were made in homes and people found with any Christian literature were severely punished.

By the end of 1966, religion was officially dead in China. Silence fell on the Christian scene for ten years. Marxism appeared to have triumphed. Survival of the gospel in China seemed impossible. It was indeed dark as midnight for Christians in China, yet, in their extremity, the grace and mercy of God were with them. It was not the end of the story. Christ was building His church.

18. From midnight darkness into light, 1966–76

Christians and Christianity in China had been exposed to ever-increasing persecution since the birth of the People's Republic of China in 1949. For ten years, between 1966 and 1976, a militant, ruthless, atheistic state was determined on the permanent eradication of all forms of Christianity from China. During this period it was a criminal offence to hold religious beliefs. There was no institutional church in China. But the power of Christ was at work, unseen to the world. He preserved His church of believers, hidden. Not only that, Christ demonstrated His mighty power in revival. The church emerged from its period of sorrows stronger than ever.

THE CULTURAL REVOLUTION, 1966–76

The Cultural Revolution was Mao Zedong's ten-year political and ideological campaign aimed at reviving revolutionary spirit throughout China. At the same time, Mao was strengthening his own personal position. In 1966, he unleashed mass action against the apparatus of the Chinese Communist Party itself. The Cultural Revolution ended with his death in 1976. In its time, it had produced massive social, economic and political upheaval and disaster.

Mao Zedong's power base was the People's Liberation Army, controlled by Lin Biao and the hero-worshipping students. Millions of middle-school and university students were called upon for fervent political demonstrations. In August 1966 no less than fourteen million students took part in nine mass rallies in front of Tiananmen Gate in Beijing. These teenage students became known as the Red Guards. They acted as 'shock troops' for the movement. Mao had an obsessive belief in violence as being the transforming power for good in society. His ideas were popularized

Statue of Mao Zedong typical of many erected during the Cultural Revolution

in the *Quotations of Chairman Mao,* or the *Little Red Book* as it is popularly known. An all-pervasive Mao personality cult took over China. The *Little Red Book* was to be found everywhere and was freely brandished during demonstrations. The goal was the destruction of the 'Four Olds' — old thinking, old customs, old habits and old culture. Christian institutions were attacked with violence and Christians humiliated, because they were considered part of the old culture and old thinking.

The result of this unfettered criticism of established organs of society by China's exuberant youth was civil disorder on a grand scale. Millions suffered ritual humiliation and beatings at their hands. This disorder was increased by clashes among rival Red Guard gangs and between the Red

Guards and local authorities. The party organization was shattered from top to bottom. Red Guards terrorized the streets, as many ordinary citizens were deemed counter-revolutionaries. Education and public transport came to a halt. The moderates, such as Deng Xiaoping, were humiliated and purged as 'capitalist rail-roaders'.

Christians were targeted for vicious torture and beatings, as a result of which some died, or were maimed for life. Crucifixion was not unknown. Women were not spared the worst of outrages. Many Christians were imprisoned, leaving no breadwinner in the family and having had all their earthly goods looted.

The PLA re-established order in 1969 and became the *de facto* political authority in China under Mao. The Red Guards were disbanded and sent to work in the countryside, where they became disillusioned and bitter. Their educational opportunities had been disrupted and lost. Nevertheless, the Cultural Revolution and its goals remained official dogma. The 'Down to the Countryside' programme involved millions of young people during 1969–74. They had no choice.

The turning point in the Cultural Revolution was the abortive coup attempt by the radical Lin Biao. This ended in September 1971 when he died in a plane crash as he fled China. His closest supporters were purged and the moderates began to gain ground, among whose number was Deng Xiaoping. In 1971 the People's Republic of China, on the mainland, replaced the Republic of China in Taiwan as China's representative on the Security Council at the United Nations. As a counterweight to the perceived expansionist aims of Soviet Russia in the late 1960s, rapprochement with the USA led to the visit of President Nixon to China in February 1972. In September of the same year, China established diplomatic relations with Japan.

The Cultural Revolution era did not come to a complete end until after the deaths in 1976 of both the veteran revolutionaries, Zhou Enlai and Mao Zedong. Within a month of the death of Mao Zedong, on 9 September 1976, members of the radical clique most closely associated with him were arrested. The 'Gang of Four', as they were known, included Mao's wife Jiang Qing. There was jubilation in the streets. It has been calculated that 'Maoist thought' cost the lives of over seventy million people during the twenty-seven years of Mao Zedong's despotic rule in China.

THE CHURCH OF CHRIST IN CHINA, 1966—69

During the worst periods of 1966–69, when the Red Guards were rampant, believers had to remain 'hidden', virtually isolated. They remained silent about their faith beyond the confines of the home. Even there they were not safe. The homes of known, or suspected, Christians were constantly searched and spied upon. Bibles were hidden away or divided up. The severity of the persecution sometimes brought even clandestine house-church gatherings to a halt. Believers in the countryside would gather together for worship and prayer on hillsides and in caves, wherever they could find reasonable safety from spying eyes. The drive for fellowship among believers could not be denied, and ways and means were found, even if only in small groups or confined to families.

Persecution can destroy organizations, but can never destroy faith. This was the fundamental factor that ensured the survival of the faith. Most Christians remained true to their faith, but, as in all times of extreme persecution, some weakened and yielded to threats and demands for them to renounce their faith. God knows the heart, and He is merciful towards all who truly belong to Him.

The strength of character and calm demeanour of the Chinese Christians spoke many a sermon to observant and thoughtful souls. It was impossible to stop the praying and the caring. Caring for neighbours in trouble or affliction, and praying with them, won many to faith in Christ. This practical involvement often stood out, in contrast with the indifference shown by the Communists. Witness for Christ was through enquiries, family relationships and close friendships. Fearless gospel witnessing by the very brave led to conversions because of the transparent honesty and joy of those proclaiming the message. But bold witness led to imprisonment. In prisons, humiliation and torture could not break these valiant hearts, and fellow prisoners were converted. At times even persecutors were made to reflect and finally yield their lives to Christ. What the Communists feared most were the prayers of Christians. The hotter the persecution, the more fervently the Christians prayed. They prayed with hearts of love for the salvation of their persecutors and for the success of the gospel.

The home fellowships were bereft of hymnals. When safe to do so, they quietly sang portions of Scripture to Chinese tunes. Where there were no Bibles to read, members shared passages they had committed to memory. Often whole chapters, or even whole books of the Bible, were memorized. Where trained men and leaders had been imprisoned, noble women stepped forward to meet the need of leadership. Courageous women also took the lead in witnessing for Christ. They had easier access to their neighbours' homes and could care for the needy.

The Little Flock influence was strong among believers, both in the cities and in the countryside. It has been noted that the Little Flock congregations were well adapted to survive the persecutions of the 1950s. This was equally true for survival during the Cultural Revolution. Their focus was on close Christian fellowship, on study of the Scriptures and on freedom from external control. These were the very practices that were needed in order to survive. Their evangelical doctrinal stance remained unchanged. Their emphases continued to be on the direct headship of Christ over each local gathering, separation from the world and the doctrine of the imminent Second Coming of Christ. These distinctives were generally taken on by the house-church movement as it emerged.

Radio broadcasting and Bibles

The Far Eastern Broadcasting Corporation played a part in keeping Christianity alive in China during the dark days of the Cultural Revolution. FEBC broadcast readings of the New Testament in Mandarin Chinese from the Philippines. These were given at dictation speed. Around 1970 the Chinese government greatly reduced the price of radios throughout China. This meant that many poor country folk could afford to buy them. Many from the remotest corners of China listened to gospel radio programmes from overseas and some found faith in Christ through them.

Douglas Sutphen (Brother David), who worked with the FEBC from 1965, had a particular burden concerning the shortage of Bibles in China. He set about organizing teams of couriers to carry Bibles into China from all possible routes. In 1970 he met with Brother Andrew, whose organization had a successful history of smuggling Bibles behind the 'Iron Curtain', into Eastern Europe. Douglas hit upon an ingenious scheme. He had New Testaments printed, virtually identical on the outside with Mao Zedong's *Little Red Book*. Fifty or so could quite easily be carried in a suitcase. The 25,000 copies of the first printing were in China within a few months. Contacts within China pleaded for a million Bibles. Brother David then began to plan ways and means for more spectacular numbers of Bibles to be taken into China.

An early sign of revival, Henan province, 1966–70

Tony Lambert reports at length on the report given to him by a house-church leader. It shows how the gospel not only survived, but flourished, in Henan province during these dark days of the Cultural Revolution:

> In the late 1960s the arm of the Lord was revealed in the villages of Henan. There were countless villages where meetings sprang up almost simultaneously. This was virtually unthinkable, as believers were under constant surveillance and even exchanging a few words of Christian comfort between friends, if overheard, could lead to political persecution. The dictatorship of the proletariat was extremely effective in repressing Christians. Yet God was able to work even within the system. When the wives of Communist cadres fell ill, they sought out medical help, even visiting doctors in Beijing, but often to no avail. So many of these women came home to Henan to die. In the villages there were many elderly Christian women who had not been able to go to church for nearly twenty years. Although all their Bibles had been confiscated they were still strong in faith and knew how to pray. They went into the homes of these commune cadres and production brigade secretaries, bringing the love of Christ and preaching Jesus, the Great Healer. Many of those women received Christ as their Saviour. Those that recovered asked for further instruction from those elderly Christian women, who were simple peasants. So, many meetings actually started in the homes of local Communist cadres!

All this was happening away from the limelight of any publicity or campaign. It was the Sovereign Lord, pouring out His Holy Spirit. It was the first fruits of the harvest to come.

THE GOSPEL IN CHINA, 1970–76

After the visit of President Nixon to China in 1972, news slowly began to emerge from China concerning the underground church.

Shanghai

A Hong Kong Christian visited Shanghai for a month in the winter of 1973 to find that the house churches were already growing. Many meetings of up to thirty or forty people were held in homes in China's largest city and sometimes they met quietly in corners of parks. Great care had to be taken with security and the introduction of new members. Passages of Scripture would be copied and distributed because of the shortage of Bibles and the risk of being caught taking them to meetings. The chosen passage would be studied verse by verse. Hymns, often of their own composition, would be sung very quietly and to Chinese folk tunes to avoid suspicion. Great emphasis was made on prayer. The focus of prayer was on their own growth in grace, imprisoned Christians and greater freedom to preach the gospel. Prayer would be by the leader, or in turn, or all together very quietly.

Wenzhou

In 1974, Hong Kong Christians were taking advantage of the new freedom to visit relatives in the Wenzhou area in the coastal province of Zhejiang. On their return to Hong Kong stories circulated that there were 50,000 active Christians in the Wenzhou area. These stories turned out to be true. The power of the gospel had been sealed by God in a remarkable way. One of the house-church leaders explained: 'We never stopped meeting [during the Cultural Revolution]. The China Inland Mission had laid a good foundation here. The old Christians knew how to pray.' David Aikman adds:

Wenzhou

Wenzhou had a good foundation for growth from the Cultural Revolution onward because the biblical and theological teaching by the city's evangelical pastors had been very thorough before 1949 and continued to be so even when the Cultural Revolution forced all Christian teaching to go underground.

One man used of God was Miao Zhitong (b. 1942). He was brought up by Christian relatives. He became a full-time preacher in 1967, at the height of the Cultural Revolution. He started mobilizing the Christians in the eastern part of Zhejiang province (including the area around Wenzhou) in 1972. On one occasion, only the presence of a sympathetic crowd prevented his being beaten to death. On another, he was handcuffed behind his back and instructed to stand on the parapet of a bridge in order to be pushed over it. A violent storm blew up at that very instant and he was taken back to prison.

Zhen Datong, the son of Christian parents in Wenzhou, was another of the Wenzhou house-church leaders who worked zealously for the Lord during the Cultural Revolution.

Fangcheng house-church movement, Henan

Fangcheng County is in the south-west of Henan province, a part of the very heartland of ancient China. In 1974 a remarkable event took place in a village there. The authorities got wind of a secret meeting for training Christians. They broke it up and arrested almost all of the 4,000 attending! Where had all these Christians come from? They were the fruit of the revival already in progress.

The story began in the 1940s, when a captain in Chiang Kai-shek's Nationalist Army named Gao Yongjiu was converted and became a zealous and effective local evangelist in his native Fangcheng County. The area was then a CIM field, with well-taught congregations. Gao was brother-in-law to Li Tianen. When Li Tianen (b. 1928) was released from prison in 1970, he agreed to help Gao with the rapidly expanding work in Fangcheng County. Li Tianen travelled throughout Henan, training a new generation of Christian leaders from the network of itinerant evangelists and preachers. These workers were constantly on the move ministering to the rapidly growing number of Christians. The work stretched right across Henan into adjacent provinces. David Aikman comments:

> It is difficult to overestimate the part Li played in training the next generation of China's Christian leaders. It was his dedicated training and travelling that helped raise an entirely new generation of 'uncles', the current leaders of China's largest house church networks. Li often lived in the home of fellow Christian workers, training up to twenty young people at a time.

Li was to train Zhang Rongliang, the most influential of the current leaders of the church in China, the man who was the main influence behind the *Confession of Faith* of 1998.

After the arrest of the 4,000 at the secret training meeting, Li Tianen became the prime target of the Public Security Bureau. He was arrested in 1975, sentenced to death and transferred to a prison in Zhengzhou, to be put on death row. A huge flood in Henan forced postponement of the execution. The new date was set for the spring of 1976, but this too had to be postponed because of infighting in the Communist Party in Henan after the death of Zhou Enlai in January 1976. After the arrest of the 'Gang of Four', party cadres were scared of being labelled 'leftists', or followers of the 'Gang of Four'. As a result, Li Tianen's sentence was reduced. In 1979, along with many other Christian leaders, he was released with all charges dropped.

SOUTH-WEST CHINA

The Lisu people

With the coming of the Communists, the churches of the 15,000 strong Lisu church were closed and the pastors imprisoned. Many Lisu believers fled across the the mountains into nearby Burma. For two decades all seemed lost. Then one elderly Lisu evangelist was released from a labour camp in the early 1970s. He began to preach the gospel along the banks of the Salween River, close to the border of Burma. Revival

broke out among the Lisu people who had remained. Not only were believers restored to faith, but the work prospered. By the end of the decade it was reckoned that the number of believers was over 30,000. This was only the beginning.

Miao people in Yunnan province

On 10 July 1998 Queen Elizabeth II attended a service in Westminster Abbey, London, to commemorate ten Christian martyrs of the twentieth century. One of the ten statues unveiled above the Great West Door was that of the Chinese martyr Wang Zhiming (1907–73). Pastor Wang Zhiming was a Miao Christian from Yunnan province. He was born in 1907 in Wuding and was educated in Christian schools. Later he became a teacher in one, and remained in this post for ten years. In 1944 Wang was elected chairman of the church council of Wuding. He was ordained in 1951 and

Statue of Wang Zhiming, Westminster Abbey

pastored the church in Sapushan. He signed the Three-Self Manifesto but refused to be a party to denunciation meetings. In 1955 he was received by Mao Zedong in Beijing.

With the onset of the Cultural Revolution. the Miao churches were closed. 'Cultural centres' were set up to indoctrinate Miao believers into atheism. Pastor Wang was labelled a counter-revolutionary and was arrested and imprisoned in 1969, with at least twenty other Christian leaders. Many other Miao Christians were sent to labour camps during the days of the Cultural Revolution. On 29 December 1973 Wang Zhiming was executed at a mass rally of more than 10,000 people. The largely Christian crowd was not cowed into submission by the spectacle. They rushed onto the platform and berated the prosecuting officials. Wang Zhiming became the only Christian martyr of the Cultural Revolution to have an official monument erected at his grave-site (in 1981). The church multiplied.

Miao people in Guizhou province

By 1965 there was a flourishing house-church movement among the Miao people in Guizhou province. In Weining alone, there were twenty times the number of independent preachers than of official ordained preachers. During the Cultural Revolution, the message of the Miao Christians was:

> The more you forbid Christianity, the more we will cling to the church. If you confiscate our churches, we will worship in caves. If you announce the extermination of the church, we will develop even more secret meetings. If you attack ordained pastors, we will use even more independent house-church preachers instead. If you take action against us on Sundays, we will multiply our meetings to every day of the week and into the night.

In 1979 a researcher from the Chinese mainland reported:

> Zhang Youxue, a China Inland Mission evangelist from Hezhang, and his relative Yang Derong went to Stone Gateway to evangelize. The commune there held a struggle-accusation meeting against them. Afterwards Zhang was forced to commit suicide. His two sons, Zhang Mincai and Zhang Mincan, jumped into a river and also committed suicide. This incident caused the mass of the Miao people to return to the church.

SUMMARY 1966–76

Believers were freed from Western denominationalism and from financial, ecclesiastical and ideological dependence on anyone. They found that the spiritual character of a Christian community was capable of authentic existence without an elaborate organization. They were led by the Bible and prayer. Love and the faithfulness of believers towards each other were very strong. Through fiery persecution, the church emerged with a truly indigenous voice to its own people. 'The hotter the crucible, the more refined the church.' The historian Gu Changsheng estimates that 250,000 Christians of all persuasions died from persecution during the Cultural Revolution.

1976 marked a watershed for the gospel in China. During the next twenty-five years, up to the end of the twentieth century, China was to experience one of the mightiest revivals in the whole history of the church. The foundations were strong. Christ had prepared His church in China for the task.

19. Christ out in the open, 1976–85

In 1949 there had been at most one million Protestant believers in China. Forty years later, in 1989, there were estimated to be between twenty and fifty million Protestant believers there. This was in spite of all the opposition of a hostile atheist state. So there had been an increase of between twentyfold and fiftyfold in forty years! This could not be hidden.

PEOPLE'S REPUBLIC OF CHINA, 1976–85

On the deaths of Zhou Enlai and Mao Zedong in 1976, the 'Gang of Four', led by Mao's widow, made a bid for power. They were arrested and convicted of crimes against the state. This represented the final putting to bed of the Cultural Revolution and Maoist thought.

In multitudes disillusionment had set in by then. Harsh reality and bitter experience had overtaken and destroyed idealism. It was a time of opportunity for the gospel.

From 1977 Deng Xiaoping, who had been purged during the Cultural Revolution, re-emerged as leader of the moderate pragmatists. By 1978 he was the *de facto* leader of China, and remained so until his death in 1997.

The Third Plenum of the Chinese Communist Party's Eleventh National Party Congress, held in December 1978, is considered a major turning point in modern Chinese history. Deng affirmed a number of reforms based on uniting the nation behind a programme of the 'Four Modernizations' — of industry, agriculture, science and technology, and national defence. The goal was to bring China into the community of advanced industrial nations by the start of the new millennium. In future, economic progress was to be put above the Maoist goals of class struggle and permanent revolution. From 1978 tourists were allowed into China under carefully controlled supervision.

By 1982, in less than fifty years, the population had doubled to over a billion, so the change in policy was timely and essential. A policy of one child per family had already been adopted in 1979, with some tragic social consequences.

REOPENING OF CHURCHES AFTER THE CULTURAL REVOLUTION

The more liberal policies of Deng Xiaoping undid Mao's extremist policies, including the outright persecution of believers. However, in January 1979 the Religious Affairs Bureau resumed its work of government control of all religion. In April 1979 the first TSPM church was reopened in Ningbo. The Three-Self Patriotic Movement was reconstituted in March 1980, and the China Christian Council (CCC) became a recognized religious body in October 1980. The leadership of both the TSPM and the CCC was entrusted to Bishop Ding Guangxun. The remit of the CCC was to handle the church organization, theological education and delegations to go overseas. The leadership of the CCC remained firmly in the hands of convinced Communists who vigorously opposed the expansion of Christianity in China. They opened as few TSPM churches as they could get away with. The CCC in due course took its seat as a member of the World Council of Churches.

Between 1978 and 1980 thousands of Christians who had been arrested in the 1950s were released and allowed back into secular occupation. These were those who had opposed the TSPM or had been caught up in the 1957–58 Anti-Rightist Campaign. The good effect that the testimony and example of these thousands of released Christian sufferers had on the emerging house-church movement can hardly be over-emphasized. Many of these Christians were older pastors and leaders, and had been well trained in theology before 1949. They were ready and willing to take teaching and leadership roles among the growing community of young believers and itinerant evangelists.

In 1980 the Chinese press grudgingly admitted that there was 'a mass of believers' in China. They recognized an un-precedented upsurge of Christian belief in China, especially among young people. Not a few members of the Communist Party had been affected.

In March 1982 a new, but ambiguous, religious policy statement of the Communist Party emerged. This was *Document 19*, which declared that 'The State protects legitimate religious activities' — that is to say, the TSPM and CCC. Thus, the activities of house churches who would not register were regarded as illegal, as was open evangelism conducted out-side the limit of a registered TSPM building. Yet there was an acknowledgement that it is 'fruitless and extremely harmful to use simple coercion in dealing with people's ideological and spiritual questions'. This policy document is a rejection of Mao Zedong's extremist religious policy. Yet, 'All the patriotic religious organizations should obey the leadership of the party and the government.' 'We must strengthen the organs of government controlling religious affairs.' Nothing had changed fundamentally. The target was the suppression of the emerging unregistered house churches. Arrests could be made on the grounds of 'illegal criminal activity' and for 'being unpatriotic'.

The fundamental dilemma was, and still is, that both the State and the TSPM, for ideological reasons, cannot tolerate what they cannot control. The TSPM did not hesitate to call upon the police and the Public Security Bureau to enforce its decrees.

'A MASS OF BELIEVERS'

The first concrete news of the real Chinese church had emerged in 1973. By 1980 it had become clear that a remarkable revival was in progress. There were 20,000 Christians in Fuzhou alone! In the whole of Fujian province, reliable reports stated there were 600,000 Christians. In one area, in that year alone, there had been 6,000 new believers baptized.

In Zhejiang province the remarkable revival in Wenzhou continued unabated. In one mountainous region of 10,000, one in three were Christians, meeting in fifteen places. The services lasted for four hours. In some communes the majority of the members were Christian. In one commune, production teams were named, 'Jesus Team No. 1, Jesus Team No. 2', and so on. Leslie Lyall noted that 'In some rural areas, over 90% of the population are Christian — a totally unprecedented statistic in the history of the Church in China ... one semi-official estimate is that in Zhejiang alone there may be as many as five million Christians.'

Leslie Lyall (OMF) in the 1980s

In Jiangsu province it was the same story. Shanghai had a million believers. 4,000 house groups held special Christmas services in 1982. This was in addition to those held in the open churches. In Nanjing, Suzhou and elsewhere there was rapid growth. An old pastor said, 'The fire of the gospel has been lit, and it is going to keep on burning like a prairie fire.'

In Guangdong province, in a small town near Guangzhou, a church of a hundred members actually baptized 300, three times its own membership! In Shantou, where the church had suffered severely in 1966, the membership had nearly doubled, and of these most of the additions were young people. 200 students met regularly for Bible study at one university.

What about inland? It was discovered, almost by accident, that the revival was not confined to the coast. In Henan province, mostly made up of farmers, it emerged that astounding numbers were turning to Christ. In the words of one pastor, 'It is God who is mightily at work today! We are doing nothing.' What was really impressive was the godliness and the Bible knowledge of the young Christians, in spite of all the handicaps of the lack of Bibles and good Christian literature. 3,000 baptisms *every day of the year* had been taking place in Henan province! Just think of Robert Morrison and his colleagues, with their ten converts in twenty-seven years, at the time of the beginnings of the gospel in China!

Likewise, revival was reported in the six provinces bordering on Henan. These were Anhui, Hubei, Shaanxi, Shanxi, Hebei and the northern coastal province of Shandong. Growth in Jiangxi was said to be 'astounding', and in Shandong 'tremendous'. In the martyr province of Shanxi, so bruised by the Boxers in 1900, there were so many recent conversions that they were described as 'innumerable'. In contrast, in Beijing there were very few Christians. In the south-west, among the minority tribes, Christians among the Miao and the Lisu were said to number 100,000, and their religion was officially described as 'Christian'. There was a huge limestone cavern which held as many as 2,000 worshippers. All the other provinces had experienced some growth as well, even if not as spectacular as that of the revival centres. The vast majority of these converts remained outside the TSPM. The house churches boomed.

THE HOUSE-CHURCH NETWORKS

The largest house-church networks that developed were in Henan and Anhui provinces.

The largest network of all was the Fangcheng Fellowship in Fangcheng County, Henan. This saw itself as a church, and its founders were Gao Yongjiu and Li Tianen.

The second largest network was the Tanghe Fellowship in Henan (also known as the China Gospel Fellowship or China Evangelical Fellowship). This viewed itself as a loose-knit fellowship, and its founders were Xing Liaoyuan, Feng Jianguo and Shen Xianfeng.

The Local Church (also known as the Shouters) consisted of the Little Flock fellowships that gravitated to the teachings of Witness Lee. They were strong in Henan and also in the south-eastern coastal provinces.

The Born-Again Movement (also known as Way of Life Church, Full Gospel Church, or the Weepers) was another large network. They emphasized the importance of discipling converts, and their founder was Xu Yongze.

In Anhui, one of the provinces hardest hit by flood and famine, house-church networks flourished in Fengyang County, Fuyang Prefecture, Mengcheng County and Huoqiu County. Over three million are associated with the house churches of Anhui. In 1949, there were about 50,000 Christians in the whole of Anhui province.

In addition, networks were developing in major cities in the coastal provinces, where there had been long association with the missionary works of the past. The most notable of these were in Fuqing County, Fujian province and Wenzhou and its environs in Zhejiang province. The latter prospered under the leadership of Miao Zhitong and Zhen Datong.

Traditional village scene in Anhui province

Around 1978 the sect of the True Jesus Church, though completely disbanded by 1966, was re-established almost single-handedly in seventeen provinces by the remarkable Wang Yuansong. After 1979 the sect mushroomed.

RADIO BROADCASTING

Listening to foreign radio broadcasts became legal in 1979, after the restoration of diplomatic relations with the USA. Then a flood of letters began to come in to the Far Eastern Broadcasting Company and Trans-World Radio. These letters came from all the provinces of China. They confirmed that many had found a living faith in Christ through their programmes and many had also found their faith sustained by them over the years.

In coastal Jiangsu province:

> A woman could not eat or sleep, but was drawn toward Christ after listening to gospel radio programmes.

She went in search of a church and found none. Finally she came to a village that had previously been a labour camp and saw a cross painted above the door of a house. She went in and discovered two elderly Christians. They introduced her to another couple who preached the gospel to her and led her to Christ. She returned home and shared the gospel with many others. The church in that area grew from just six believers to over two hundred in the space of only two years. They meet in three house churches and listen regularly to gospel radio for spiritual support.

In north Shanxi 3,000 had come to faith through listening to gospel broadcasts.

BIBLES

As we saw in the previous chapter, in the 1970s Brother David had managed to get 25,000 New Testaments into China in driblets, inside travellers' suitcases. He also managed to have a further 30,000 Bibles taken in by business people attending the twice-yearly Guangzhou Trade Fair. The project was called Operation Rainbow and went flawlessly. Encouraged by this, Project Pearl was put into operation. This was an audacious plan to ship one million Bibles into China in one go!

On 18 June 1981, one million Bibles, weighing 232 tons and divided into one-ton blocks, were smuggled by a barge towed by tugboat to a prearranged beach. This was a 300-yard stretch of beach near Shantou, on the coast of China's Fujian province. The three-day journey was nerve-racking but successful. Unloading the barge by moonlight took two hours by means of multiple trips to shore in three rubber boats. Each one-ton block held forty-eight waterproofed boxes of ninety Bibles. These were swiftly distributed to 2,000 Chinese Christians, who took the Bibles by bicycles, cars and lorries to locations in almost every province in China. By the time the

Fishermen on a beach in Fujian province

army turned up, only a few boxes were left on the beach for them to dump at sea. Fishermen reclaimed most of these, dried them and then sold them to the local Christians! The tug and barge arrived safely back at base. Two Fujian Christians were sentenced to three years of imprisonment.

Project Pearl received sensational worldwide news coverage and predictably drew widespread criticism from both within and outside China. Yet, by drawing attention to the scandalous shortage of Bibles in China, it brought pressure to bear on the TSPM. As a result, the officially sanctioned Amity Press was set up in Nanjing in 1987. Amity was permitted to print Bibles in large numbers, with the help of the United Bible Society and with funding from outside China. By the year 2005 as many as forty million copies had been produced. This is still only a third of the number of Bibles needed for Chinese Christians alone! The shortfall has had to be made up from other sources, or not at all. Distribution of Bibles is mainly through TSPM outlets, and they put obstacles in the way. Importation of Bibles is not technically illegal, but is forbidden for ideological reasons. It would be a best seller in bookshops! Printing of Bibles illicitly inside China is severely punished.

RISE OF THE ITINERANT EVANGELISTS

In the latter years of the Cultural Revolution and the early post-Mao years of 1974–82, China saw the rise of itinerant evangelists. 1981 was a turning point for the Fangcheng Fellowship. 'This was when the church moved from being underground to open meetings in full view of the police,' says Wu Baixin, a Henan intellectual. The emerging house-church networks had developed a pattern of evangelism. They would train young Christians and send them out in pairs. These were told to evangelize everyone. They were not to pass anyone on the street, or in the course of their journey, without sharing the gospel. Tracts were given out in public places. The police were very surprised to see these bold, dedicated young men and women. It was something new. Inevitably some of these young evangelists were arrested, beaten, jailed and tortured. This prospect did not dampen their zeal.

A graphic account of the bravery and persecution of some of these young evangelists was sent in a long letter to Christians overseas from Fangcheng County, Henan province, dated 6 May 1982. This is reproduced in full from Tony Lambert's book *China's Christian Millions*:

ALL WHO LIVE GODLY LIVES IN CHRIST JESUS WILL SUFFER PERSECUTION

Dear brothers and sisters,

On behalf of the brothers and sisters in Henan I send greetings to the members of the Body overseas! Today the church in Henan is being greatly blessed by the Lord and the number of those saved increases daily. The gospel of God is flourishing. All this is done not without your prayers and contributions.

Wherever there is revival, there are also trials. The revival in Henan has flourished in such a situation. If Jesus had not been crucified, nobody today could be saved — if there were no testing by fire, then true faith would not be revealed. Suffering is the means for promoting spiritual life and the ingredient for revival of the church.

Dearly beloved, most recently the cause of the gospel in Fangcheng County, Henan, has been greatly promoted. A dozen young Christians have been imprisoned, beaten and bound, and this is the cause. They have regarded suffering for Christ as more precious than the treasure of Egypt. They started preaching the gospel in the poorest, most desolate regions. One day they went to Yangce Commune in Miyang County. No one seemed to listen, so they prayed and were greatly inspired by God. They split into groups and went preaching to many different places. As soon as they started to preach, the power of God came down. They preached with tears streaming down, so that passers-by and street-vendors, both Christians and non-Christians, stopped to listen. Even the fortune-tellers were moved by the Holy Spirit to burst out crying. Many people forgot their food, forgot their work or even forgot to return home. Even by evening people had not dispersed. They preached until they were exhausted but still the crowd would not let them leave. When the shops and factories closed, their employees also came to listen.

However, then Satan made his move. The authorities suddenly dragged them away one by one, binding them with ropes and beating them with electric stun-truncheons. They also kicked them in the face with their leather shoes, beating them unconscious. But when they came to, they continued to pray, sing and preach to the bystanders. One girl who was only fourteen was beaten senseless. But when she came to and saw that many people were sympathetic, she started to preach again. Her words were few and spoken in a low voice but the street-acrobats and actors could not refrain from crying out, repenting and believing in Jesus. As they were being bound and beaten, many people noticed a strange expression on their faces. Amazed, they saw that they were smiling. Their spirit and appearance was so lively and gracious that the crowd asked why they, themselves, did not feel ashamed. They were so young, so where did this power come from? Their example caused many people to believe in Jesus.

When the Christians in that area saw them bound and forced to kneel on the ground for more than three days without food or water, beaten with sticks until their faces were covered with blood, and their hands made black by the ropes, but still singing, praying and praising the Lord — then they too wished to share their persecution. So the flame of the gospel has spread throughout Yangce Commune. There had never been revival here before, but through this persecution the seeds of life have been truly planted. May everyone who hears of this give thanks and praise for the revival of the church here.

Dearly beloved, in men's eyes this was an unfortunate happening, but for Christians it was like a rich banquet. This lesson cannot be learned from books, and this sweetness is rarely tasted by men. This rich spiritual life cannot be had in a comfortable environment. Where there is no cross, there is no victory. If the spices are not refined to become oil, the fragrance of the perfume cannot flow forth. If the grapes are not crushed in the vat, they cannot become wine. Dearly beloved, these saints who went down in the fiery furnace, far from being harmed, have been glorified. Their spirits have been filled with power to preach the gospel with far greater authority and to enjoy a far more abundant spiritual life. Satan was unable finally to force them to give up their faith, so they were released.

The Christian workers in Fangcheng, Sheqi and Miyang Counties have all been emboldened to preach the gospel. Those who were not imprisoned felt ashamed and saw the marks of the Lord Jesus upon their bodies. They also desired to suffer that the Lord's name be glorified. Dearly beloved, the Lord wishes to add to the number being saved working through us. Let us seize the opportunity to work for Him as there are many souls still unsaved. There are many lambs wandering on the mountains without anyone to seek and to find them. May the Lord Jesus place a burden to preach the gospel on every Christian's heart. May He give a spirit of prayer to every Christian so they will become a prayer-warrior. May our brethren overseas strive to meet the need for Christian literature which is so lacking within China, as God has given you the perfect environment to do this. May God grant you to be faithful unto death until He comes. The Lord is coming soon. Lord Jesus, I desire you to come! May the Lord give us hearts to pray for each other until that day. Emmanuel!

From the weak brethren in Fangcheng, Henan.
6 May 1982

In 1983 and 1984 there were major crackdowns on the house churches. These crackdowns started in Henan and Anhui provinces and spread nationwide. This was as a result of a nationwide 'anti-spiritual pollution' campaign. These persecutions continued until mid-1984. Many house-church Christians were arrested, fined, given long-term prison sentences, and some were even executed by the authorities.

Christ was coming out into the open in China. He could not be ignored.

20. The house-church movement from 1970

We have traced in earlier chapters the story of the rise of the Protestant house churches. Now we will look at them in more detail. By 1998 the house-church movement was to claim eighty million believers in fellowship with them. Since then the numbers have continued to rise.

FANGCHENG FELLOWSHIP IN HENAN

The Fangcheng Fellowship is referred to as the 'Mother Church in Fangcheng' and the 'Bethlehem' of the whole house-church movement. The rapidly growing numbers of Christians in Fangcheng County became a headache for Communist Party officials from the 1970s onwards. Cadres called Henan province the 'Jesus nest'. This name has become a badge of honour. Likewise the revival taking place across country areas in China was called by the cadres 'Christianity fever'.

Zhang Rongliang (b. 1950) has for many years been the senior leader of Fangcheng Fellowship. He was trained by Li Tianen. The second generation of house-church leaders are given the honorary title of 'uncles'. Zhang's family lived in the small rural village of Sun Lu Zhuang, isolated in the mountains of Henan province. He was converted in 1963, before the age of thirteen. With only a few years of elementary education, yet highly intelligent, Zhang is one of a number of largely self-taught men who have risen to be great leaders in the history of the church. Zhang Rongliang kept his faith a secret in the commune, even becoming a party member. Nevertheless he was denounced in 1974 and sentenced to seven years in the Xihua labour camp in Henan. His televised trial was shown to schools all over Henan. On his part he refused to give any information about fellow believers and, of course, was cruelly treated with beatings by officials from the Public Security Bureau.

In the labour camp Zhang Rongliang came to be put in charge of a work team and given the freedom to choose new members from the incoming prisoners. As a result he met up with the older Feng Jianguo from Tanghe County. Feng had been brought up in a Christian family and had been converted at a young age. He was arrested for his faith in 1975. Zhang and Feng became close friends. Through planting apple orchards in the countryside around the camp, they witnessed for Christ and new churches sprang up to ring the labour camp! These years in prison camp honed the faith and the leadership skills of both men, as similar trials did to other faithful men and women elsewhere in China.

On his release in 1980, Zhang Rongliang's leadership qualities were to excel in the areas of personal relationships and organization. These were much needed to equip the burgeoning house churches with the measure of harmony among themselves that they have since enjoyed. Zhang is the 'uncle' that all the leaders in the house-church movement look up to. He was the guiding light behind the 1998 *Confession of Faith*. He was arrested again in July 2006 and sentenced to seven and a half years' imprisonment.

TANGHE FELLOWSHIP IN HENAN

Feng Jianguo (b. 1926?) is the senior leader of the second largest Henan-based house-church network, along with Xing Liaoyuan (b. 1964) who was converted in 1978. The Tanghe Fellowship, also known as the China Gospel Fellowship, emerged as a result of the work of the many Christians who were released between 1978 and 1980. Feng Jianguo was released in 1980 after five years' imprisonment along with Zhang Rongliang. Tanghe County is a part of Henan that had a number of Christian traditions before 1949 and, as such, sees itself as a loose-knit fellowship. In 1997 Shen Xianfeng was arrested and the house-church network in Xinyang County was called a cult organization. He complained that the unregistered house churches are labelled as cultic just because they do not join the TSPM.

THE LITTLE FLOCK

The Brethren remaining true to the original ideals of Watchman Nee continued to be called by the name of the Little Flock. In Zhejiang province alone, in 1984 nearly all the recorded 63,000 Christians in Xiaoshan County belonged to the Little Flock. Many Little Flock devotees joined the house-church movement, much to its spiritual enrichment. Some branches of the Little Flock have come to be removed from the list of illegal organizations. These have been granted recognition within the TSPM.

THE LOCAL CHURCH

After the death of Watchman Nee in 1972, the acknowledged leader of the Little Flock, his mantle fell upon Witness Lee. Though living in America from 1962, he came to enjoy much prestige in China. However, he was very autocratic and had developed his own idiosyncratic ideas, which included release of the Spirit by shouting. Hence his followers in China became known as the 'Shouters'. His movement in China was called the Local Church movement and fundamentally they remained true to the doctrines and practices of the Brethren. In 1983, when the Shouters had a following of 200,000 in twenty provinces, the authorities called them a heretic cult and repressed them violently. Nevertheless, in the *United Appeal* (see Appendix IV, paragraph 2) the Local Church has been recognized as orthodox and as a branch of the House Church.

THE BORN-AGAIN MOVEMENT

Peter Xu (Xu Yongze, b. 1940) had a strong Christian faith from childhood. A disciple of Li Tianen, Xu began to emerge as a preacher and leader in his own right by 1978. Xu thought that in the excitement about all the accounts of healing miracles, the rapidly emerging house-church networks were not doing enough to disciple solid Christian lives. His emphasis was on the need for personal holiness, through daily repentance for sin. Yet the evangelistic fervour was maintained and the network grew rapidly. At spiritual retreats, for which there was a long tradition in the Chinese church, exhortations were made for people to repent of their sins. It soon became normative to weep at these meetings as evidence of the work of the Holy Spirit. The Born-Again Movement became known as the 'Weepers' and they were officially regarded as a heretic sect. The authorities cracked down on them in 1988, and Xu was caught and imprisoned in 1997. Samuel Lamb of Guangzhou regarded them as a sect, but it was not so according to Li Tianen, Zhang Rongliang or Jonathan Chao. Xu Yongze is on record as rejecting weeping as a requirement of salvation and he also states that weeping has no theological value in itself.

It needs to be noted that the last three of the church groupings listed above are recognized as orthodox Christians in the *United Appeal*, and the first two were signatories to the *Confession of Faith* (see Appendices IV and V).

HOUSE CHURCHES AFTER 1989

Ever since the development of the Chinese indigenous church in the 1900s there has always been a Pentecostal presence, though a minority one. With the rise of the house-church movement, this strand of Christianity has become more mainstream in China, especially in rural areas.

By the early 1990s Fangcheng Fellowship of Henan had sent evangelistic teams to over thirty provinces and municipalities, including China's largest cities of Shanghai, Beijing and Chongqing.

In March 1994 the Tanghe Fellowship of Henan commissioned and sent out seventy young, single, evangelists. They went to twenty-two out of the twenty-eight Chinese

Aerial view of Shanghai

provinces and regions. The mission turned out to be richly blessed. The period 1994–96 was the time of greatest growth for Tanghe. The missionary vision took hold and by 2002 ninety-eight couples and 120 single men had migrated to every other province to take the gospel there. Now the vision is to take the gospel beyond China, westward, all the way to Jerusalem.

From 2002 onwards there has been a marked slowdown in the growth rate of the rural house churches as a result of the mass emigration of people to the cities. Many people have moved without permission of the authorities. It is estimated that at least 18% of the inhabitants reside illegally in the large cities. The new challenge is to evangelize and plant churches and fellowship groups among these largely disenfranchised citizens. Many house churches in the cities are linked to local networks or are independent and have no allegiance to any house-church grouping.

There are a hundred or so small clandestine training seminaries for house-church workers, in both rural and urban areas throughout China. These supplement teaching done at the local church level.

An extremely gifted and prolific hymn and Christian song-writer is the charismatic Lu Xiaomin (Sister Ruth, b. 1970) of Hui descent. Her hymns and songs were published in a book called *Songs of Canaan*. They are now sung all over China and in Chinese Christian communities overseas.

THE DANGER OF CULTS

The history of China is full of peasant rebellions that have originated in secret societies and cults. We have come across an example in the case of the Taipings in the nineteenth century. They nearly brought down the ruling dynasty. So the authorities today are extremely nervous of cults and un-authorized sects who claim a higher allegiance than to the state. A present-day example is the Falungong sect. The ancient meditation system had been hijacked by a cult leader called Li Hongzhi. In 1992, with a blend of Buddhist and Daoist doctrine, he claimed to have borne the sins of mankind. World attention was focused on this sect when a demonstration by his followers was brutally put down by the authorities in Beijing.

On the margins of authentic Christian expression, there have always been false teachers who prey on the churches and the superstitious, in order to gain a personal following for themselves and their teaching. The danger of this in China is increased by the fact that the Communists have sought to limit the circulation of the Bible and also to suppress unregistered Christian teachers. In the countryside, in particular, there are a multitude of peasants still steeped in native Daoist and Buddhist folk-beliefs, which have occult beliefs and practices. This is fertile ground for Christian cults, merging the native with a half-baked and dimly understood Christianity. The danger has been the more real because of Pentecostal practices among the house churches in rural areas together with their prevalent apocalyptic millenarian views. Two questions arise: How genuinely Christian is the understanding of millions of professing Christians? Are they attracted by the miraculous, rather than by Christ Himself? Every effort needs to be made to teach and disciple properly. This is especially true for the more marginal and vulnerable members.

THREE MAJOR CHINESE CHRISTIAN CULTS

The Eastern Lightning cult emerged in 1993 and gained worldwide publicity as a result of its recruitment practices. These included deceit, immoral inducements, kidnapping for brainwashing and beatings. They teach that Christ has come again in the form of a Chinese woman called Deng. Mysteriously unapproachable, her direct commands, prolific visions and writings supplement the Bible as the Word of God. The end of the world was to have been in 1999. They now have an international following. There is no connection with the True Jesus Church sect, which continues to thrive worldwide. The TJC had used the same biblical text (Matthew 24:27) in defining its world mission fifty years earlier. Both groups claim to be the answer to the 'Last Day' prophecy of Jesus that 'The lightning that comes from the east is visible in the west.' They see this as meaning that, from China, the gospel is to go westward around the world through them.

The Disciples' Society, or the Narrow Gate in the Wilderness, was founded by Ji Sanbao (1940–97) around 1989. The TSPM was the 'wide gate that leads to destruction'; they were 'the narrow gate that leads to life'. They set dates for the end of the world. Recruiters were rewarded with food. By 1995 the society had more than 300,000 followers, when the Public Security Bureau launched a nationwide campaign against them. The cult persists across China, particularly in the north-west.

The Three Ranks of Servants (after the parable of the talents — the five, three and one) is a cult founded by Xu Shuangfu (1946–2006). Xu was seen as the key to salvation. He presided as the 'great servant' over 'the small servants'. Extreme penitential actions were exacted. Dates were set for the end of the world. These are in constant revision. The movement has claimed a million followers.

THE HOUSE CHURCHES AND THE CULTS

Persecution of the unregistered house churches is more than just a simple case of Communist dogma put into practice and the determination to control every aspect of life. It is also an expression of a deep fear, the fear of a fanatical uprising by the masses. Counter-revolution can also breed in secret, from meetings which the authorities do not control. It is the view of the Chinese government that the house-church movement falls into the category of a being a secret cult movement, subversive of government authority and control.

The house churches have been faced with the problems of cults from the beginning. On one hand, the leaders had to protect their congregations from flamboyant cults, heresies and demonic delusions. On the other hand, they had to convince the authorities that they themselves were not a cult. To meet the dilemma, the need was recognized among the leadership of the largest house-church groupings for a doctrinal statement to be issued on a biblical basis. This was done in 1998.

THE 1998 CONFESSION OF FAITH

The purpose of the confession was to demonstrate that the house-church movement represented mainstream Protestant Christianity, as recognized by Christians internationally. They are not a sect, and should not be treated as one. Also, in order to maintain orthodoxy and unity in the house-church movement, cult doctrines and false prophetic claims are refuted and rejected.

Jonathan Chao (Zhao Tianen, 1937–2004) was the leading authority on the church in China under the Communists. He was born in China but his Christian family fled from China in 1949. Chao became an American citizen in the 1950s. He received a master's degree in divinity from Westminster Theological Seminary, the leading Conservative Protestant Reformed training institution in America. He also obtained a Ph.D in Sinology from the University of Pennsylvania. Chao was founder and president of China Ministries International until his death. In 1978 he founded the Chinese Church Research Center in Hong Kong and made his first trip into post-Mao China with David Adeney. Chao built up a database from interviews of Chinese Christians leaving China and of Christian visitors returning from China. In the 1980s Chao formed close links with many of the house-church leaders.

In the spring of 1996, Jonathan Chao began to work with the house-church leaders on the different aspects of theology emphasized by each group. David Aikman says, 'The result of his theological counsel, nudging, and cajoling was the *United Appeal* and the *Confession of Faith*. Undoubtedly Chao's theological counsel was crucial in persuading them to realize that they had far more in common than in difference.' Certainly, in this writer's view, they could not have had a better adviser to guide them into the fold of the mainstream Protestant confessions.

The core group of house-church leaders behind the *United Appeal* and the *Confession of Faith* called themselves the Sinim Fellowship (Sinim = China; see Isaiah 49:12). The fellowship continued to meet until 2004 under the name of Shen Zhou.

THE UNITED APPEAL, THE CONFESSION OF FAITH, AND THE HOUSE-CHURCH POLICY

On 22 August 1998 the *United Appeal of the Various Branches of the Chinese House Church* was issued. It is reproduced here in Appendix IV. This was followed on 26 November 1998 by the *Confession of Faith*, which is reproduced here in full in Appendix V. Issued along with the *Confession of Faith* was a document stating *The Attitude of House Churches toward the Government, its Religious Policy, and the TSPM*. This is reproduced here in Appendix VI.

The *United Appeal* makes the statement that 'The House Church represents the mainstream of Christianity, as recognized internationally.' It also says that the TSPM cannot make that claim because it is only an eighth of the size of the house-church movement and 'in many spiritual matters there is serious deviation' from the Scriptures. The *United Appeal* states that the House Church therefore ought not to be treated as a cult. It recognizes as valid the expression of the gospel by those of their number who are called Presbyterian (Calvinists), the Charismatic Church, the Local Church and the Little Flock (both Brethren), the Way of Life or Full

Gospel Church (Born-Again Movement), Pentecostals, Lutherans and Baptists. They all represent orthodox Christianity (evangelicalism). It states that persecution should stop and all orthodox Christians imprisoned for their faith should be released from the labour camps.

The *Confession of Faith* issued three months later defines the orthodox Christianity of this large segment of the Chinese house-church movement. It is thoroughly evangelical. Its premillennialism reflects the majority view of house-church Christians, as does its moderate Pentecostalism. The confession confronts cult doctrines that had sprung up, and rejects them through its negative assertions. It asserts the separation of church and state as distinct spheres.

The statement concerning *The Attitude of House Churches toward the Government, its Religious Policy, and the TSPM* makes for fascinating and edifying reading. It is thoroughly Christian in tone and content. It is an honourable statement. It has been dismissed out of hand by the authorities. Yet, make no mistake, the statement represents the heartbeat and heart-cry of Christianity. It stands in the proud succession of faithful witnesses since the days of the apostles. Just reading this statement gives valuable insight into the real issues being played out in China today.

The house-church movement does not constitute a denomination in itself. It recognizes biblical Christianity as its basis of unity, not denominations. Yet it is evident that the House Church acknowledges that some groups ('various branches') hold loyally to the distinctives of some of the historic Protestant denominations, such as the Presbyterians, Lutherans and Baptists.

In the opinion of this author, if 'unity' is to be maintained successfully among the evangelical groupings, then that unity must be based on the biblical fundamentals. At the same time 'diversity' — that is, differences of view — must be allowed concerning secondary matters. These latter ought not to cause division. An adequate doctrinal basis is an imperative.

Does the *1998 Confession of Faith* constitute an adequate basis for the unity of evangelicalism? It certainly does constitute a good foundation, but a major weakness is that it does not admit a non-Pentecostal evangelicalism. By failing to do so, it is out of step in this regard with a large segment of mainstream evangelical Protestantism worldwide, and also with the Reformation confessions. Perhaps this can be put right at some future date. Nor does it recognize the validity of other interpretations than its own premillennial view concerning the details of the Second Coming of Christ.

What hope is there for future union of this large segment of the House Church with the Three-Self Church? Certainly, as we shall see, the majority of the grass-roots members of the Three-Self churches now share their evangelicalism. But the prospect of a union seems only a very remote possibility. Doctrinally there is the divide over the issue of the separation between church and state. There is also the barrier to overcome created by the theological liberalism of the entrenched leadership of the TSPM. In addition, the history of persecution and betrayal of the leaders and members of the house churches by the TSPM, often working in close collaboration with the Public Security Bureau, has left deep wounds and created a climate of suspicion. Memories are long.

In some big cities of China certain unregistered churches are permitted their own buildings and flourish. However, their continuance is not guaranteed.

It must also be said that today many house churches in the coastal areas and cities have not even heard of the existence of the *Confession of Faith*. Nevertheless its issue constitutes an important historical event in Chinese church history. With the accompanying statements, it ought to be known and studied by all Christians in China.

21. The gospel in China since 1985

After the Tiananmen Square incident of May 1989, 'Christianity fever' was to break out in even greater measure. In the next ten years the church nearly doubled in size! In spite of continued persecution, the following twenty years saw the establishment of the gospel in China as a revival church, with explosive growth and dynamic spiritual power.

In 1989 there were estimated to be between twenty and fifty million Protestant believers in China. In 1998 the house-church leaders claimed that there were ninety million Protestant believers in China. Eighty million of these were to be found in the variety of house churches scattered throughout the land, and ten million worshipped in the registered Three-Self Patriotic Movement churches and meeting points. The TSPM official figure claimed that they had twelve million members, a figure excluding all under the age of eighteen. By 2006 the official TSPM number had grown to fifteen million members and to twenty-three million in 2010.

On 7 September 2007, the 200th anniversary of the landing of the pioneer missionary Robert Morrison on the soil of mainland China, there must have been approaching 100 million professing evangelical believers in China.

These can only be approximate figures, as statistics in China are notoriously unreliable. If the overall figures are anywhere near accurate, then the Protestant church in China had grown by a hundredfold in the fifty years under the Communist regime, from the official figure of 834,000 communicants in 1949. Since 2007 there has been an indication of slackening of the increase, in terms of overall numbers, in some places — mainly in the countryside — yet in other places the remarkable growth continues.

PEOPLE'S REPUBLIC OF CHINA SINCE 1985

Between 1986 and 1989, China's 'open-door policy' opened the country to foreign investment and technical knowledge. This encouraged some development of a market economy and a private sector. It was to be 'Socialism with Chinese characteristics'. In 1989 stock markets opened in Shanghai and Shenzhen.

In May 1989 student demonstrators camped for weeks in Tiananmen Square in Beijing to demand the posthumous rehabilitation of the former moderate CCP general secretary Hu Yaobang. They also wanted a crackdown on corruption within the Communist Party and a government engagement

Tiananmen Square, Beijing

towards democracy. Already Communism was in danger of collapsing in Eastern Europe and in the USSR. The Chinese leadership feared the same for China. Troops were sent in on the evening of 3 June. Many hundreds of students and Beijing citizens were killed. Many students were arrested nationwide in the aftermath. International outrage led to sanctions.

After the Tiananmen Square incident, Deng Xiaoping retired from public view but kept overall control. Power passed to Jiang Zemin as general secretary of the Communist Party, and then to his successor Hu Jintao in 2002. The economy continued to grow at an impressive rate, but at the cost of many social problems and tensions. In 1997 Hong Kong reverted to Chinese control, as did Macau in 1999. In 2001 China gained accession to the World Trade Organization. The 2008 summer Olympics were held in Beijing. As a permanent member of the UN Security Council, China is in the centre of world politics. It uses its economic and political clout to forward its interests in developing countries.

Since 1989 the Communist Party has held firmly onto power, with antipathy towards all major political and religious reforms. Economic growth has averaged at least 8% per annum. This, together with the emergence of a middle class and pride in China's growing influence on the world stage, has kept the lid on disaffection. The modern Chinese psyche is proudly nationalistic and accepts the Confucian mode of governance, with its emphasis on strong central government, hierarchy and the fact that people should not expect to be empowered politically in their own right. Wealth is more important. People can now get rich, and that is the main thing. The general acceptance of the ruthless repression of the democracy movement at Tiananmen Square reflects all this.

IN THE AFTERMATH OF TIANANMEN SQUARE

Across China, after the Tiananmen Square incident, urban churches noticed a new development. Thousands of students, previously uninterested in religion, were coming to church or openly wanting to discuss the Christian faith. This added a new dimension to the revival already taking place. In Fuzhou (capital of the province of Fujian) over 800 students came to a meeting to learn more about Christianity. The gospel was now reaching the new intelligentsia, the university students, a phenomenon last seen in the revival during and after World War II.

Reaching the intelligentsia with the gospel can be seen as a step forward in the maturing of the revival church in China and progress in its reach into all levels of society. Behind the staggering increase in numbers enquiring and joining both the official church and the house churches was a hunger for Bibles and Bible teaching.

OFFICIAL CHURCH POLICY AFTER 1989

Since 1989 there has been a marked increase in repression of nonconformist Christian activity.

In 1991 President Jiang Zemin called for tighter controls on religion. *Document Number 6* was issued by China's State Council. It reinforced the restrictions laid out in the 1982 *Document Number 19* and demanded that religious activity in the whole of China be registered at the local level with the Religious Affairs Bureau or the TSPM. In November 1993 Jiang Zemin ordered that all religion must 'adapt to socialist society'. In 1994, documents numbered 144 and 145 again demanded the registration requirement and also prohibited foreigners from carrying out any kind of religious activity in China without previous permission at national level. This was aimed at preventing the return of 'foreign missionary' activity, in the persons of foreign pastors and teachers who were giving assistance to the rapidly expanding house-church networks.

All these initiatives led to crackdowns aimed at tighter control at grass-roots level. Unregistered house churches have been subjected from the mid-1990s onwards to closures, arrests, beatings, fines and imprisonments. Many preferred to disband and reconstitute themselves in another guise or in smaller groups. Whenever there is a major political campaign or a crackdown on crime, unofficial church leaders and their members become an easy target and prey for the security forces, however unjustly. They are a soft touch for fines and extortion. Christians in general are still open to be discriminated against, at all levels of society. When they are reckoned to be a potential threat to the authority of the Communist Party, they are carefully monitored by the police and security forces. Contacts with evangelical Christians from abroad are enough to put a person on the list.

200 delegates from the house churches sought to attend the Third Lausanne Congress on Global Evangelization in Cape Town, South Africa, in October 2010. All 200 were prevented from leaving China, whatever route they had individually chosen.

In 1997, Jiang Zemin, then China's president and leader of the Communist Party, visited Wenzhou. He was shocked by the visibility of religious symbols in public and, following his visit, hundreds of unauthorized Christian churches and Buddhist temples were summarily demolished. This was followed up in 2002 by an edict from the city's Religious Affairs Bureau abolishing all Sunday school teaching as illegal. In the end the RAB had to back down on this issue. The weight of Christian opinion and influence counted locally. By 2007 it was estimated that 14% of the population in the Wenzhou area were professing Christians. Some estimates double that number. The influence of the Christians has been felt there. As a result, some house churches have been exempted from registering with the TSPM/CCC and have been allowed to register with the local authorities instead. It is to be hoped that this avenue to legal status will turn out to be a pattern adopted throughout China. Other house churches have refused to register on principle and are very suspicious of those who have. Since 1980 Wenzhou has seen remarkable economic expansion and prosperity. The merchants of Wenzhou, with their wares, are to be found not only all over China but all over the world. Now, wherever their merchants go abroad, Chinese churches spring up. This is evidence of the profound effect of the Christian gospel in Wenzhou.

Persecutions are sporadic and depend on local conditions, but they constitute a grim reality. In June 2004, Jiang Zongxiu was arrested in Guizhou province for distributing Bibles. Through mistreatment and torture she died in custody. Yet persecutions have played an important role in the remarkable growth of the evangelical Protestant church. These persecutions continue. In a report in June 2006 by China Aid Association, it was recorded that 1,958 Chinese house-church pastors and other believers were arrested in the year to May 2006. The crackdown in 2006 was as a result of the revelation to the State Council in 2005 that a large number of Communist Party members attended Christian worship and that believers were becoming so numerous in eleven provinces and municipalities that the local authorities did not know what to do about them. As a matter of record these localities were Guangdong, Shanghai, Jiangsu, Beijing, Fujian, Zhejiang, Hunan, Hubei, Hebei, Henan and Chongqing.

The numbers reported to have been arrested for religious reasons have increased annually since 2006, according to China Aid Association.

THE THREE-SELF PATRIOTIC MOVEMENT

The TSPM was led between 1980 and 1996 by Bishop Ding Guangxun and since his official retirement he continues to lead the China Christian Council, the TSPM and Nanjing Union Theological Seminary — all of these posts with the title 'emeritus'. As an Anglican bishop he had international clout. He used this influence to forward the Communist doctrines and cause both at home and abroad. He was also an implacable enemy of all things evangelical, like his predecessor Y. T. Wu. Under Wu's direction, Ding had been the hatchet man on Wang Mingdao. Ding had followed President Zemin's 1993 order that religion must 'adapt to socialist society' by issuing a campaign to impose his own 'theological reconstruction' on the Chinese church, in which all progressive social and political movements of mankind are equated with the redemptive work of Christ. Of course Marxism takes pride of place. This attempt to create a Marxist indigenous social Christian theology has met with almost total rejection in the TSPM churches, at grass-roots level.

The current situation is that the TSPM still operates under the direct orders of the Religious Affairs Bureau, now renamed the State Administration of Religious Affairs (SARA). All SARA officials are Communist Party members and have to be atheists. They have overall control of the training and disposition of pastors and also of the number of meetings permitted monthly. Since 1995 the director general of SARA is Ye Xiaowen. He is a militant atheist, vigorously opposed to the expansion of Christianity.

There are twenty-three seminaries and Bible schools open for the training of pastors, with about 1,200 full-time students. There are fifty applicants for each place. Little effort is made to expand the seminaries. Many of them exist on a shoestring budget and academic standards vary. Liberal leaders determinedly sideline evangelicals when they can. In 2006 there were more than 16,000 TSPM churches led by only 3,000 accredited clergy. With a membership of twenty-three million to cater for, it can easily be seen that most preaching and pastoral work must actually be in the hands of lay persons, who are now predominantly evangelical.

The insatiable demand for Bible commentaries, books on church history, biographies and devotional books is not being met by the TSPM. Whatever has been provided by them is strictly limited and controlled. Some private publication of Christian books is happening within the TSPM. This is an encouraging sign.

One noticeable change in the TSPM churches can be seen with reference to the organization's magazine *Tianfeng*. In the 1950s its contents were mostly political and replete with liberal theology. Now its contents are mainly evangelical and devotional.

At the grass roots, in the churches, Christian volunteers engage in all manner of social and public services. They have set up medical clinics and advice centres. They repair roads and bridges. They help out the locals after floods and earthquakes with relief such as blankets, food and medicines. They continue to help well after media attention has moved on. They witness at the same time.

Christianity is not viewed by the general population as subversive, but rather as a force for good in society. It is to be hoped that the authorities will recognize this too and grant full toleration.

THE EVANGELISM EXPLOSION CONTINUES

The explosion in evangelistic activity in the 1980s among the house churches was to reap a great harvest in the 1990s. Even when there was tighter control by the authorities after 1989, ways and means for effective evangelism were found by prayerful and determined Christians and churches. The emergence of the mobile phone and of the Internet was of assistance, in spite of determined censorship and official control of these media.

As always, evangelistic activities come under criticism even from some professing Christians. The TSPM leadership have an antipathy for these zealous activities. They have always co-operated with the official CCP policy in banning all evangelism. However, the CCP has seldom been able to prevent the gospel being preached within the TSPM churches and meeting places, nor has it been able to prevent explosive growth in the membership of TSPM churches. In 1995 the pastor of a TSPM church in north China saw over 1,000 come to faith, be baptized and added to the membership in that year. In 1997 a TSPM church in Zhejiang province conducted special evangelistic services for two evenings. From one service alone, over 600 signed up for baptismal classes.

In Jiangsu province, the number of Christians grew from 50,000 in 1949 to 125,000 in 1985, to 400,000 in 1989, and then to over 1,000,000 by 1998! This figure is derived from the detailed statistics compiled by Tony Lambert in his book *China's Christian Millions*. Making all allowances for the unreliability of such figures, there can be no hiding from the fact that a remarkable spiritual awakening and revival has taken place in Jiangsu province.

Farmhouse in Jiangsu province

According to Lambert, other provinces in China that have participated in spiritual blessing on the same scale proportionally are Anhui, Heilongjiang, Henan, Guangxi, Guizhou, Inner Mongolia, Jilin, Liaoning, Jiangxi, Yunnan and Zhejiang. All the other regions have seen some increase, but not nearly of that order. Indeed, vast tracts of the country are still unevangelized pioneer missionary situations. Overall, the reality of widespread increase in Christian converts is confirmed by the strength of official reaction at government level.

OVERSEAS CHRISTIANS

It has been natural for as much help as possible to be given to the Chinese church by foreign Christians, churches and organizations. Yet great harm can be done by well-meaning but ill-advised actions. Wisdom is needed. Overseas Chinese Christians naturally want to help. However, in particular, financial aid in plenteous amounts is dangerous to the spiritual life and can be accompanied by hidden agendas, such as the promotion of democracy in China. Fortunately, foreign para-church organizations have largely found no place in China, and where they have, their help is strictly at the invitation and control of the Chinese churches. The best practical help that can be given is from visiting pastors and by the supply of good teaching materials. Apart from that, the best policy is to let the Chinese church stand on its own feet and trust in God for provision.

THE PASSING OF A PATRIARCH

Allen Yuan was released from his twenty-one years of imprisonment in 1979. He continued to live in Beijing to the end of his life. He refused to join the TSPM. He continued to preach and teach at worship meetings held at his home. He never hid anything that he did publicly. He welcomed foreign visitors, which included Billy Graham in 1994. In June 1998 he was given international prominence during the visit of President Clinton to China. Allen Yuan held annual baptismal services for converts, which numbered many hundreds over the years. At first these were held in a local swimming baths; then, as the numbers grew, the baptisms were held in a river outside Beijing. He remained energetic and faithful in his ministry as a pastor to the end. He baptized more than 700 new believers in 2005 alone! This was just before he was taken to be with his Master on 16 August 2005, at the age of ninety-one!

SURVIVING PATRIARCHS

Moses Xie now lives quietly in Beijing.

Samuel Lamb was released from his twenty years' imprisonment in 1978. He lives in Guangzhou. After his release, Samuel Lamb started to teach English in 1980, and within weeks had formed a house church of converts from this

Aerial view of part of modern Guangzhou

English class. The house church grew and grew, and now the church holds four main services a week, with estimated total attendance of 4,000–5,000. Because Samuel Lamb has the most international recognition of all the house-church leaders, he has been afforded a greater measure of liberty, though he is not free from harassment. He remains determined to do everything in a straightforward and completely open way.

Li Tianen (b. 1928) now lives in Shanghai. He has preached and taught in all the provinces and municipalities of China, except Tibet, Guizhou and Xinjiang.

What changes and what events the surviving elderly Christian patriarchs have seen in the course of their lives! They can recollect the calibre of the Chinese Christian leadership and powerful evangelists of their youth. They remember the sharp conflict with the liberal, rationalistic, humanistic theology imported from abroad in the name of Western enlightenment and scholarship. They saw God's own answer in the major revival among university students in the 1940s. They witnessed the rapid expulsion of the whole foreign missionary movement when the Communists came to power in 1949. They experienced the full weight of the Communist efforts to extinguish their faith. They remember the days of the Cultural Revolution and the onslaught of Mao Zedong's Red Guards. They look back in gratitude to God for His grace that enabled them to endure years of imprisonment and, with countless other believers, to keep the faith. They pass on a good confession of Christ.

22. Looking to the future

As the Protestant church, both official and unofficial, looks to the future, it can do so with encouragement. The power of the gospel of Christ will continue to bless China with spiritual and social good. Official church buildings remain packed with keen worshippers and enquirers and there is a demand for new church buildings. As far as the house-church movement goes, confidence is evident in their missionary vision.

AN EMERGING MISSIONARY CHURCH

With the rapid expansion of the house-church movement in the 1990s, the missionary vision to take the gospel of God's saving grace beyond the Chinese borders was rekindled. Up to that time, the days had been so dark for believers in China that their prayers and energies had been taken up with just seeking the survival of the faith. Now their prayers and energies could embrace the Great Commission of Christ to take the gospel to everyone in the world.

In 1981, when Simon Zhao was released from prison in Kashgar after surviving thirty-one years of appalling circumstances and cruelties, nobody was waiting for him. He had nowhere to go and had no money. However, he was looked

Simon Zhao in 1988

after by the local Christians in Kashgar. In 1988 some workers from the Henan network of house churches were in Kashgar. They heard about this original 'Back to Jerusalem' worker and leader. They were eager to meet him and learn from him. The vision for Chinese churches to take the gospel to the nations west of China, all the way along the ancient silk road to Jerusalem, had originated with Mark Ma as far back as 1942.

A group of house-church leaders then visited Simon Zhao. He looked like a wizened old sage. They could not persuade him to travel east to speak to the churches in Henan. He just wanted to be left in peace and quiet. Certainly he dreaded becoming the centre of attention. This was the understandable reluctance of one who had suffered so much and was now over seventy years of age. This reluctance was finally broken around 1995 by the very patient and prayerful arguments of Xu Yongling, sister to the Tanghe Fellowship leader Xu Yongze. She persuaded Simon Zhao to go to Henan, 'where thousands of new troops need training and equipping if the "Back to Jerusalem" mission is to be rekindled in the life of the Chinese church'. His ministry turned out to be very powerful, and many tears flowed as he gave his moving testimony and shared the original vision.

Just how successful his ministry proved to be can be measured by the fact that many Christians within China today know and pray for the 'Back to Jerusalem' vision to be

The original Back to Jerusalem Band (Mark Ma is in the centre of the front row)

realized. A motivation for many is the belief that Chinese Christians should be present in Jerusalem to witness the Second Coming of Christ, as a reward for their evangelizing the nations between China and Jerusalem. Wenzhou Christians see a second route back to Jerusalem, the ocean route to the Persian Gulf.

Simon Zhao died on 7 December 2001, rejoicing in the faithfulness of God and the perfection of His ways.

The majority of the nations west of China are Muslim, and the Chinese Christians with missionary vision have taken this to heart. They consider that this constitutes a special call for them to do the evangelizing. Rightly or wrongly, they believe a Chinese Christian will be more acceptable than a Western Christian. In their view, the legacy of the Crusades has raised an insuperable barrier of prejudice against Westerners. The Chinese do not have this particular millstone around their necks.

Missionary vision is not confined to 'Back to Jerusalem'. That has been a catalyst. It is a beginning. As Chinese Christians are able to be more mobile within China, there are 520 people groups within the borders of China to be reached, including Muslims. That is a starting place for mission. The task cannot be easy, but a start has been made.

When they are able to link up and work in partnership with strong Chinese churches already established abroad, they will be a spiritual force to reckon with. They could evangelize south-east Asia and re-evangelize the West. The vision for 100,000 Chinese missionaries on a global scale is already in circulation within China! That would represent just one in a thousand of the Protestant believers in China. It is only a dream under present circumstances, but a noble one.

If ever the time comes to implement the task of overseas missionary work seriously, then biblical standards will need to be upheld. It must be realized that it is not a human programme, but a divine purpose and calling to be followed. For all missionary workers it is spiritual quality, and not numbers, that is of paramount importance. Good candidate selection is crucial for the success of any mission endeavour. Thorough training and mature character are essential. A local church should do the sending. Lessons can be learned from the story of foreign missionaries to their land of China. The lives of the pioneer missionaries to China, in particular, have good lessons to teach, as well as being excellent models for inspiration.

A popular and sensational book is called *The Heavenly Man*. It describes the life and views of Brother Yun. He now lives abroad and is a popularizer of the 'Back to Jerusalem' vision. Despite the claims, he does not represent the house churches in China. His ideas for sending abroad ill-prepared young peasant missionaries are unbiblical. It is sending lambs to the slaughter. This matters because much harm is done and the name of Christ is brought into disrepute.

A MORAL CHURCH

Many Christian families have received government awards as model households, and many individual Christians have received rewards for the quality of their contribution in the workplace. Christians demonstrate a healthy lifestyle and set a good example. The reason is that they have to answer to God, a higher authority than that of the state. Their self-sacrificing care often puts to shame the empty slogans and, only too often, the callous indifference of Communist Party members.

The 1998 *House Church Policy* (reproduced in Appendix VI) made the claim that 'the persecuted Christians have a heart that loves their country and people', and 'have high moral integrity'. 'As a matter of fact', they state, 'wherever there are more believers, there is also greater social stability.' 'We only do what is beneficial to the people.' Jesus said that it is spiritual character that produces such good disciples (Matthew 5:3-12). They are the 'salt of the earth' and 'the light of the world' (Matthew 5:13-16). 'Love your enemies' and 'Overcome evil with good' must continue to be the standard.

CONCLUSION

China is a huge country. The extraordinary variety of conditions mean that a complete overview of current conditions of the church in China is difficult to achieve. Strictness by the authorities in one part of China is matched by toleration in another. We need to be cautious. Two extremes are to be avoided; one, an over-optimistic, starry-eyed triumphalism; the other, a cynical detachment that sees only the faults of human imperfection and a future impending doom. The real question is: what is God doing in China? The answer is: He has done much and is doing much today.

What is God yet going to do in China? The fact is that Christianity is a minority religion in China and still marginal in the life of the nation. The remarkable spiritual revival in China needs to continue to grow unabated. The key is in the word 'unabated'. Historically, when a genuine revival has progressed unchecked for over a hundred years within a nation, that nation has been radically changed for the better — spiritually, morally and socially — whatever the obstacles.

There have been no exceptions to this rule. Britain and the USA have been privileged to experience such periods, but have known no genuine revival of extensive length in the last 150 years.

Our prayer must be:

• that the revival will continue and retain its spiritual power
• that the revival will remain pure as to doctrine and practice
• that the revival will continue to mature the church
• that the revival will renew China spiritually, morally and socially
• that out of the revival will come a host of missionaries to the rest of the world

This would be the fitting repayment of the debt that the Chinese owe, in love and in the providence of God, to Robert Morrison, the pioneer of the gospel to China, and also to all who have given their lives in the service of the gospel to China, whether they be Chinese or foreigners, whether known or unknown.

Jesus said, 'I will build My church, and the gates of hell will not prevail against it.' In China today Christ is building His Church. The power of God to save is at work.

Timeline

1939–45	Second World War; Japanese defeated
1939–49	Spiritual revival among university students
1946–49	Civil war in China; Chiang Kai-shek loses, flees to Taiwan
1 October 1949	People's Republic of China declared by Mao in Beijing
1950	Three-Self Patriotic Movement formed to control the church
20 July 1953	The last foreign missionary leaves China
1958–60	The Great Leap Forward; twenty to thirty million people starve
1966–76	The Cultural Revolution — launched by Mao, a disaster for China.
1966	All churches closed; the church goes underground for thirteen years
1976	Death of Mao signals the end of the Cultural Revolution
1978	Deng Xiaoping; 'Four Modernizations' policy; rehabilitation policy
1979-80	TSPM re-established; churches reopen; many Christians released
1983	Persecution of house churches resumes
1989	Tiananmen Square incident — crackdown on student protesters
	A massive increase in church attendance follows
1989–2002	Jiang Zemin, general secretary of CCP, succeeds to power
1997	Hong Kong returned to China
1999	Macao reverts to China; Falungong sect outlawed
2001	China joins World Trade Organization
2002 to date	Hu Jintao, general secretary of CCP, succeeds to power
2003	Launch of first manned space flight from China
2006	Three Gorges Dam completed
2008	Olympic Games held in Beijing

Appendix I
Old and modern names of the provinces of China

THE TWENTY-TWO PROVINCES, FIVE AUTONOMOUS REGIONS AND FOUR MUNICIPALITIES OF CHINA
(see maps on page ii)

Modern name	Old name (where different)
The north-east *(known as 'the Rust Belt')*	
Heilongjiang province	Manchuria
Jilin province	Manchuria
Liaoning province	Manchuria
The north *(including the Yellow River Basin — the heartland of China)*	
Hebei province	Hopeh or Zhili/Chihli (means 'direct rule')
Beijing municipality	Peking, capital of China
Tianjin municipality	Tientsin, city of Hopeh province
Shandong province	Shantung
Inner Mongolia region	
Shanxi province	Shansi
Henan province	Honan

Modern name	Old name (where different)

The north-west *(grasslands, deserts, nomads, Islam)*

Shaanxi province	Shensi
Ningxia region	Ninghsia
Gansu province	Kansu
Qinghai province	Tsinghai (constituted 1928)
Xinjiang region	Sinkiang (part was called Chinese Turkestan)

The south-west *(exotic, spectacular scenery, minority groups)*

Tibet (Xizang) region	
Yunnan province	
Guangxi region	Kwangsi
Guizhou province	Kweichow

Central *(farming areas)*

Sichuan province	Szechwan
Chongqing municipality	Chungking, city of Szechwan province.
Hubei province	Hupeh
Hunan province	
Jiangxi province	Kiangsi
Anhui province	Anhwei

South-east *(coastal, traditional trading centres)*

Hainan (Island) province	The province, constituted since 1988, was formerly part of Kwangtung
Guangdong province	Kwangtung
Fujian province	Fukien

East *(coastal, the new economic centre)*

Zhejiang province	Chekiang
Shanghai municipality	city of Jiangsu/Kiangsu province
Jiangsu province	Kiangsu

Appendix II
A *summary history of the Chinese dynasties, 2500 BC — AD 1912*

A braided silk belt, silk threads and woven silk have been discovered at the Liangzu culture site at Qianshanyang in Wuxing district, Zhejiang, which has an approximate dating of 2500 BC. Early Chinese civilization developed roughly contemporaneously with the Indus Valley civilization but later than the early Mesopotamian.

THE XIA DYNASTY (2205–1766 BC)

The Xia is the first dynasty to be described in ancient historical documents with some historical basis. (For convenience I follow the traditional dating for the early dynasties.)

The first ruler, Yu the Great, was a gifted organizer and was greatly praised for largely eliminating the scourge of flooding in his kingdom by setting in motion the construction of many canals. In the course of time, canal systems came to be built extensively across the plains of China and were to prove one of the distinctive hallmarks of China's civilization. Hudson Taylor and other missionaries used these networks extensively in their travels and evangelistic endeavours in the nineteenth century. Yu also introduced the hereditary system of dynastic rule.

Biblically this dynasty is contemporary with the early patriarchs, Abraham, Isaac and Jacob.

THE SHANG DYNASTY (1766–1122 BC)

The Shang dynasty ruled over the core Chinese civilization of the Han people in the Bronze Age. Its cradle area was in the plains and hills of what are now the Yellow River provinces of Hebei, Henan, Jiangsu, Shanxi and Shaanxi. All people living outside this area were regarded as barbarians and savages fit only to be subject peoples.

The Shang civilization was based on agriculture and animal husbandry. They moved their capital at least six times. Bronze was used mainly for cultural objects rather than for weaponry. The king was head of the cult of ancestor and spirit-worship. Hundreds of commoners were buried alive with the royal corpse. Forms of Chinese-character writing developed during this period.

This period also saw the development of the people of Israel, their slavery in Egypt, their deliverance under Moses and Joshua and the period of the judges.

THE ZHOU (CHOU) DYNASTY (1122–246 BC)

In the late Bronze Age and Iron Age which followed the Shang dynasty, the Zhous added to their rule the Yangtze River Basin, the great fertile basin of Sichuan to the west and some of Manchuria to the north-east. They invoked the concept of 'the Mandate of Heaven', a form of ruling by divine right, to legitimize their rule. This concept was to be adopted by almost every succeeding dynastic ruler in China.

The Zhou were especially marked by the development of schools of thought. In the sixth century BC Taoism and Confucianism made their appearance. In 140 BC the works of Confucius were made the official philosophy.

Biblically this long period spans from the days of the prophet Samuel through the period of the kings of Israel, right to the end of Old Testament times.

THE QIN (CHIN) DYNASTY (221–206 BC)

Though short in length, the Qin dynasty has been regarded as the real start of the Chinese Empire. It set the pattern for the next two millennia. The major contribution of the Qin was the concept of central government, which led to the unification of the legal code, standardized writing, a currency for China and harmonization of weights and measures. The name 'China' has its origin from this Qin dynasty.

The first emperor of imperial China, Qin Shi Huang (Chin Chi Wung), reigned for twelve years and was responsible for building the original Great Wall of China, which ran for a length of over 3,000 miles and a height of up to thirty feet. Little of this has survived. This wall was further north than the present-day Great Wall.

When Qin Shi Huang died in 210 BC, he was buried with the famous terracotta army of 8,000 soldiers with 130 terracotta chariots and 670 terracotta horses. The lavish tomb and complex were built near his capital Xianyang, in Shaanxi province, half an hour's travel from modern Xian. There is still much being discovered there.

THE HAN DYNASTY (206 BC – AD 220)

The Han dynasty was contemporary with the founding and heyday of the Roman Empire and the establishing of the Christian church. The Han dynasty is rightly considered within China to have been one of the great periods of their history. It is the Han people who regard themselves as the truly authentic Chinese.

During this period China officially became a Confucian state and prospered domestically. Cai Lun invented papermaking in AD 105. Agriculture, handicrafts, art, science and commerce all flourished and the population reached over fifty-five million. The empire extended its political influence over Mongolia, much of Korea, Vietnam and central Asia before finally collapsing. During this dynasty some huge landed estates were abolished and the land was nationalized and divided up among the peasantry, but this reform did not last. Emperor Wu (141–87 BC) started a school to teach future administrators the Confucian classics.

THE TANG DYNASTY (AD 618–907)

The Tang dynasty introduced a new age of prosperity after hundreds of years of political fragmentation and chaos. Xian, their capital, is thought to have been the world's largest city at that time. Under this dynasty the 'equal field system' was introduced, which granted lands based on family need rather than wealth. To this day, China is a country full of smallholdings. The drinking of tea became a national habit. Trade prospered and many foreign traders settled in China. Poetry and painting flourished. Entrance examinations for the imperial civil service were introduced in AD 605. Woodblock printing was established and the first newspaper was published in Beijing in AD 700.

THE SONG DYNASTY (960–1279)

This dynasty was to succumb eventually to the Mongols. Their rule extended only a very little beyond China proper and their hold over the north became more and more eroded as time progressed. Yet the Song period was one of striking cultural and technological achievements. Porcelain and painting were notable. Gunpowder weapons gave military advantage, especially in naval warfare. The compass was used on ships by 1050. Moveable wooden type was invented in 1041. Printing developed to such an extent that enormous literary works were published, including histories. The professional civil servants took the lead in scholarship.

THE YUAN DYNASTY (1279–1368)

The Yuan was a foreign dynasty established by the Mongol, Kublai Khan. He was the grandson of Genghis Khan (Chingis Khan) and under him all China became part of the Mongol Empire. The Mongols took over a rich China and left behind an impoverished one. A census held in 1300 reported a Chinese population of about sixty million, compared with about 120 million before the Mongol invasion. The cultural differences between the Mongols and Chinese proved too much to bridge, and the practice of using non-

Chinese in government positions cemented the wedge between them.

The Chinese nobility were left free to pursue art and literature. Notable advances were made in the realms of theatre, opera and the novel. The Mongols welcomed foreign traders and this explains the kind treatment and promotion of Marco Polo in the service of Kublai Khan.

The last years of the dynasty were marked by plague, famine, feuds and outlawry. The fourteenth-century epidemics of plague reduced the population further to about fifty million.

THE MING DYNASTY (1368–1644)

The Ming was a Han Chinese dynasty founded by Zhu Yuanzhang, who was also known as the Hongwu (Vast Military) Emperor. He was the third of only three peasants ever to become an emperor in China. He developed a military class that ranked higher than any civil servant. A standing army of between one and two million was maintained. A large navy was built. The Forbidden City and Beijing were built for the emperor's use in 1420. After 1449 the Great Wall was reconstructed and modernized over a distance of 4,160 miles. The Grand Canal was also repaired and extended to a length of 1,144 miles, from Beijing to Hangzhou, capital of Zhejiang province, to the south.

Under the Hongwu Emperor the movement to establish China as an agricultural society of independent peasant landholders, with town markets as the hub, was begun. New crops were cultivated and cottage industries specializing in paper, silk, porcelain and textiles also restored prosperity across China. The population recovered rapidly and towards the end of this period was estimated at between 100 million and 150 million.

What brought about the downfall of the dynasty was a combination of internal power struggles, acute debasement of the currency and, between 1616 and 1644, the ultimately successful invasion from Manchuria by the Manchus (formerly known as the Jurchen). An estimated twenty-five million Chinese died during this final struggle.

THE QING (CH'ING) DYNASTY (1644—1912)

The Qing was a foreign dynasty of Manchus who quickly adopted the Confucian norms of traditional Chinese government. However, they enforced the adoption by the Han Chinese of Manchu-style clothing and the queue hairstyle. The penalty for not complying was death.

In an attempt to avoid assimilation into Chinese society, they set up an elite military system called the 'Eight Banners' system. Banner membership was open to Manchus and was based upon the traditional Manchu skills such as archery, horsemanship and frugality. The Manchu language was to be used by them. Bannermen were given economic and legal privileges in Chinese cities. The Manchus consolidated control of areas originally under that of the Mings, including Yunnan, and extended their influence over Xinjiang, Tibet and Mongolia.

The eighteenth century

This century saw both the height of the Qing power and the beginning of its decline. The latter came about as a result of the rampant corruption of court officials and the White Lotus Rebellion (1796–1804). The rebellion, in a part of central China, was instigated by a secret society with the aim of toppling the Manchus in order to set up a native Chinese dynasty. The White Lotus tradition was an amalgam of Daoist and Buddhist elements in popular religion. The Mother of No-Birth promised to send the Matreiya Buddha during a period of end-time chaos to save humanity and remake the world. Though eventually this rebellion was crushed, it shattered the myth of the Manchus' invincibility. The next century was to see the multiplication both of secret societies and of rebellions.

The nineteenth century

This century saw Qing control weaken as China faced increasing international trade pressures, massive social strife, huge national disasters, constant economic stagnation and unremitting defeats in the trade and territorial wars forced on the nation by foreign powers. All this was too much for an antiquated bureaucratic government, and the Qing dynasty fell into terminal decline and was overthrown early in the next century.

Among the woes of the century was the iniquitous and illegal opium trade carried on openly by Western traders in collusion with corrupt officials. The cost to China was a massive increase of drug addiction throughout the land and a large outflow of silver from the treasury. The source of the opium was British India. Britain twice went to war with China to protect this lucrative trade. In these wars, the First Opium War (1839–42) and the Second Opium War (1856–60), China was ill equipped to fight and was defeated and nearly bankrupted by the indemnities imposed. Hong Kong was ceded to Britain and a number of ports, known as 'treaty ports', were opened to foreign traders. Inland China was also opened to foreigners in a limited way after 1860. The treaties ending these wars, and others which followed, came to be known by the Chinese as 'unequal treaties' because they were imposed upon the nation by foreign powers.

Four major rebellions led to major loss of life and devastated areas of countryside across most of China. These were the Taiping Rebellion (1850–64), the North-West Muslim Revolt (1856–73), the South-West Muslim Revolt (1862–73) and the Nien Revolt (1856–68).

The Taiping Rebellion was finally quelled with the help of a special elite trained force called the 'Ever-Victorious Army' founded by the American F. T. Ward. It had a European officer corps which was later commanded by Major Charles George Gordon ('Chinese Gordon'). Twenty million died during the course of the Taiping Rebellion alone!

The Nien Revolt arose after the Yellow River flooded in 1851 and then again in 1855, when many were drowned. No repairs had been carried out because there was insufficient money available. The flood damage and the revolt devastated the richest provinces in China, which had largely escaped the Taiping ravages — all of which added to the woes of the Qing regime.

The last quarter of the century saw foreign powers encircle China like jackals, ready to strike at any weak point for their own advantage. France's interest was to take over Indo-China and she went to war successfully with China in 1884–85. Russia penetrated into Chinese Turkestan. Japan, having modernized itself, picked a quarrel with China and defeated her conclusively in the war of 1894–95. China had to cede Taiwan and the Penghu Islands, pay a huge indemnity, permit Japanese industries to be set up in four ports and recognize Japanese hegemony over Korea. In 1898 Britain got a ninety-nine-year lease of the New Territories, on the mainland opposite Hong Kong.

The Qing emperor, Guangxu (r. 1875–1908), ordered a series of sweeping reforms known as the Hundred Days' Reform. This attempt at modernization was too late to save the dynasty. There was a backlash from the ultra-conservatives led by the formidable Empress Cixi, and in a coup d'état she took over the government and cancelled the reforms, In addition she encouraged the anti-foreign and anti-Christian movement of secret societies called Yihetuan, better known in the West as the Boxers. In 1900 Boxer bands spread across north China killing all foreigners, missionaries and Chinese Christians. In June 1900 the Boxers besieged the foreign concession areas in Beijing and Tianjin. By August allied troops from Austria-Hungary, Britain, France, Germany, Italy, Japan, Russia and the United States, known by the Chinese as the 'United Force from Eight Countries', restored order in Tianjin and Beijing and then the Boxers were systematically put down.

The end of the Qing dynasty (1900-1912)

Failure of reform and the quashing of the Boxer Uprising convinced many that the only remedy for China's ills lay in outright revolution. The chief advocate was Sun Yat-sen, and his influence rapidly increased. The republican revolution broke out on 10 October 1911 and the Qing dynasty collapsed. When the Empress Dowager Long Yu abdicated in the name of the child, and last emperor, Pu Yi on 12 February 1912, imperial China came finally to an end and the Republic of China was born.

Appendix III
The provinces of China in the time of Hudson Taylor

The seven provinces with resident missionaries by 1865			Residence
Kwangtung	(Guangdong)	Canton (Guangzhou)	1807
Chekiang	(Zhejiang)		1843
Kiangsu	(Jiangsu)		1843
Fukien	(Fujian)		1846
Shantung	(Shandong)		1860
Hopeh	(Hebei)		1860
Hupeh	(Hubei)		1861

The eleven unevangelized inland provinces in 1865		Residence
Anhwei	(Anhui)	1869
Kiangsi	(Jiangxi)	1869
Honan	(Henan)	1875
Kansu	(Gansu)	1876
Shansi	(Shanxi)	1877
Yunnan		1877
Kweichow	(Guizhou)	1877
Shensi	(Shaanxi)	1879
Szechwan	(Sichuan)	1881
Kwangsi	(Guangxi)	1894
Hunan		1897

Appendix IV
United Appeal of the various branches of the Chinese House Church

(Translation revised and polished, after consultation with Chinese scholars, by Jonathan Chao, 12 October 1998)

1. We call on the government to admit to God's great power, and to study seriously the new trends of development of Christianity. The government should ask itself, if it were not the work of God, why would so many churches and Christians be raised up in China?

Therefore, the judicial branch of the National People's Congress and the United Front system should readjust their policies and regulations on religion lest they violate God's will to their own detriment.

2. We call on the legal authorities to release unconditionally all House Church Christians presently serving in labour reform camps. These include Presbyterians (who believe that if one is saved once, he or she is always saved), the Charismatic Church, the Local Church (incorrectly called the 'Shouters' Sect'), the Way of Life Church (also called the Full Gospel Church), the Little Flock Church, the Pentecostal Church, Lutherans who do not attend the Three-Self churches, and the Baptist Church. They should be released from prison if they are orthodox Christians — as recognized by Christian

churches internationally — and have been imprisoned for the sake of the gospel.

3. There are approximately ten million believers in the Three-Self Church, but eighty million believers of the home churches in the House Church. The House Church represents the mainstream of Christianity in China. Therefore the government should face reality as it is. If Taiwan, with its population of twenty-two million, cannot represent China but the mainland can, with its population of 1.2 billion, then the Three-Self Church cannot represent the Christian church in China. The Three-Self Church is only one branch. Moreover, in many spiritual matters there is serious deviation in the Three-Self Church. The government should clearly understand this.

4. We call on the central leadership of the Chinese Communist Party to begin a dialogue with representatives of the House Church in order to achieve better mutual understanding, to seek reconciliation, to reduce confrontation, and to engage in positive interaction.

5. We call on the government to spell out the definition of a 'cult'. The definition should be according to internationally recognized standards and not according to whether or not people join the Three-Self Church.

6. We call on the legal authorities to end their attack on the Chinese House Church. History has proven that attacks on Christians who fervently preach the gospel only bring harm to China and its government. Therefore, the legal system should end its practice of arresting and imprisoning House Church preachers and believers, confining them in labour camps, or imposing fines as punishment.

7. The Chinese House Church is the channel through which God's blessings come to China. The persecution of God's children has blocked this channel of blessing. Support of the House Church will certainly bring God's blessing.

We hope the government will have a positive response to this united appeal by the House Church. The Holy Spirit has awakened our hearts. May God bless China!

Henan province, 22 August 1998

Appendix V
Chinese Christian Confession of Faith, 1998

Issued by four major house-church groupings (Fangcheng, Tanghe, Born-Again and Anhui) on 26 November 1998, after nearly two years of discussion

In order to arrive at a common standard of faith among house churches in China, in order to establish a common basis for developing unity among fellow churches in China and overseas, in order to let the government and the Chinese public understand the positions of our faith, and in order to distinguish ourselves from heresies and cults, top leaders of a few major house groups have come together in a certain village in north China in November 1998, to pray together, to search the Scriptures, and to draft the confession of faith as shown below.

1. ON THE BIBLE

We believe the sixty-six books of the Bible to be inspired of God and written by the prophets and apostles under the inspiration of the Holy Spirit. The Bible is the complete truth and without error; it will allow no one to change it in any manner. The Bible clearly describes God's plan of redemption for man. The Bible is the highest standard of our faith, life and service.

We are opposed to all those who deny the Bible [as the Word of God]; we are opposed to the view that the Bible is out of date; we are opposed to the view that the Bible has error; and we are opposed to those who believe only in selected sections of the Bible.

We want to emphasize that the Scriptures must be interpreted in the light of their historical context and within the overall context of scriptural teachings. In seeking to understand Scripture, one must seek the leading of the Holy Spirit and follow the principle of interpreting Scripture by Scripture and not taking anything out of context. In interpreting Scripture, one ought to consult the traditions of orthodox belief left by the church throughout the history of the church.

We are opposed to interpreting Scripture by one's own will, or by subjective spiritualization.

2. On the Trinity

We believe in only one true God, the eternally self-existing triune God, Father, Son, and Holy Spirit, who are the same in substance, equal in honour and glory, each having different functional roles in the work of redemption: the Father plans salvation, the Son accomplished salvation, and the Holy Spirit implements salvation. However, there is no division among the Father, the Son, and the Holy Spirit, and the three are one in unity; the Son manifests the Father, the Holy Spirit manifests the Son; Father, Son and Holy Spirit all receive our worship. We pray to the Father through the Son and in the Holy Spirit. God the Son and God the Holy Spirit are both eternal; the Son is eternally begotten of the Father and is not created; the Holy Spirit is sent by the Father and the Son. God is a spirit; He has no visible shape or form. Christians worship Him in spirit and in truth. Aside from the Trinity, Christians have no other objects of worship.

We believe that God created all things, and He created man according to his own image. God controls and sustains all things; He is the Lord of human history. The almighty God is just, holy, faithful and merciful. He is omniscient, omnipresent and omnipotent. He manifests his sovereignty in all of human history.

We refute all mistaken explanations of the Trinity, such as one entity with three modes of manifestation (such as water, ice and steam); or one entity with three identities (such as [that] a person can be a son, a husband, and a father; or as the sun, its light and heat).

3. ON CHRIST

We believe that Jesus Christ is God's only begotten Son; He came to the earth by way of incarnation (the Word became flesh). In His perfect humanity He was tempted, though without sin. He allowed himself to be crucified on the cross of His own will and there shed His precious blood in order to redeem those who believe in Him from sin and death. He arose from the dead, ascended into heaven and sat at the right hand of God the Father from whom He received the promise of the Holy Spirit, whom He gives to all who believe in Him. In the last day, Christ shall come again the second time to judge the world.

Christians receive the status of sonship, but they remain humans; they do not become God. No one knows the specific dates of the Second Coming of Christ, but we firmly believe that Christ will come again. We can also know some signs of his Second Coming.

We are opposed to the teaching that Christ has come again the second time, in his incarnated form. All who claim that Christ has already come the second time should be declared heretics.

We are opposed to all who claim to be Christ.

4. ON SALVATION

Anyone who repents, confessing his or her sins, and believes in Jesus as the Son of God, that He was crucified on the cross for our sins and that he rose again on the third day for the remission of our sins and for receiving the Holy Spirit, will be saved through being born again. For by grace are we saved through faith; we are justified by faith; we receive the Holy Spirit through faith; and we become the sons of God through faith.

We believe that God will preserve His children in Christ to the end, and we also believe that believers should firmly believe in the truth to the end. We believe that receiving the Holy Spirit is the assurance (evidence) of being saved, and the Spirit of God bears witness with our spirits that we are the children of God.

We are opposed to all who take specific phenomena or personal experience as the objective criterion for being saved.

We are opposed to the belief that one can sin because one is under grace [that is to say, 'once saved, always saved' means one may sin freely].

We are opposed to the idea of multiple salvation [that is, salvation can be lost, so those who fall away must go through repentance and faith again in order to be saved again].

We are also opposed to the belief that we can be saved by keeping the law.

5. ON THE HOLY SPIRIT

We believe that the Holy Spirit is the third person in the Trinity. He is the Spirit of God, the Spirit of Christ, the Spirit of truth and the Spirit of holiness. The Holy Spirit illuminates a person, causing him to know sin and repent, to know the truth, and to believe in Christ and so experience being born again unto salvation. The Holy Spirit leads believers into the truth, to understand the truth and obey Christ, thereby bearing abundant fruit of life. In Christ, God grants a diversity of gifts of the Holy Spirit to the church so as to manifest the glory of Christ.

The Holy Spirit gives all kinds of power and manifests the mighty acts of God through signs and miracles. The Holy Spirit searches all things. Through faith and thirsting, Christians can experience the outpouring and the filling of the Holy Spirit. We do not believe in the cessation of signs and miracles or the termination of the gifts of the Holy Spirit after the apostolic period. We do not forbid the speaking of tongues, and we do not impose on people to speak in tongues; nor do we insist that speaking in tongues is the evidence of being saved.

We refute the view that the Holy Spirit is not a person in the Trinity but only a kind of influence.

6. ON THE CHURCH

The church is composed of all whom God has called together in Jesus Christ. Christ is the head of the church and the church is the body of Christ. The church is the house of God built on the foundation of truth. The church is both local and universal; the universal church is composed of all churches of orthodox faith currently existing in all parts of the earth, and all the saints throughout history.

The administration of the church should be conducted according to principles laid down in the Scriptures. Its spiritual ministry shall not be directed or controlled by secular powers. Within the church all brothers and sisters are members of the same body, each fulfilling his or her role, and in love grow up in all things into Christ who is the head. In the Spirit, the universal church should come to the unity of the faith and be united into one in Christ.

The mission of the church is: proclamation of the gospel, teaching and pastoring the believers, training and sending them, and defending the truth by refuting heresies and bringing them to the correct path. Christians meeting in the name of Christ shall not be limited by number or location. All believers are priests, and they all have the authority and responsibility to preach the gospel to the ends of the earth.

We are opposed to the unity of the church and state or the intermingling of the church and political power.

We are opposed to the expansion of the church by relying on political power, whether domestic or international.

We are opposed to the church taking part in any activities that seek to destroy the unity of the people [of China] or the unification of the Chinese state.

7. ON THE LAST THINGS

We believe in the Second Coming of Christ and the bodily resurrection of those who are saved. Aside from the heavenly Father, no one knows the date of the Second Coming of Christ.

When Christ comes again, He will come down in the clouds from heaven with power and glory. The angels will blow the horn and those who are asleep in Christ shall be raised from the dead, and the bodies of those Christians who have been born again and saved will be changed, and they will be lifted up to meet the Lord in the air, and they will receive glorified bodies.

The saints and Christ will reign [on earth] for a thousand years. During this period of a thousand years, Satan will be cast into the bottomless pit. After the thousand years, Satan will be temporarily released to deceive all the peoples until he is cast into the lake of fire and brimstone. Then Christ will sit on His throne and judge all nations and peoples. All the dead will be raised again and they will stand before the judgement seat.

All those whose names are not written in the book of life will be cast into the lake of fire, and heaven and earth will be consumed by fire, and even death and hell will be cast into the lake of fire. Those whose names are written in the book of life will enter into the New Jerusalem and be with God for ever.

We believe that as believers wait for the Second Coming of Christ, they should be diligent doing the work of the Lord, preaching the word of life, shining for the Lord on earth, and bearing abundant fruit in word, deed, faith, love and holiness. Those who do these things will receive all kinds of rewards.

As to whether Christ will come before or after the tribulation, we acknowledge there are different views among different church groups, and we cannot absolutely endorse any view.

The responsibility of Christians is to be alert and be prepared to welcome the Second Coming of Christ.

CONCLUSION

We praise and thank our almighty heavenly Father for leading us to draft this confession of faith. May the Holy Spirit work among

more brothers and sisters to accept it, identify with it, and pro-
claim this confession of faith in church meetings.

We pray that this confession will strengthen the faith of the
brothers and sisters, enable them to resist heresies and cults, and
cause them together to forward the great revival of the church in
China.

May the Lord bless the unity of the house churches in China.
May the Lord bless China, the Chinese peoples and the Chinese
church. May praise and glory be unto our triune God. Amen.

(Signed 26 November 1998)
Shen Yiping,
representing China Evangelistic Fellowship (Tanghe), China
Zhang Rongliang,
representing the Mother Church in Fangcheng, China
Cheng Xianqi,
representing the Church in Fuyang, Anhui Province, China
Wang Chunlu,
representing one of the house churches in China

[translated by Jonathan Chao, 18 December 1998].

Appendix VI
House-church Policy

[THE] ATTITUDE OF CHINESE HOUSE CHURCHES TOWARDS THE GOVERNMENT, ITS RELIGIOUS POLICY, AND THE THREE-SELF MOVEMENT

(Statement issued together with the Confession of Faith on 26 November 1998 by the four major house-church groupings, Fangcheng, Tanghe, Born-Again and Anhui)

I. OUR ATTITUDE TOWARDS THE GOVERNMENT

1. We love the Lord, the Chinese people, and the state; we support the unity of the nation and the unity of the peoples.

2. We support the constitution of the People's Republic of China and the leaders and the government of the people that God established.

3. Even though we are often misunderstood and persecuted by the government, yet we do not show a reactionary attitude, nor have we taken any reactionary action.

4. We have never betrayed the interest of the Chinese people; we only do what is beneficial to the people.

II. OUR ATTITUDE TOWARDS THE RELIGIOUS POLICY OF THE GOVERNMENT

Why do we not register?

1. Because the state ordinances on religion and demands of regulations for registration are contrary to the principles of the Scripture, such as the 'three-designates' policy:

> a. *Designated location:* only in registered places are we allowed to conduct religious activities; otherwise such activities are considered illegal religious activities. But the Scriptures tell us that we meet anywhere and that so long as we meet in the name of the Lord, He will be with us.
> b. *Designated personnel:* only those who have been issued preaching licences by the Religious Affairs Bureau are allowed to preach. But according to the teachings of the Scriptures, so long as preachers are called by the Lord, recognized and sent by the church, they may preach.
> c. *Designated sphere:* preachers are restricted to preaching only within the district for which they are assigned; they may not preach across villages or across the provinces. But the Bible teaches us to preach the gospel to all the peoples and throughout the ends of the earth, and to establish churches.

2. Because the state policy does not permit believers to preach the gospel to those under eighteen, or to lead them to Christ and be baptized. But Jesus said, 'Let the little children come unto me and forbid them not.' Therefore, those under eighteen should have the opportunity to hear and to believe in the gospel.

3. Because the state policy does not permit believers to pray for the sick, to heal them, and to exorcise demons out of them.

4. Because the state policy does not allow us to receive fellow believers from afar, but the Bible teaches us that elders should receive brothers and sisters from afar.

5. Because the state policy does not allow us to have communication with churches overseas, but the Bible teaches us that the church is universal and that there is no division between Jews or Gentiles, and hence no division between Chinese and foreigners, for Christ has redeemed His people from all nations with His blood,

and believers are to love each other and to have communion with each other.

III. WHY WE DO NOT JOIN THE THREE-SELF PATRIOTIC MOVEMENT

Chinese house churches do not join the TSPM for the following reasons:

1. The heads of the two are different:

    a. Three-Self churches accept the state as their governing authority: their organization and administration are governed by the government's religious policy.

    b. House churches take Christ as their head, and they organize and govern their churches according to the teachings of Scripture.

2. The way church workers are established is different:

    a. Religious workers in the TSPM churches must first be approved by the Religious Affairs Bureau before assuming office.

    b. The house churches set apart their workers by the following qualifications: spiritual anointing, being equipped in the truth, possessing spiritual gifts, approved by the church, and having spiritually qualified character.

3. The foundations of the two are different:

    a. The Three-Self churches are products of the Three-Self Reform Movement, which was initiated by the government; they were started by Wu Yaozong [Y. T. Wu], who propounded [a] liberal social gospel type of theology; some of the initiators of the TSPM were not even Christians.

    b. House churches take the Bible as the foundation of their faith; they developed from the traditions of the fundamentalists and evangelicals.

4. The paths of the two are different:

   a. The Three-Self churches practise the unity of politics
and the church; they follow the religious policy of the state,
and they engage in political activities.
   b. House churches believe in the separation of the church
from the state. They will obey the state when such obedience
is in accordance with the Scriptures. When the two are in
conflict with each other, they will 'obey God rather than man'.
For such obedience they are willing to pay the necessary price,
which is known as 'walking the pathway of the cross'.

5. The missions of the two are different:

   a. The Three-Self churches can preach the gospel and
conduct pastoral ministry only within the designated places
of religious activities.
   b. House churches obey the Great Commission of preaching the gospel and planting churches.

IV. OUR ATTITUDE TOWARDS PERSECUTION

1. House churches are persecuted not because of political or
moral issues, but solely because they refuse to register with the
government and refuse to join the TSPM.
2. When house churches are persecuted, they do not hate the
government but accept suffering as permitted by the Lord; they
endure suffering silently; they yield to the government, and they
intercede for the government and bless it.
3. When leaders of house churches are persecuted, fined,
interrogated, sent to labour instruction camps or labour reform
camps, they do not complain; they still love their country and the
government, waiting for God to grant them mercy.
4. The grassroots cadres who persecute the church can testify
that the persecuted ones are innocent; these cadres have to execute
their duties without choice.
5. The two reform institutions have high regard for the believers
and pastors under their authority; they trust them and are sympathetic to them. These all testify that the persecuted Christians

have a heart that loves their country and people; they also testify that Christians have high moral integrity.

6. The faith of the house churches is orthodox; their model of ministry is in accordance with Scriptures, and they enjoy the presence of God. Therefore, although persecuted, the number of believers has increased rapidly — a force that cannot be resisted. The number of believers in all of China is by far larger than that in the Three-Self churches. This is God's confirmation for us.

OUR SINCERE APPEAL TO THE GOVERNMENT

1. We appeal to the government to know the facts clearly and, in a truthful manner, correctly understand the nature of our faith and the purpose of our preaching, and no longer mistake us for cults.

2. We sincerely ask the government to stop its persecution against house churches, such as brutal beating, house searches, fines, detention, and labour-camp sentences; we sincerely petition the government to truly implement freedom of religion.

3. We ask the government to free all Christians and evangelists who are detained in the labour camps because of their faith or for preaching the gospel, and to do so as soon as possible.

As a matter of fact, wherever there are more believers, there is also greater social stability, higher spiritual civilization, better social atmosphere, and the enjoyment of greater blessings from God. May there be peace in China and among her people. May God bless China abundantly.

By the representatives of the house churches in China
26 November 1998

[Translated by Jonathan Chao, 18 December 1998]

Bibliography

MAJOR SOURCE MATERIAL

Aikman, David. *Jesus in Beijing,* Monarch Books, 2006

Billy Graham Center Archives, Collection 393, *Audio interview with David H. Adeney,* 1988

Billy Graham Center Archives, Collection 472, *Audio interview with Paul A. Contento,* 1992

Broomhall, A. J. *Hudson Taylor and China's Open Century,* Books 1-7, Hodder & Stoughton, 1981 onwards

Broomhall, Marshall. *Hudson Taylor, The Man who Believed God,* CIM, 1929

Kinnear, Angus. *Against the Tide, The Story of Watchman Nee.* Kingsway ed., 1979

Lambert, Tony. *China's Christian Millions,* Monarch Books, 2000

Latourette, K. S. *A History of Christian Missions in China,* Macmillan, NY, 1932

Latourette, K. S. *A History of Modern China,* Pelican, 1954

Lyall, Leslie. *Come Wind, Come Weather,* Hodder & Stoughton, 1961

Lyall, Leslie. *Three of China's Mighty Men,* OMF, 1973

Partners International website, partnersintl.org/history/complete history/links with *Calvin Chao*

Taylor, Dr & Mrs Howard. *Hudson Taylor in Early Years,* Morgan and Scott, 1919 edition

www-chaos.umd.edu/history, articles on *The People's Republic of China*

Xi, Lian, *Redeemed by Fire — Rise of Popular Christianity in Modern China*, Yale University, 2010

IN ADDITION TO THE ABOVE SOURCES

Chapter 2
Budge, E. A. Wallis. *The Monks of Kublai Khan,* London, Religious Tract Society, 1928

Chapter 3
Townsend, William John. *Robert Morrison, the pioneer of Chinese Missions,* LMS ed., 1892

Chapter 4
Lutz, Jessie and R. Ray. 'Karl Gutzlaff and the China Union', in *Christianity in China. From the 18th Century to the Present,* Daniel H. Bays (editor), Stanford University Press, 1996

Chapter 5
McNeur, G. H. *Liang A-Fa,* Oxford University Press China Agency, 1934
Murray, Iain. *The Puritan Hope,* Banner of Truth Trust, 1971 (essential reading towards understanding the eschatology and motivation of the evangelical missionaries)

Chapter 6
Coad, F. Roy. *A History of the Brethren Movement,* Paternoster Press, 1968

Chapter 7
Miller, R. Strang. 'William C. Burns', Banner of Truth, *Five Pioneer Missionaries,* 1965
Orr, J. Edwin. *The Second Evangelical Awakening in Britain,* Marshall, Morgan & Scott, 1949 (see pages 223-9 for fascinating evidences of the direct and indirect impact of the 1858–60 revival in North America and the United Kingdom on the mission fields of the world, including China)

Chapter 8

Bebbington, David W. *The Dominance of Evangelicalism, The Age of Spurgeon and Moody*, IVP, 2005

Thompson, R. Wardlaw. *Griffith John, The Story of Fifty Years in China*, Religious Tract Society, 1907

Chapter 9

Bebbington, David W. *The Dominance of Evangelicalism, The Age of Spurgeon and Moody*, IVP, 2005

Glover, A. E. *A Thousand Miles of Miracle in China. A Personal Record of God's Delivering Power from the Hands of the Imperial Boxers of Shan-si*, Hodder & Stoughton, 1904

Thompson, R. Wardlaw. *Griffith John, The Story of Fifty Years in China*, Religious Tract Society, 1907

Chapter 10

Blair, William and Bruce Hunt, *The Korean Pentecost*, Banner of Truth, 1977

Goforth, Rosalind. *Jonathan Goforth*, Bethany House Publishers, Minneapolis, 1986

Kendall, R. Elliott. *Beyond the Clouds, The Story of Samuel Pollard of South-West China*, Cargate Press, 1948

Whitaker, Colin. *Great Revivals*, Marshall Morgan & Scott, 1984

Chapter 11

Broomhall, Marshall. *The Answer of God, A Doxology on the Seventieth Anniversary of the China Inland Mission*, CIM & Religious Tract Society, 1935

Goforth, Rosalind. *Jonathan Goforth*, Bethany House Publishers, Minneapolis, 1986

Renwick, A. M. and A. M. Harman. *The Story of the Church*, IVP, 1985

Whitaker, Colin. *Great Revivals*, Marshall Morgan & Scott, 1984

Chapter 12

Ming-Dao, Wong. *A Stone Made Smooth*, Mayflower Christian Books, 1981.

Woods, Grace W. *The Half can Never be Told, The Shanghai Revival 1925*, Marshall Brothers Ltd

Chapter 13
Bosshardt, Alfred. *The Guiding Hand,* Hodder & Stoughton, 1973
Burgess, Alan. *The Small Woman,* Evan Brothers, 1957
Ming-Dao, Wong. *A Stone Made Smooth,* Mayflower Christian Books, 1981.
Monsen, Marie. *The Awakening, Revival in China 1927–1937,* CIM, 1961
Taylor, Geraldine. *The Triumph of John & Betty Stam,* OMF Books, 1978

Chapter 14
Cheng, Marcus. *Lamps Aflame,* CIM, 1949
Keddie, John W. *Running the Race, Eric Liddell — Olympic Champion and Missionary,* EP, 2007 (Since the publication of this book, the Chinese authorities have revealed that, in a prisoner exchange, Eric Liddell gave up his place to a pregnant woman. This great sacrifice was news even to his own family.)
Orr, J. Edwin. *Through Blood and Fire in China,* Marshall, Morgan & Scott, undated

Chapter 15
Back to Jerusalem website/history
Gih, Andrew. *His Faithfulness. The Story of the Evangelize China Fellowship,* Marshall, Morgan & Scott, 1955

Chapter 16
Gih, Andrew. *His Faithfulness. The Story of the Evangelize China Fellowship,* Marshall, Morgan & Scott, 1955
Thompson, Phyllis. *The Reluctant Exodus,* Hodder & Stoughton and OMF, 1979

Chapter 17
Adeney, David H. *China, The Church's Long March,* OMF, 1985
Lyall, Leslie. *God reigns in China,* Hodder & Stoughton and OMF, 1985
Wang, Mary. *The Chinese Church that Will Not Die,* Hodder & Stoughton, 1971

Wangzhi, Gao. 'Y. T. Wu', in *Christianity in China from the 18th Century to the Present*, Daniel H. Bays (editor), Stanford University Press, 1996.

Whitaker, Colin. *Great Revivals*, Marshall, Morgan & Scott, 1984

Chapter 18

Adeney, David H. *China, The Church's Long March*, OMF, 1985

Chao, Jonathan. *Christian Community Life in Communist China, 1949–1979*, pamphlet in Evangelical Library, 1980

Lyall, Leslie. *God reigns in China*, Hodder & Stoughton and OMF, 1985

Chapter 19

Adeney, David H. *China, The Church's Long March*, OMF, 1985

Chao, Jonathan. 'China — Growth through Suffering', *Reformation Today*, no. 178

Lyall, Leslie. *God reigns in China*, Hodder & Stoughton and OMF, 1985

Chapter 20

Lyall, Leslie (editor), *The Phoenix Rises — Eight Chinese Churches*, OMF, 1992

Chapter 21

Hattaway, Paul. *Back to Jerusalem — Three Chinese Leaders*, Piquant, 2003

Index

190, 201, 203, 205, 226, 233, 239, 244, 245, 250, 252, 253-4, 265, 275, 289, 298, 302, 308, 318
   missionary conferences at, 123-5, 129, 137, 143-4, 146, 155
Shansi (Shanxi) province, 122, 132, 137, 138, 140, 141, 176, 177, 185, 188, 200, 233, 244, 252, 253, 276, 279, 317, 320, 327
Shantou (formerly Swatow), 243, 276, 279
Shantung (Shandong) province, 145, 153, 157, 167-8, 177, 188, 189, 201, 204, 276, 317, 327
Shen Xianfeng, 287
Shensi (Shaanxi), 30, 147, 181, 183, 207, 224, 276, 318, 320, 321, 327
Shouters — see Local Church
Sinkiang (Xinjiang) province, 183, 208, 224, 225, 318, 324
Song dynasty, 322
Spiritual Food Church, 201
Spiritual Food Quarterly, 176, 197, 248
Stam, Helen Priscilla, 181-2
Stam, John and Betty, 181
Stearns, Thornton and Carol, 188-9
Stone, Mary, 170
Stone Gateway, 148, 271
Stott, George, 115
Studd, C. T., 127
students, 164-5, 174, 236-7, 251, 256, 300
   conferences, 215-19, 243
   opposition to Christianity, 164-5, 218
   work among, 189, 195, 201, 204, 205-9, 211-19, 227, 250, 276, 308, 316
summer resorts (conferences), 157, 188
Sun Yat-Sen (Sun Yixian), 26, 151-3, 163, 326
Sung, John, 170-71, 189, 190-93, 200
Sutphen, Douglas — see Brother David

Suzhou, 276
Swatow (Shantou), 97-8
Szechwan (Sichuan), 147, 207, 318, 320, 327
Taiping Rebellion, 62, 73-4, 89, 90, 91, 96-7, 103-4, 115, 117, 290, 315, 325
Taiyuan, 138, 139, 244
Tang dynasty, 27, 322
Tanghe Fellowship, 277, 287, 289-90, 310, 330, 336, 337
Taoism (Daoism), 24-5, 26, 33, 230, 291, 320, 324
Taylor, Amelia (Amelia Hudson, mother of Hudson), 80, 82-3, 90
Taylor, Amelia (later Amelia Broomhall, Hudson's sister), 80, 82, 83, 84, 85, 88, 101
Taylor, Howard, 134
Taylor, (James) Hudson, 68, 78-135, 155, 254, 319
   adopts Chinese dress, 94-5
   arrival in China, 91, 235, 315
   belief in the power of prayer, 83-4
   early years, 78-90
   founds the CIM, 68, 87, 104-19
   reliance on God alone, 87, 98, 106, 116
Taylor, James (father of Hudson), 80-81
Taylor, James (great-grandfather of Hudson), 78-9
Taylor, Jennie, 117, 121, 134
Taylor, John, 79, 80
Taylor, Maria (née Dyer), 99-100, 117, 134
Thompson, Phyllis, 234
Three Ranks of Servants, 292
Three-Self Movement (TSPM), 199-200, 231-2, 237-8, 239, 243, 246, 247-9, 251-4, 256, 273-5, 277, 280, 287, 292, 294, 296, 297, 300, 301, 302-5, 306, 316, 328, 329, 341

Bob Davey gives us a detailed account of the works of God in China from the nineteenth century onwards. It will inform and encourage believers in its depiction of the fire of God's Spirit spreading through China unquenched by persecution and suffering... May the Lord continue His work of biblical reformation and spiritual revival in China to the blessing of the whole world!

Joel R. Beeke, President, Puritan Reformed Theological Seminary,
Grand Rapids, Michigan

Bob Davey must be congratulated on gathering together a wealth of material, providing a good overview of missionary endeavour in China down fourteen centuries and the exciting emergence of a vibrant, growing church, despite persecution and setback.

Ronald Clements Ph.D, writer and researcher

In 1951 the Communist government expelled my missionary parents from the Chinese town where they were working. Only ten trembling believers remained... Today there are hundreds of Christians in that place. In *The Power to Save*, Bob Davey traces the unconquerable power of the gospel through the years in that land. Despite all opposition, and in answer to the prayers of many generations, God is at work. This thrilling account encourages us to pray again for such mighty acts of God even here in the West.

Faith Cook, author and biographer

Bob Davey is to be deeply thanked for this succinct, deeply helpful overview of the progress of Christianity in China. By and large, the church in the West is woefully ignorant of what God has done in China and this work will certainly rectify that. It is also a great reminder of what we see in the book of Acts: the power of God's Word is unstoppable once unleashed. As such, this history is reason for deep praise of the triune God.

Dr Michael A. G. Haykin, Professor of Church History and Biblical
Spirituality, The Southern Baptist Theological Seminary

The history of the gospel in China from the tiniest beginning in 1807 until the present is packed with encouragement. The outstanding feature is the fulfilment of Christ's words: 'I will build my church, and the gates of hell will not prevail against it.' ... Vigorous and protracted persecution has not succeeded in stopping the multiplication of believers. In fact ... persecution has had the opposite of the effect intended by those opposed to the gospel. Today the potential for the Chinese church to play a major role on the world stage of missions is greater than ever... In the future there will be millions of Chinese who will value this history of how they have emerged through the last two hundred years to become a mighty spiritual army.

Erroll Hulse

China is an important country to watch, and it has just overtaken Japan as the second largest economic power in the world after the US. This book by Bob Davey chronicles the history of transformation of this great giant and the political, social and spiritual changes that were divinely ordained of God over the past few centuries... I will heartily recommend this book for anyone who desires to have a proper appreciation of the spiritual dynamics of this fast-changing world power and the gospel impact it has experienced over these decades. Read, study and relish it, and be awakened and revived for Christ and for the souls of men in China and beyond.

Jack Sin, Pastor of Maranatha BP Church, Singapore, and Lecturer at the Emmanuel Reformed Bible Lectures

What we call 'Bible truth' came to China in 1807 with Robert Morrison. Now China is a world power. This book traces the history of the enormous advance of the gospel there. In this way it inspires us to glorify God!

Tom Wells, author of A Vision for Missions

In this book, the author offers a detailed description of key persons and comprehensive coverage on Chinese events, movements and leaders, with a concise summary from the author's painstaking work... May the Chinese church stand up to the current challenges and not deviate from it!

Yang Ye, Chinese lay leader